Grails 1.1 Web Application Development

Reclaiming Productivity for Faster
Java Web Development

Jon Dickinson

[PACKT] PUBLISHING

BIRMINGHAM - MUMBAI

Grails 1.1 Web Application Development

Copyright © 2009 Packt Publishing

First published: May 2009

Production Reference: 2190509

Published by Packt Publishing Ltd.
32 Lincoln Road
Olton
Birmingham, B27 6PA, UK.

ISBN 978-1-847196-68-2

www.packtpub.com

Cover Image by Vinayak Chittar (vinayak.chittar@gmail.com)

Credits

Author
Jon Dickinson

Reviewers
Harshad Oak
Xinyu Liu

Acquisition Editor
Douglas Paterson

Development Editor
Dhiraj Chandiramani

Technical Editor
Shadab Khan

Copy Editor
Leonard D'Silva
Sumathi Sridhar

Indexer
Monica Ajmera

Production Editorial Manager
Abhijeet Deobhakta

Editorial Team Leader
Akshara Aware

Project Team Leader
Lata Basantani

Project Coordinator
Leena Purkait

Proofreader
Angie Butcher

Production Coordinator
Dolly Dasilva

Cover Work
Dolly Dasilva

About the author

Jon Dickinson is an independent software development consultant based in the UK. He has been delivering web applications on the Java platform over a range of business domains covering finance, tourism, energy, education, and transport, for the last ten years. He uses a mix of agile methods, pragmatism, and software craftsmanship to deliver valuable software that helps achieve the goals of real users.

He is the principal consultant and founder of Accolade Consulting Ltd. (`http://www.accolade-consulting.co.uk`) and can be contacted at `jon@accolade-consulting.co.uk`.

Acknowledgement

I would like to thank the people that have helped me on my way to writing this book.

My thanks goes to the people at Packt involved in this project: Douglas Paterson, Usha Iyer, Dhiraj Chandiramani, Leonard D'Silva, Sumathi Sridhar, Leena Purkait, and Shadab Khan. They have been very supportive and patient throughout the process, putting up with my ongoing restructuring of the book and the occasional missed deadline. I have come to realize that it is much easier to refactor code than prose.

The comments of my reviewers have been invaluable in the creation of this book. I can't imagine the end product without them. Thank you to Harshad Oak for invariably being right regarding issues of the books structure, Michael Galpin for his input to the early chapters, Xinyu Liu for some excellent technical review points in the later chapters and Phil Parker for reinforcing structural issues and convincing me to upgrade the book to the latest version of Grails.

To Graeme Rocher and the Grails development team, thank you for taking the issue of productivity in Java web development seriously and doing something about it. To the Grails community at large, and it is getting pretty big, keep up the great work on those plug-ins.

To my wife, Georgia, thank you for your patience and putting up with the lost weekends and evenings. To Amelia and Oliver, thank you for the constant interruptions that put everything else in perspective.

About the reviewers

Harshad Oak is the founder of Rightrix Solutions and the editor of IndicThreads. com. He is the author of three books which include Oracle Jdeveloper 10g: Empowering J2EE Development, Pro Jakarta Commons, and J2EE 1.4 Bible. He has also written several articles on Java topics. For his contributions to technology and the community, he has been recognized as an Oracle ACE Director and a Sun Java Champion.

Rightrix Solutions works in the field of technology media and research. It runs the Java portal **IndicThreads.com** and hosts the annual **IndicThreads.com** conference in Pune, India.

Xinyu Liu had graduated from the George Washington University. As a Sun Microsystems certified enterprise architect and developer, he has intensive application design and development experience in Java and SOA environments. He is a writer for Java.net and Javaworld.com and covers various topics including JSF, Spring Security, Hibernate Search, Spring Web Flow, and the new Servlet 3.0 specification. He also has a background in physics PhD with several publications in both, high energy and condensed matter fields.

Table of Contents

Preface

The expectations of our users are increasing, and rightly so. The Internet is no longer the playground of geeks and nerds. Businesses use it to communicate with and support their customers; families use it to keep in touch while whole communities share their experiences with like-minded people. The democratization of the Internet has brought a new wave of software into the lives of people who would otherwise rarely use computers. The most successful of the new generation of web applications have not been written for the expert user, but for the casual user, focusing on ease of use. Web application development frameworks that focus on developer productivity have improved the ability of developers to respond to the demands of their users. Simpler and more intuitive frameworks have allowed the rapid development and refinement of new features.

Java web application development has something of a checkered history; simple isn't it. There may be more than one way to skin a cat, but there are almost infinite numbers of ways to build a Java web application. The options that are available are mind-boggling. Which database server to use? What about the application server? You also better choose an MVC framework while you're at it. Should you use a persistence framework, or hand code SQL statements? If you use an ORM framework, which one is best? Don't forget to choose a logging library. How should the project be laid out? Once you've finished making all these decisions, it's time to start on the configuration to get all of these disparate frameworks working together. Now, eventually you are ready to start coding! No wonder the latest and greatest web applications are built in PHP and Ruby on Rails.

Java still has a lot to offer. It is faster than most other languages that are used for web application development. It is an extremely mature platform, with lots of high quality libraries available. Moreover, its static, strong typing gives you less rope to hang yourself with. However, Java developers need to find technologies that deal with the common activities of web development. Sometimes we need a few choices taken away to help us focus on the problem at hand, creating great software that provides value to our users at less cost to the people paying the bills.

Grails does just this. It removes the need for reams of configuration through a convention-based approach that constrains developers in a healthy way. The decisions concerning project layout and which frameworks to use are removed. This leaves the developers free to use their creative talents for producing great software, rather than tweaking configuration files.

Throughout this book, you will learn how to build a web application using Grails and a number of key plug-ins. You will see that it is possible to achieve a great deal with very little code. Who knows, you may even rediscover your passion for web development on the Java platform!

What this book covers

Chapter 1 presents a short state of the nation of Java web development and makes the case for a framework like Grails. At the end of the chapter, we will install and create a Grails project.

Chapter 2 covers the use of Grails scaffolding to generate some simple pages to manage users and roles for our application.

Chapter 3 shows how to post messages, where we write the first basic functionality for the application by allowing users to post messages that can be shared with other users. This chapter introduces a number of basic concepts for Grails development including: controllers, validation, Groovy Server Pages (GSP), and Grails Object-Relational Mapping (GORM).

Chapter 4 covers an introduction to Groovy. Here we take a short break from the Grails framework to get a better understanding of the Groovy programming language. We will cover just enough of the language to be able to proceed through the rest of the book.

Chapter 5 shows how to use our first external plug-in to add authentication and authorization to the application.

Chapter 6 covers testing, where we introduce the different levels of automated testing that are available in the Grails framework. We see how to write unit tests with new support for testing in Grails 1.1. We also cover integration tests, and install a functional testing plug-in.

Chapter 7 covers file sharing, where we allow users to share files through the application by introducing file uploads.

Chapter 8 covers some advanced querying techniques, using Hibernate criteria support in GORM, to implement file version history.

Chapter 9 introduces Grails services in more depth. We see how to extract logic from our controllers into services to keep the application maintainable.

Chapter 10 introduces more advanced GORM techniques, such as: persisting inheritance and performing polymorphic queries to enable tagging. We also delve into GSP a bit more by using templates to encapsulate view components.

Chapter 11 covers AJAX and RIA Frameworks—Where we improve the user experience with AJAX to allow users to edit tags in-line and use the RichUI plug-in to create tag clouds and perform auto suggestion when editing tags.

Chapter 12 shows us how to use the Searchable plug-in to add a search feature to our site in a matter of minutes. We also provide an RSS feed and a REST based API for managing messages.

Chapter 13 show us how to build our own plug-in, where we follow the example of the Grails plug-in community and extract our tagging code into a plug-in that we can use on future projects.

Chapter 14 shows how to package and deploy the application to a production ready for use in a production environment. We then discuss some next steps that may be worth investigating to handle real world situations.

What you need for this book

To implement the example code in this book, you will need the Java SDK 5 or above. More importantly, you will need to have some experience of web development on the Java platform.

Who this book is for

This book is aimed at Java web developers looking for ways to speed up development of web applications on the Java platform. If you are frustrated with integrating the many different frameworks that are available for web development and want to get on with building slick web applications for your users, then this book is for you.

Grails is built on the Groovy language, but experience in Groovy is not required, as you will learn enough about Groovy to understand how to use Grails.

Conventions

In this book, you will find a number of styles of text that distinguish between different kinds of information. Here are some examples of these styles, and an explanation of their meaning.

Code words in text are shown as follows: "Create the `saveNewVersion` method to link the usage of the `createNewVersion` and `applyNewVersion` methods."

A block of code will be set as follows:

```
def saveNewVersion( params, multipartFile ) {
    def version = createVersionFile( params, multipartFile )
    def file = applyNewVersion( params.fileId, version )
    file.save()
    return file;
}
```

When we wish to draw your attention to a particular part of a code block, the relevant lines or items will be shown in bold:

```
package app

class FileController {

    def fileService

    def save = {
        def multipartFile = request.getFile('fileData.data')
```

Any command-line input or output is written as follows:

```
# grails create-domain-class app.User
```

New terms and **important words** are shown in bold. Words that you see on the screen, in menus or dialog boxes for example, appear in our text like this: "clicking the **Next** button moves you to the next screen".

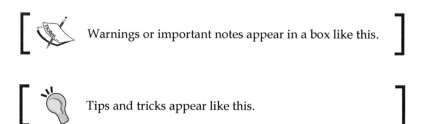

Warnings or important notes appear in a box like this.

Tips and tricks appear like this.

Reader feedback

Feedback from our readers is always welcome. Let us know what you think about this book—what you liked or may have disliked. Reader feedback is important for us to develop titles that you really get the most out of.

To send us general feedback, simply drop an email to feedback@packtpub.com, and mention the book title in the subject of your message.

If there is a book that you need and would like to see us publish, please send us a note in the **SUGGEST A TITLE** form on www.packtpub.com or email suggest@packtpub.com.

If there is a topic that you have expertise in and you are interested in either writing or contributing to a book, see our author guide on www.packtpub.com/authors.

Customer support

Now that you are the proud owner of a Packt book, we have a number of things to help you to get the most from your purchase.

Downloading the example code for the book

Visit http://www.packtpub.com/files/code/6682_Code.zip to directly download the example code.

The downloadable files contain instructions on how to use them.

Errata

Although we have taken every care to ensure the accuracy of our contents, mistakes do happen. If you find a mistake in one of our books—maybe a mistake in text or code—we would be grateful if you would report this to us. By doing so, you can save other readers from frustration, and help us to improve subsequent versions of this book. If you find any errata, please report them by visiting http://www.packtpub.com/support, selecting your book, clicking on the **let us know** link, and entering the details of your errata. Once your errata are verified, your submission will be accepted and the errata added to any list of existing errata. Any existing errata can be viewed by selecting your title from http://www.packtpub.com/support.

Piracy

Piracy of copyright material on the Internet is an ongoing problem across all media. At Packt, we take the protection of our copyright and licenses very seriously. If you come across any illegal copies of our works in any form on the Internet, please provide us with the location address or website name immediately so that we can pursue a remedy.

Please contact us at `copyright@packtpub.com` with a link to the suspected pirated material.

We appreciate your help in protecting our authors, and our ability to bring you valuable content.

Questions

You can contact us at `questions@packtpub.com` if you are having a problem with any aspect of the book, and we will do our best to address it.

1

Getting Started with Grails

Grails is a dynamic web development framework on the Java platform for rapid application development. It has taken the coding by convention approach popularized by Ruby on Rails, and applied it as a wrapper over long established open source Java frameworks such as Hibernate and Spring. It uses the flexibility of Groovy to provide a **Domain-Specific Language (DSL)** for web development.

The goal is to be able to develop web applications with the minimum amount of effort without having to repeat yourself. Grails provides a consistent and reliable environment between all of your projects.

Why Grails?

Web development is a tricky business. Even a simple web application has a number of context changes ready to trip up the unwary developer. HTTP requests must be parsed and converted into internal code representations. Once parsed, the data must be validated to make sure no invalid or dangerous information has been sent. The data extracted from these requests is then persisted to rows in database tables. To send a response back to the user, data must be retrieved from the database and converted into the domain model. It is then rendered from the domain model into HTML format and sent back over HTTP. With every user action going through all these different conversions, we can see how web development can become expensive, and this is just the server side. We haven't even considered all the client-side coding that goes into web applications with the rich user experiences that are becoming the norm in the Web 2.0 era.

Over the years, there have been a number of frameworks created to alleviate the cost of building web applications. Web frameworks such as Struts, Spring MVC, Stripes, and JSF help in mapping the HTTP requests to code logic. Object to relational database mapping frameworks allow domain objects to be persisted directly to the database, Hibernate being the most notable. These frameworks have allowed larger and more complicated web applications to be implemented by reducing the workload of the application developer. Unfortunately, a side effect of multiple frameworks is an increased level of configuration that needs to be produced and maintained. The level of knowledge required to create framework configuration files is probably less than writing the code. However, it is notoriously difficult to debug and test the configuration.

Grails helps application developers provide value faster by:

- Requiring less configuration
- Faster setup
- Shorter develop/test cycle
- Consistent development environment
- Domain-specific language for web development
- Fewer dependencies

Less configuration

The first benefit Grails provides is a convention-based approach to remove the need for reams of configuration, while still leveraging the power of the mature underlying frameworks. In practice, this means that you don't spend a lot of time wiring your code together in XML configuration files, or muddy your code with endless annotations. Instead, if a class is created, according to the convention in the correct location, it will be wired into Spring as needed or will be treated as a Hibernate entity ready to be persisted in the database.

Faster setup

The convention based approach applies to your development environment as well as the code. As soon as you create a Grails project, you have a defined structure and a set of scripts already available to compile, test, run and package your project. Having all these scripts managed in a consistent and conventional manner greatly reduces the time required to get a project up and running.

Grails also comes configured with a bundled database and application server. So once you have Grails installed, and your project created, there is nothing else you need before you start development.

No longer do you need to spend time setting up a development environment for each project. Tweaking your Ant build scripts slightly for each new environment is a thing of the past, and so is configuring an application and database server for development.

Shorter develop/test cycle

Grails uses a bundled Jetty (`http://www.mortbay.org/jetty/`) installation for the application server, which is configured to execute against the working code base of your application. Grails is also built on top of Groovy — a dynamic language for the JVM that adds powerful new features to Java. Groovy compiles down to the Java bytecode, which allows it to integrate with any existing Java code. Chapter 4 introduces you to the Groovy language, if you have not used it before.

In development mode, Grails provides an auto-reloading feature (`http://www.grails.org/Auto+Reloading`), which allows you to make changes to your code and see the changes in your browser with the next refresh. There is no need to restart the application, or to re-deploy to an application server.

Consistent development environment

It is best practice in software development to try and ensure that all developers in a project are working in the same way and have a common environment on each machine. In reality, there are often conflicts between the configurations of different team member's development environments; team members may configure their application servers differently or use different database versions. You can waste valuable time debugging false problems in your software just because another team member has a configuration slightly different from yours.

Grails comes with a pre-defined application structure. This ensures that all developers will be working in the same way with the same environment configuration.

Domain-specific language for web development

Any experienced Java web developer will be familiar with the Servlet Specification, which provides a standard set of interfaces for working with HTTP. Grails builds on this specification and provides a DSL for developing web applications. The underlying specification is still available to developers, if they wish to use it, but in- depth knowledge is no longer required. By leveraging the flexibility of the Groovy language, Grails provides an intuitive and simple domain language specific to the web development, upon which you can build great web applications.

Fewer dependencies

The cost of getting up and running with Grails is remarkably low. You will need to download and install the following:

- Java 1.5 or greater
- Grails 1.1 or greater

Note that there is no need to download Groovy; it comes bundled with the Grails download.

Compare this to getting set up on a normal Java web project, where the typical download and install list would look something like this:

- Java
- DB server (for example, MySQL, HSQL DB)
- Application server (for example, Tomcat)
- Hibernate
- Spring
- Web framework (for example, Struts, Spring MVC)
- View rendering framework (for example, Velocity, Freemarker)
- Logging framework (for example, commons logging and Log4J)

You will eventually need to download and install an application server and a database server. Fortunately, this work can be put off until later down the line when you are thinking about deployment.

Installing Grails

Now that you have had the salesman's pitch for Grails, it's time to see if it can live up to the hype. So, let's get started.

Download Grails from `http://www.grails.org` and extract the downloaded files to your `development` folder. Create an environment variable called `GRAILS_HOME` and point it to the extract location.

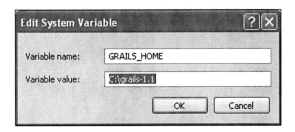

You will then need to add the `%GRAILS_HOME%/bin` to your path. It's that easy!

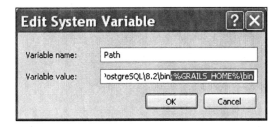

While working on a Mac, you can modify the `environment.plist` file in the `.MacOSX` directory as shown in the following screenshot:

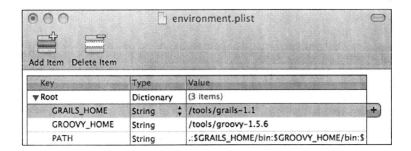

Although Grails is built on top of Groovy, there is no need to install Groovy separately. Grails comes with the `groovy-all-x.x.x.jar` bundled and executes your Groovy code directly.

The first step is to create a new Grails application with the Grails script, 'create-app'. You will create a new application called 'teamwork'. Open up your command line, go to your development area and run:

```
>grails create-app teamwork
```

You should see something like the following output:

```
Welcome to Grails 1.1 - http://grails.org/
Licensed under Apache Standard License 2.0
Grails home is set to: /tools/grails-1.1

...

Created Grails Application at <your_development_location>/teamwork
```

This will create a folder called `teamwork` and will set up your application structure within this folder. Verify that the application has been configured correctly. Go to the `teamwork` directory and check that you have a folder structure as shown in the following screenshot:

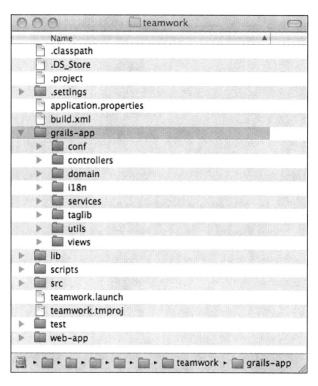

The **grails-app** folder will contain the main source code for your application. By examining the layout of this folder, you can see the beginnings of the convention for the layout of your application. The **Model View Controller (MVC)** (`http://java.sun.com/blueprints/patterns/MVC-detailed.html`) pattern is enforced through this convention.

Here is the breakdown of the layout:

- The **domain** directory contains the `Model` classes.
- The **views** directory contains the view code.
- The **controller** directory contains the controller files.
- The **conf** directory contains any configuration code that we need to implement.
- The **i18n** directory contains message bundles to support internationalization.
- Helper **services** will reside in the classes that go into the `services` directory.
- Tag libraries, which are refreshingly trivial to be implemented in Grails, reside in the **taglib** directory.

Once you have confirmed that the structure of your project directory is correct, go into the `teamwork` directory in your command line and run:

```
>grails run-app
```

Wait for the message, **Server running. Browse to http://localhost:8080/teamwork**, to appear in your command line. Then you can open a browser, and you will see the default Grails start page as shown in the following screenshot:

This is an equivalent of your "Hello World" example, when using any other framework. The result is a Java application server running on port 8080 with your application deployed to the context `teamwork`. This is not bad going for a five-minute job.

Grails comes with Jetty and HSQLDB already configured, which is why we have been able to get an application up and running so quickly. Jetty is a Java application server that can be ran as an embedded component within any Java application. HSQLDB is a lightweight Java SQL database engine that can be run in-memory with minimal configuration.

Grails applications are packaged as a WAR file for deployment, and so, are not limited to running under Jetty. But developing in this environment provides several benefits including:

- Fast deployment time
- Pre-configured setup
- Automatic reloading of code changes during development

Build a team communication portal

Now that we have installed Grails and the default page is up and running, it is time to start creating our application. The aim of this book is to build a communication portal for teams. The application will allow team members to share messages and files with the rest of the team. You will need to implement the following:

- Manage the users of the application
- Control access
- Allow users to send messages
- Allow team members to share files
- Improve organization of data through tagging
- Add an XML API via a **REST (Representational State Transfer)** web service
- Allow messages and files to be searched
- Add RSS feeds

Once you have finished implementing the application, you will see how to deploy the application into a production environment using Tomcat and MySQL.

Finally, you will finish up with some additional areas to consider and investigate further, which have not been discussed in this book.

Summary

There is a common set of problems associated with web development. There has been a constant progression of frameworks that have gradually made life easier for web developers by pulling more and more common tasks into framework code, allowing us to focus on the implementation of application logic. Grails is the next link in the chain. It applies a Domain-specific language for web development to the most mature and popular frameworks and enforces some best practices along the way.

By setting up the Grails version of the "Hello World" application, we have seen that the cost of setting up your development environment is almost nonexistent. In the next chapter, we will see how to use the power of scaffolding to perform basic user management tasks without having to write any logic at all.

2

Managing Users with Scaffolding

We are going to create a web application that will allow members of a team to communicate with one another. We will need to be able to make each of the team members a user of the application, so that in future iterations they can log in and collaborate. In this chapter, we will create a domain class to represent a user and a role in the application. We will add constraints to these domain classes to enforce the integrity of the data that is entered. By the end of this chapter, we will use Grails scaffolding to generate a user interface that allows users and roles to be managed within the application.

What is scaffolding?

Scaffolding is a mechanism used in Grails to allow developers to generate web pages that perform basic **CRUD** (**Create, Read, Update, Delete**) operations on the classes that make up the domain model of the application. These "scaffolded" pages are a very useful low-cost mechanism that allows you to verify whether your domain classes are capturing all the necessary information. It is however, extremely rare for a scaffolding to be used in a version of the application released to users, as most web applications require more complex usage scenarios that can be provided through default scaffolding.

scaffolding purpose & fate

When scaffolding is enabled for a domain class, the following pages and actions will be available to work with that domain object:

- List
- Create
- Edit
- View
- Delete

Scaffolding will handle:

- Creation of the web pages
- Mapping user input to the domain class
- Validating the user input
- Persisting the data to the database

We will see that it is possible to get a significant amount of value from these screens without needing to implement any application logic.

Create the domain classes

Grails uses the **Model View Controller** (MVC) pattern for web development. We will work on our model first. To allow the application to manage users, we will need a User class and a Role class. These must be created as domain classes in Grails. Domain classes constitute the domain model for the application. They are mapped directly to database tables by the Grails framework and form the central structure of an application. You can create new domain classes by using the supplied Grails command line tool.

[handwritten: misleading at best]

Go to your console and enter:

```
>grails create-domain-class app.User
```

The output of this command should look like this:

```
Welcome to Grails 1.1 - http://grails.org/
Licensed under Apache Standard License 2.0
Grails home is set to: /tools/grails-1.1

Base Directory: /workspace/books/effective-grails/code-1.1/chapter02/
teamwork
Running script /tools/grails-1.1/scripts/CreateDomainClass.groovy
```

```
Environment set to development
    [mkdir] Created dir: /workspace/books/effective-grails/code-1.1/
chapter02/teamwork/grails-app/domain/app
Created DomainClass for User
    [mkdir] Created dir: /workspace/books/effective-grails/code-1.1/
chapter02/teamwork/test/unit/app
Created Tests for User
```

Now, enter:

```
>grails create-domain-class app.Role
```

You should see from the messages in the console that both the `User` and `Role` classes have been created, along with a test class for each of them. The new classes will be created in the `app` package.

> Always put your Grails classes in a package. Otherwise, you may have compilation problems if you implement utility classes in Java code that use your application classes. The Java compiler, as of JDK 1.4, does not allow classes from the unnamed or `default` package to be imported into classes under a package (`http://bugs.sun.com/bugdatabase/view_bug.do?bug_id=4361575`).

Good Point ←

Create the User domain class

Go to the `grails-app/domain/app` folder and open up the `User.groovy` class. The vanilla class will be a simple empty Groovy class:

```
package app
class User {
    static constraints = {
    }
}
```

Add the following properties to the `User` class:

- The username of the user, for authentication.
- The title of the user.
- The first name of the user.
- The last name of the user.
- The password the user must enter to be authenticated.
- The date the user was created.
- The date the user was last updated.

```
package app
class User {
    String username
    String title
    String firstName
    String lastName
    String password
    Date dateCreated
    Date lastModified

    static constraints = {
    }
}
```

The given code looks a lot like Java code (there is a package and class definition and the properties have been declared as Java objects). However, there are a few issues that would stop this class compiling as Java code, namely:

- There are no semicolons marking the end of a statement
- The Date class is not imported
- The class definition is missing the public keyword

This is all fine because it is not a Java class; it is a Groovy class. It is a reassuring fact that there is very little difference syntactically between Java and Groovy code. We will cover Groovy in more depth in Chapter 4.

Create the Role domain class

Open the Role.groovy file and add a property to this class to capture the human readable name of the Role:

```
package app
class Role {
    String name

    static constraints = {
    }
}
```

Creating controllers to enable scaffolding

A controller is used to handle all web requests related to a given domain class. For example, the UserController class will handle all default actions for the User domain class (create, edit, list, delete and so on). Once a controller is created, there is no configuration needed to make it accessible to users. All the actions that are declared on the controller are available through a URL based on the controller and action name. The base URL for UserController is http://localhost:8080/ teamwork/user. The action that allows a user to be created is accessible through the URL, http://localhost:8080/teamwork/user/create.

explanation of url of correlation to controller

It is time to get Grails to create a readymade application by generating scaffolding for the User and the Role domain classes. Scaffolding is made available through a controller for each domain class. To create the controllers, go back to your command line and run:

```
>grails create-controller app.User
>grails create-controller app.Role
```

why not just use generate-controller. if scaffolding purpose & tete are legit.

This will create two controller classes in the app package under the grails-app/ controllers/app directory.

The new UserController class will contain the following code:

```
package app

class UserController {
    def index = { }
}
```

While the RoleController will contain:

```
package app

class RoleController {
    def index = { }
}
```

*it will also create unit tests
UserControllerTests
RoleControllerTests
note: generate-controller does not create
tests. does generate-all?*

In `UserController.groovy` remove the line `def index = {}` and add the `scaffold` property to enable scaffolding for the `User` domain class.

```
package app

class UserController {

    def scaffold = User

}
```

The highlighted line in the code above creates a publicly available `scaffold` property on instances of the `UserController` class. The `def` keyword declares a variable of dynamic type, while the assignment of `User` is giving the scaffold property the value of the `User` class. The equivalent Java code would look something like this:

```
private Object scaffold = User.class

public void setScaffold( Object scaffold ) {
    this.scaffold = scaffold;
}

public Object getScaffold() {
    return this.scaffold;
}
```

Member variables without a scope definition are also published as `public` properties in Groovy. This is covered in more detail in Chapter 4.

Now, in the `RoleController.groovy` file, remove `def index = {}` and add the `scaffold` property to the controller to enable scaffolding for the `Role` domain class.

```
package app

class RoleController {

    def scaffold = Role

}
```

Now, restart the application from your command line and go to the home page at `http://localhost:8080/teamwork`. You will be greeted by the default home page, as before, but this time there will be two new links:

- **app.RoleController**
- **app.UserController**

By clicking on the **app.UserController** link, you will see that you now have a basic set of screens for listing, viewing, creating, editing, and deleting users.

~~not shown~~ no you don't see that, but you can presume it.

The list page shows a table of users, which is of course empty at the moment, with headings for some of the properties of a user. Let's take a moment to consider the elements of the page and examine how the Grails scaffolding has managed to create them from our `User domain` class. The following elements are dynamically generated:

- The page title (**User List**)
- The navigation (**New User** link)
- The table title (**User List**)
- The table headers

part of
convention
over configuration

The page title, navigation, and table title are all generated from the name of the domain class. The table column headings come from converting the property names into readable text by assuming that your properties will be in camel case and using the capital letters to denote word breaks. So, the firstName property is displayed as **First Name**.

not always

At this point, you might be wondering where the **Id** column has come from, as you did not give the User domain class an id property. Each domain class has a dynamic property called id added to it at run time by Grails. This is the database identifier of the object that is assigned when instances of the class are saved to the database.

If you click on the **New User** link in the navigation on the list page, you will be taken to the **Create User** page as shown in the following screenshot:

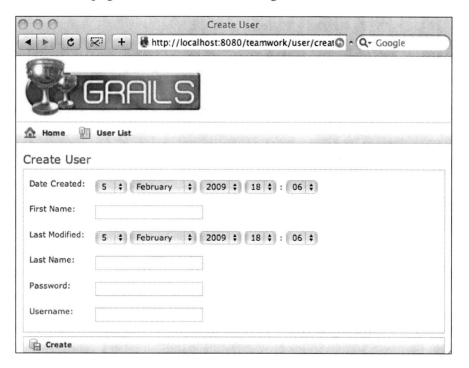

The **Create User** page uses the same conventions as the **User List** page for displaying the page title, navigation, form heading, and property names. In addition, the scaffolding will render an input field based on the data type of the property. You can see that the input fields for the dateCreated and lastModified properties have been rendered differently because they are Date objects rather then String objects.

Grails applications will startup with an in-memory HSQLDB database by default. If you fill in the fields on the **Create User** page and click on the **Create** button at the bottom of the form a new user will be saved in the database. You can verify this behavior by going back to the **User List** page; you should see the details of the new user displayed as a row in this table.

Just as controllers are able to handle web requests by virtue of existing in the `controllers` folder, domain classes can be persisted to the database without any need for configuration. This allows the scaffolding code to persist the data entered by the user to the database without requiring any additional information from us.

Part of convention over configuration

Control through constraints

While this in itself is pretty impressive, with a few minor changes to your domain class, you can control the order in which the fields are displayed. You can also perform some basic validation to make sure that the users aren't entering rubbish into the application. Add the following highlighted code in the `User.groovy` class file:

```
package app

class User {
    String username
    String title
    String firstName
    String lastName
    String password
    Date dateCreated
    Date lastModified

    static constraints = {
        username(blank: false, size: 4..20, unique:true)
        title(blank:false, inList:["", "Dr", "Miss", "Mr", "Mrs"])
        firstName(blank: false, size:1..20)
        lastName(blank: false, size:1..30)
        password(blank: false, size:6..20, password:true)
        dateCreated(nullable: true)
        lastModified(nullable: true)
    }
}
```

shows blank though blank not allowed

This is your first introduction to the DSL that Grails provides for web development. Defining constraints on the domain class using the above syntax provides a simple and readable way of specifying rules for your domain objects.

The definition of the `constraints` property may look unfamiliar at this point. The `constraints` property references a closure (or code block). Each line in the code block declares the constraints for an individual property. You will notice that the methods being called in the code block have not been declared anywhere. This is possible because a Groovy Builder is being used to intercept the method calls. The builder uses the arguments as the constraints for the property that matches the method name. You will learn more about Groovy Builders in Chapter 4.

The first use of constraints, with regard to scaffolding, is the order. Grails scaffolding uses the order in which the constraints are declared in the domain class to determine the display order of fields on the scaffolded screens. This ordering applies to the create, edit, and list screens.

The second use of constraints within scaffolding is to determine which input type is used when rendering a form. The **username**, the **firstName** and the **lastName** fields will all be rendered as simple text inputs, while the **password** field is now rendered as a password input. By using the `inList` constraint for the **title** field, scaffolding will render an HTML **select input** field containing the options specified in the constraint.

The main use of constraints is to enforce the validity of the data in our application. We can set rules regarding whether a property is required, how many characters are allowed, and whether the property must be unique. If we take the constraints we have added to the user class as an example, we have specified that:

- The **username** cannot be blank. It must be between 4 and 20 characters and must be unique

- The **title** cannot be blank and must be one of these options: '**Dr**', '**Miss**', '**Mr**', or '**Mrs**'

- **First name** cannot be blank and must be in the range of 1 to 20 characters

- **Last name** cannot be blank and must be in the range of 1 to 30 characters

- **Password** cannot be blank and must be in the range of 6 to 20 characters

If you go back to the **Create User** page, you should see that the order of the fields displayed is the same as the order defined by the constraints property as shown in the following screenshot:

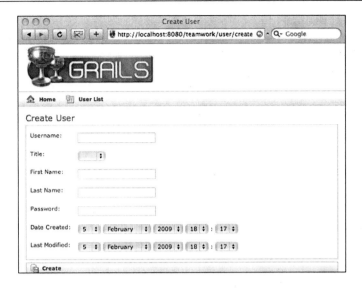

Now, try to create a user without specifying all the required information, and you will find that the Grails scaffolding automatically performs the validation checks on the data entered for a user.

As you have seen in your `User` class example, it is possible to use a number of constraints for a single property. At the time of writing this book, the following default constraints were available:

Constraint	Description	Example
`blank`	Determines whether a string can be blank.	`firstName(blank: false)`
`creditCard`	Is the string a valid credit card number?	`cardNum(creditCard: true)`
`email`	The string must be a valid email address.	`mailTo(email: true)`
`inList`	The value must be in a provided collection of values.	`title(inList: ['Mr', 'Mrs', 'Miss'])`
`matches`	Does the string match the defined regular expression?	`lower(matches: '[a-z]+')`
`max`	The value must be less than or equal to the defined value.	`age(max: 100)`
`maxSize`	The size of the value must be less than or equal to the defined value.	`username(maxSize: 20))`
`min`	The value must be greater than or equal to the defined value.	`age(min: 18)`
`minSize`	The size of the value must be greater than or equal to the defined value.	`username(minSize: 6) )`
`notEqual`	The property must not be equal to the defined value.	`agree(notEqual: 'no')`
`nullable)`	Determines whether the property can be null.	`username(nullable: false) )`
`range`	The value of the property must be within the specified range. NB. The syntax x..y denotes a range in Groovy.	`workingAge(range: 16..75)`
`scale`	Rounds floating-point numbers to the specified number of decimal places. This does not produce a validation error.	`payment(scale: 2)`
`size`	A range is used to restrict the size of a collection or the length of a string.	`username(size: 6..20)`
`unique`	Ensures the property is unique within the database.	`username(unique: true)`
`url`	Is the String a well-formed URL?	`site(url: true)`
`validator`	Allows you to implement your own custom validator in a closure.	`password(validator: { !it.startsWith('password') })`

Meeting the relations

In Hibernate, and therefore in Grails, persistent objects can be given relationships to other persistent objects. Grails supports the following types of relationships:

- One-to-one — where one instance of a class can have a relationship to a single instance of another class. For example, a person can have only one heart, so the relationship between person and heart would be one-to-one.

- One-to-many — where one instance of a class can have a relationship to a number of instances of another class. For example, a person can have many telephone numbers.

- Many-to-one — the other side of one-to-many, where many instances of a class have relationships to one single instance of another class. For example, many children can have the same father.

- Many-to-many — where many instances of a class can be related to many instances of another class. For example, a child can have many parents, and a parent can have many children.

of course, can be far more sophisticated than this

Relating roles and users

So far, you have a `Role` class and a `User` class, and you can create users and roles in the application. However, there is no relationship between the two classes; so you have no way of knowing which role a user is in. Scaffolding allows you to manage relationships between objects. All you need to do is create the relationships in the domain. You can create the relationship between the `Role` class and the `User` class by adding the highlighted code given here to the `Role.groovy` class:

misleading. only the static hasMany is necessary

```
package app

class Role {

    static hasMany = [users: User]

    String name

    static constraints = {
        name(blank: false, size: 1..20)
    }

    public String toString() {
        return name
    }
}
```

unnecessary

The relationship between a `Role` and a `User` is one-to-many, which is defined by the `hasMany` property. You have also added a constraint to the name of a role to make sure that it is not empty, and is not more than 20 characters. The `toString` method on `Role` has been overridden, so that the scaffolding can present meaningful role options when creating a user.

You should also associate the `User` class with the `Role` class:

```
package app
class User {
    String username
    String title
    String firstName
    String lastName
    String password
    Date dateCreated
    Date lastModified
    Role role
    static constraints = {
        username(blank: false, size: 4..20, unique:true)
        title(blank:false, inList:["", "Dr", "Miss", "Mr", "Mrs"])
        firstName(blank: false, size:1..20)
        lastName(blank: false, size:1..30)
        password(blank: false, size:6..20, password:true)
        role()
        dateCreated(nullable: true)
        lastModified(nullable: true)
    }
}
```

A role will apply to many users, but a user can belong only to one role. By simply adding a property of the type `Role` to the `User` class, you have created the other side of the many-to-one relationship between roles and users. You can then control where role information is displayed in the user scaffolding by adding it as a constraint.

The effect of making these changes on the scaffolding is that when a new user is created, you are prompted to select the role that they belong to. Additionally, if you edit a role, you will be allowed to add a new user to the role.

Ordering fields through constraints

repeats what is on p.26

Finally, it would be a good idea to hide the passwords of our users on the **User List** page. By default, the scaffolding for the list action displays only six columns. The first column is always the database ID of the object, which is rendered as a link to the view action. The other five columns are taken in the order specified by the constraints on the domain class. In our example, we can show the users' roles and hide the users' passwords by swapping the order of the role and password in the constraints for the `User` class. So,

```
password(blank: false, size:6..20, password:true)
role()
```

becomes:

```
role()
password(blank: false, size:6..20, password:true)
```

Once this change is made, you can see that passwords are no longer displayed on the **User List** page:

Bootstrapping demo data

You saw earlier that Grails comes pre-configured with an in-memory HSQLDB database. The benefit of this is that you don't need to configure a database server to get started. The problem is that whenever you restart Grails, all your data is lost. Grails provides a handy notion of Bootstrapping data, so a set of demo data can be loaded into your application during startup. At the very least, you will want to add the `User` and `Administrator` roles to this bootstrap to save you re-creating them each time.

The BootStrap class can be found under the grails-app/conf folder. Update the init code block to create and save the two new roles:

```
import app.Role

class BootStrap {
    def init = { servletContext ->
        def user = new Role(name: 'User').save()
        def admin = new Role(name: 'Administrator').save()
    }
    def destroy = {
    }
}
```

The BootStrap class is able to interact with the ServletContext of the application as it is passed as an argument to the init closure.

Now that the roles have been pre-configured for the application, it is possible to create users that belong to one of these roles as shown in the following screenshot:

Summary

In this chapter, you have seen that it is possible to create the skeleton of an application by simply defining the domain model. Scaffolding allows you to generate a basic application from the domain classes. Defining constraints to check the validity of the domain model is simple and concise, and best of all the constraints are encapsulated within your domain model. This makes it simpler to understand the domain model by giving extra context when working with the domain.

Constraints also allow some control over the default scaffold application, which means that it is possible to get enough mileage out of scaffolding to make it a feasible option for the first iteration of a rudimentary user interface.

In the next chapter, you will implement the first user goal for the application by allowing users to post messages.

3
Posting Messages

You have used Grails scaffolding to create some skeleton pages that manage users and roles. You will now learn the basics of web application development in Grails and implement the first of our user's goals to post messages.

The first user story could go something like this. As a team member, I want to be able to send a message to the rest of my team, so that I can share important information with my teammates.

To accomplish this goal, you are going to implement the following:

- A page to allow users to post messages
- A home page to display all messages in a chronological order

You will need to take the following steps to implement the above items:

- Create a domain class to represent messages
- Create a controller to handle user actions for messages
- Create a view to allow users to enter message data
- Create a controller to handle requests for the home page of the application
- Create a view for the home page
- Validate the message data input by the user
- Use **GORM (Grail's Object Relational Mapping)** to persist the message
- Use GORM to retrieve the messages in chronological order

Message domain class

The very first thing you need to do is create a domain class to represent messages so that they can be saved to the database. You saw how to create domain classes in Chapter 2. Go to the `grails-app/domain/app` directory and create a file called `Message.groovy` and then add the following code to this file:

```
package app

class Message {

    String title
    String detail

    Date dateCreated
    Date lastUpdated

    static constraints = {
        title( blank: false, size: 1..50 )
        detail( blank: false )
        dateCreated( nullable: true )
        lastUpdated( nullable: true )
    }
}
```

do not need to set nullable to true

There is nothing in the above code that is unfamiliar. But let's have a recap anyway. You have created a Groovy class called `Message` with the following properties:

- `title`—the title of the message
- `detail`—the details of the message
- `dateCreated`—the date on which the message was created
- `lastUpdated`—the date on which the message was last updated

You have also specified that the `title` cannot be blank and must be between 1 and 50 characters in length; notice the use of a Groovy range here. The `detail` of the message cannot be blank and the `dateCreated` and `lastUpdated` properties can be **null**.

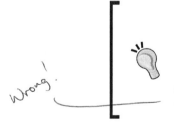

> dateCreated and lastUpdated convention
>
> There is a convention in Grails that if a domain class has a property of the type `Date` with the name `dateCreated` or `lastUpdated`, it will automatically populate these properties when the GORM persists the object to the database. When a message is first saved there should be no information in the `dateCreated` and `lastUpdated` fields, so you need to allow them to be `null` to pass the validation before saving the object.

Wrong!

Rendering a form

The first step to allow users to post messages is to present them with a form to enter the message data. To do this, you need to create a controller to handle the users request, and a view to show the form.

Message controller

Create a file called `MessageController.groovy` under the `grails-app/controllers/app` directory and place the following code in the new file:

```
package app
class MessageController {
    def create = {
    }
    def save = {
    }
}
```

Here you have created a controller for messages that can handle two actions: `create` and `save`. The following new URLs are now available in the application:

- `http://localhost:8080/teamwork/message/create`
- `http://localhost:8080/teamwork/message/save`

Of course, these URLs won't do anything yet as you have neither added any behavior to the controllers, nor created any views to render information to the user. The next step is to add the `view` for the **Create Message** page.

Groovy Server Pages

Groovy Server Pages (GSP) is the default view template language used when working with Grails. GSP provides a very similar syntax to JSP where you can use scriptlets or tags to perform logic within the pages. Like most features of Grails, there is a convention you must follow if you want to have the correct GSP used to render the result of an action.

Grails GSPs live under the `grails-app/views` directory. GSP files intended to render the results of an action on a particular controller should remain under a directory within `views` with the same name as the controller. So for `MessageController`, you will need to create the directory structure, `grails-app/views/message`.

The convention for finding a default view for an action is that Grails will look for a GSP under a directory matching the controller name and in a file matching the action name. In the case of the `create` action on `MessageController`, the default GSP page used for rendering would be `grails-app/views/message/create.gsp`.

Create message view

Create the GSP file `views/message/create.gsp` and add the following code:

```
<%@ page contentType="text/html;charset=UTF-8" %>
<html>
    <head>
        <meta http-equiv="Content-Type"
                content="text/html; charset=UTF-8" />
        <meta name="layout" content="main" />
        <title>Post Message</title>
    </head>
    <body>
        <p>Create a message form: coming soon!</p>
    </body>
</html>
```

why not use generate-views? (handwritten annotation)

By creating this simple GSP, you should now be able to request the `create` action on `MessageController` and the GSP you have just created will be rendered. The line of markup highlighted above means that the GSP will be rendered with the main layout. You will learn more about the layouts in just a second, but first of all, fire up your application and check whether you can go to the URL `http://localhost:8080/teamwork/message/create`. You should see the window as shown in the following screenshot:

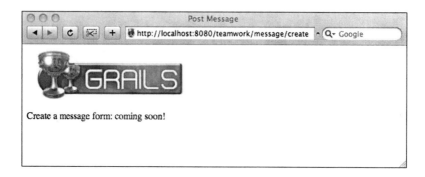

Grails layouts

Grails uses SiteMesh (`http://www.sitemesh.org`) as its rendering engine. SiteMesh leverages layouts by allowing developers to decorate their pages with a consistent look and feel. Take another look at the GSP you have just created. The line you are interested in is highlighted:

```
<meta name="layout" content="main" />
```

This tells Grails to decorate the current page with the `main` layout. Layouts can be found under the `grails-app/views/layouts` directory. Look at the `main.gsp` file in this directory and you can see that it is referencing a stylesheet, setting up the basic page structure and loading the Grails logo. There are three tags being used that are of real interest, and should be defined in all layouts. These are: `g:layoutTitle`, `g:layoutHead`, and `g:layoutBody`.

explains contents of main.gsp

Each of these tags is used to insert the contents of the page that is being rendered into the layout structure. For example, when the `g:layoutTitle` tag is called, the contents of the `<title>` element in the requested page will be rendered. The same applies to the `g:layoutHead` and the `g:layoutBody` tags.

explains how sitemesh uses tags above to decorate form

Show the form

Now that you have a very simple view associated with the create message action, you can add some markup that will allow users to enter the details of a message. Modify `message/create.gsp` as shown here:

```
<%@ page contentType="text/html;charset=UTF-8" %>
<html>
<head>
    <meta http-equiv="Content-Type"
            content="text/html; charset=UTF-8"/>
    <meta name="layout" content="main"/>
    <title>Post Message</title>
</head>
<body>
<g:form action="save" class="inputform">
    <fieldset>
        <dl>
            <dt>Title
                <span class="requiredfield">required</span>
            </dt>
            <dd><g:textField name="title" value="${message.title}"
                    size="35" class="largeinput"/></dd>
            <dt>Message detail
                <span class="requiredfield">required</span>
```

```
                </dt>
                <dd><g:textArea name="detail" value="${message.detail}"
                        cols="40" rows="10"/></dd>
        </dl>
    </fieldset>
    <g:submitButton name="Save" value="Save"/>
    |
    <g:link action="create">Cancel</g:link>
</g:form>
</body>
</html>
```

The markup above is very similar to plain HTML, with the exception of the Grails tags (with the g namespace). Grails tags are being used for the following:

- Form
- Input fields
- Submit button
- Cancel link

Grails, like many other web frameworks, provides tags to render forms and form elements, reducing the amount of HTML you need to write when creating forms.

In the g:form tag, you specify the Grails action (save, in this case) to be executed when the form is submitted. If no controller is specified, then the current controller will be used. The Grails specific attributes for the g:form tag are:

- controller—which controller to use when constructing the HTML action URL
- action—which action to use when constructing the HTML action URL
- id—which id to add when constructing the HTML action URL
- url—a map containing the controller, action and id to use when constructing the URL

In addition to the above attributes, you can also specify any other attribute which will be passed through to the rendered HTML. This is particularly useful as it allows you to retain full control over the attributes that are defined by the HTML specification.

The use of the g:textField, g:textArea and g:submitButton tags are very similar and simply allow you to specify a name and a value for the form input. Again all the standard HTML attributes for these fields are rendered if you specify them.

Finally, you render a link that will clear any data entered in the form by reloading the **Post Message** page.

To add the required behavior for the **Post Message** page it is necessary to implement the `create` action in the `MessageController` class:

```
def create = {
    return [ message: new Message() ]
}
```

The `create` action simply instantiates a new `Message` object and returns it in a model to be rendered. The model for rendering is constructed as an instance of `Map`, which contains the new `Message` object registered against the key 'message'. When you return a map from an action, the default view is still used for rendering. Additionally, each value in the map is made available to the GSP with the variable name matching its key. In the above example, `create.gsp` will receive a variable called 'message' that is assigned a new instance of the `Message` domain class.

Refresh the **Post Message** page in your browser, and you should see the form as shown in the following screenshot:

Handling user input

You have now created a page that users can enter message data into. The next step is to handle the information that is submitted from this page. The operations you need to perform when the data is received are as follows:

1. Convert the data from an HTTP request into your domain model
2. Validate whether the information entered is acceptable for the application
3. If there are problems with the information, stop executing and let the user know what the problems were
4. If the data is acceptable, persist the data to the database
5. Inform the user that the information has been saved

This is the sort of thing that slows down the development of the web application, but with Grails, it really is a breeze. Make the following highlighted changes to `MessageController.groovy`:

```groovy
package app

class MessageController {
    def create = {
        return [ message: new Message() ]
    }
    def save = {
        def message = new Message( params )
        if( !message.hasErrors() && message.save() ) {
            flash.toUser = "Message [${message.title}] has been added."
            redirect( action: 'create' )
        } else {
            render( view: 'create', model: [message: message] )
        }
    }
}
```

The `save` action performs all the work of binding the request to the domain model, validating the user input, persisting the data to the database and informing the user. Not bad going for very few lines of code!

Binding the request to the domain

On the first line of the `save` action, a new `Message` instance is created from the parameters sent on the request. The `params` property is a map that has been dynamically added to the controller at runtime by Grails. It contains all the request parameters as key/value entries in the map. The default Groovy constructor, which takes a map, is used to populate the properties of `Message` from the `params` map.

When a new instance of a domain class is created from a map, basic type checking validation takes place. If any property on the request is different from those expected by the domain class, then a new instance of the class will still be created and the details of the type conversion errors will be added to the `errors` property of the new instance.

Validate and save

The next line of code in the `save` action performs the validation and attempts to persist the users message to the database.

```
if(!message.hasErrors() && message.save() ) {
```

Grails adds a number of dynamic methods and properties to domain classes at runtime. The following are related to the validation of domain classes:

- `errors` — a property that contains an instance of the spring `Errors` interface: `http://static.springframework.org/spring/docs/2.5.x/api/org/springframework/validation/Errors.html`. This property is populated as a result of data binding or validation.
- `hasErrors` — a method to determine if there are validation errors on an instance of a domain class.
- `validate` — a method to perform validation of the data stored in an instance of a domain class against the constraints defined on the domain class.

When the `hasErrors` method is called in the `save` action, the properties of the message instance will not have been validated against the constraints yet. As mentioned above, only type conversion validation has taken place. However, when the `save` method is executed, the `validate` method is called before the domain class instance is persisted to the database.

Grails adds a `save` method onto all domain classes to persist the contents of the object to the database. This method takes two named parameters, `validate` and `flush`.

- The `validate` parameter tells the `save` method whether to validate the properties of the object against the validation constraints. If the validation fails, the method returns **null** and does not persist the data. This is set to **true** by default.
- The `flush` parameter tells Hibernate whether to make the changes directly in the database, or to batch a number of database operations up together. The default is **false**. This allows Hibernate to control when it persists information to the database.

Flash scope

If the `save` method executes without any validation errors, then our action has been successful, and we can tell the user:

```
flash.userMessage = "Message [${message.title}] has been added."
redirect( action: 'create' )
```

It is common practice to perform a redirect after making an update to persistent storage so that, if a user performs a refresh in their browser, the same data will not be sent again. The problem with this approach is that all the state that exists on the server when the operation took place has been lost because of the redirect. Enter flash scope!

Flash scope has been introduced to provide a scope that holds data between two consecutive HTTP requests. This means that you can construct a message for the user after the data has been saved, when you have the necessary context, and then add these messages to the flash scope so that they are available to the redirected request.

Redirect

Grails adds a `redirect` method, which of course sends a redirect command to the client browser, onto controller classes as syntactic sugar to simplify the operation. When performing a redirect, there are a number of options available.

You can specify the URI to be redirected to:

```
redirect( uri: "home/index" )
```

In your application, this would send the user to `http://localhost:8080/teamwork/home/index`. Or you can specify the entire URL to redirect to:

```
redirect( url: "http://grails.codehaus.org" )
```

If you specify a controller and an action, then Grails will work out the URL to redirect the users to:

```
redirect( controller: "user", action: "list" )
```

This would send the user to `http://localhost:8080/teamwork/user/list`. Alternatively, if you specify only the action:

```
redirect( action: "save" )
```

Then the current controller will be assumed. If the above example was called from an action in `UserController`, then the user would be sent to `http://localhost:8080/teamwork/user/save`. Finally, you can specify an `id` parameter, which will become a part of the URL. You can also specify any number of additional parameters as a `Map` will be converted into parameters on the query string of the URL:

```
redirect( controller: "user", action:"show", id:2, params: [order:
"desc"] )
```

Now the user will be redirected to: `http://localhost:8080/teamwork/user/show/2?order=desc`.

Going back to the application:

```
redirect( action: 'create' )
```

This will redirect the user to the **Post Message** screen once the current message has been created.

Render validation errors

If there are problems with the message, then the validation will fail when the `save` method is called. You will need to show the information back to the user so that they can correct it.

```
render( view: 'create', model:[message: message] )
```

Here, you are telling Grails to render the `create` GSP with the message object that failed the validation.

The `render` method is another dynamic method that Grails adds on to all the controllers. It provides a concise syntax to determine what should be used to render information for the user. Here are some examples:

- `render 'A basic bit of text to be displayed`: This will render some basic text to the response.

- `render(view: 'staticView')`: This will render a GSP called `staticView` under the directory for the current controller. No model has been passed to the view. So only data on the default scopes will be available to the page.

- `render(view: 'create', model: [message: message])`: From your example, the `create` GSP will be rendered with the message object available for rendering.

- `render(template: 'simpleTemplate', model: [data: myData])`: This will render a `template` GSP file with the data provided in the model.

 Templates are used to contain re-usable sections of view rendering logic. You will cover them in more detail as the application grows to a size where it is necessary to remove duplicated presentation code.

Feedback to the user

Now that the users can create messages, you need to change the form to give some feedback so that the user knows what is going on. Modify `message/create.gsp` to show the success message that is added to flash scope if the message is created. In order to show the validation errors that may have stopped a message being created, you can use the following code:

```
<%@ page contentType="text/html;charset=UTF-8" %>
<html>
<head> … </head>
<body>

<g:if test="${flash.toUser}">
    <div id="userMessage" class="info">
        ${flash.toUser}
    </div>
</g:if>

<g:hasErrors bean="${message}">
    <div class="validationerror">
        <g:renderErrors bean="${message}" as="list"/>
    </div>
</g:hasErrors>

<g:form action="save">
...
</g:form>

</body>
</html>
```

The section of highlighted code checks to see if there is a message for the user in flash scope. If so, the message is displayed. Remember that a `userMessage` is added to flash scope when a message is successfully saved by the `save` action on `MessageController`.

The second section renders a list of the validation errors that occurred when the form was last submitted. The `g:hasErrors` tag checks whether the `errors` property for the specified object contains any errors. The `g:renderErrors` tag renders the errors associated with the bean, using a default message for each error as an unordered list.

You should now be able to go back to the application and create messages as shown in the screenshot:

In addition, validation of user input should also be working:

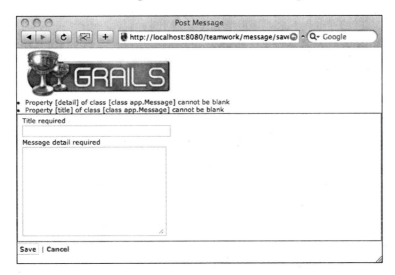

You have now implemented the first part of one of your user goals—being able to create messages that can be shared with other users of the application. You have managed it with two very simple classes and another equally simple GSP. The next step is to allow all the messages that have been created to be viewed.

Create a home page

Given that the application only allows people to create messages at the moment, you might as well just make the home page show all the messages that have been created. To get the home page up and running, you will need to do the following:

- Create a new controller for the home page to retrieve all messages
- Create a new GSP to display the messages
- Modify the main layout to use the right stylesheet for your application

HomeController

The HomeController will retrieve the information to be displayed on the home page. This needs one action, to retrieve the messages from the database in the descending order of date. Create a file called HomeController.groovy in the grails-app/controllers/app directory and add the following code:

```
package app

class HomeController {

    def index = {
        def messages = Message.list( sort: 'lastUpdated',
                order: 'desc' )
        return [messages: messages]
    }
}
```

The index action is the default action for controllers. This allows users to access the action without having to specify the action name on the URL. Both the following URLs would execute this action:

- http://localhost:8080/teamwork/home/index
- http://localhost:8080/teamwork/home

List all messages

You can query the database for instances of Message using the list method that Grails adds on to all the domain classes. By default, the list method will return all the objects of the class the method is called on. In your example, you specify that the lastUpdated property will be used for sorting, and that the sort order will be descending.

The following are valid parameters for the `list` method:

Parameter	Description	Default
max	The maximum number of results to return	none
offset	The offset from the first result to start retrieving from	0
order	The sort order to apply to results; must be either 'desc' or 'asc'	none
ignoreCase	Whether to ignore the case when sorting	true
fetch	The Hibernate fetch policy for object's associations. This is specified as a Map where the key is the name of the property on the object and the policy is defined in the value.	The default is 'lazy' for all associations.

Apart from the current usage, some examples will illustrate these parameters:

- `Message.list()`: This will retrieve all instances of the `Message` from the database.

- `Message.list( sort: 'lastUpdated', order: 'desc', max: 20 )`: This will retrieve the twenty most recently updated messages.

- `Message.list( sort: 'lastUpdated', order: 'desc', offset: 20, max: 20 )`: This will retrieve the twenty next most recently updated messages.

- `Message.list( fetch: [ user: 'eager' ] )`: This will retrieve all instances of message and populate the `user` property. When the default fetch strategy (lazy loading) is used, the `user` property on the `message` objects will not be populated. Instead, Hibernate will wait until the `user property` is accessed, and then load the related user data from the database. Currently, there is no `user` property on `Message` this will change in Chapter 5, where you will see why and when to specify the fetch strategy.

Home page view

Now to work on the **Home Page** view, you must create a GSP file called `index.gsp` in the `grails-app/views/home` directory and replace its contents with the following:

```
<%@ page contentType="text/html;charset=UTF-8" %>
<html>
<head>
    <meta http-equiv="Content-Type"
            content="text/html; charset=UTF-8"/>
    <meta name="layout" content="main"/>
```

```
        <title>Home</title>
    </head>
    <body>

    <h2>Messages</h2>
    <g:if test="${flash.toUser}">
        <div id="userMessage" class="info">
            ${flash.toUser}
        </div>
    </g:if>

    <g:each in="${messages}" var="message">
        <div class="amessage">
            <div class="messagetitle">
                ${message.title}
            </div>
            <div class="messagebody">
                ${message.detail}
            </div>
        </div>
    </g:each>

    </body>
    </html>
```

The aim of the home page is to show a list of all the messages that have been posted in the descending order of date.

You should recognize the first block of code on the home page. It will display a user message that has been added to the flash scope. This has been included because users will be sent to the home page once they have created a message in future.

The second highlighted section iterates through the list of messages that have been retrieved from the database by the index action in HomeController. It then prints out the title and the detail of the message. The Grails each tag allows you to specify the collection to be iterated over using the in attribute. You then declare the variable name to be used for each item using the var attribute.

Before viewing the home page to check that everything is working, add some messages to the BootStrap class, so that you have the test data available whenever you restart the application:

```
import app.Role
import app.Message

class BootStrap {

    def init = { servletContext ->
        def user = new Role(name: 'User').save()
        def admin = new Role(name: 'Administrator').save()

        new Message( title:'The Knights Who Say Nee',
                detail:'They are after a shrubbery.' ).save()
        new Message( title:'The Black Knight',
                detail:"Just a flesh wound." ).save()
        new Message( title:'air speed velocity of a swallow',
                detail:"African or European?" ).save()
    }
    def destroy = {
    }
}
```

You should now be able to go to the URL for the home page
(`http://localhost:8080/teamwork/home`) and see the list of messages that
have been posted so far, with the most recent message at the top.

need to restart app to pick up changes to boot strap

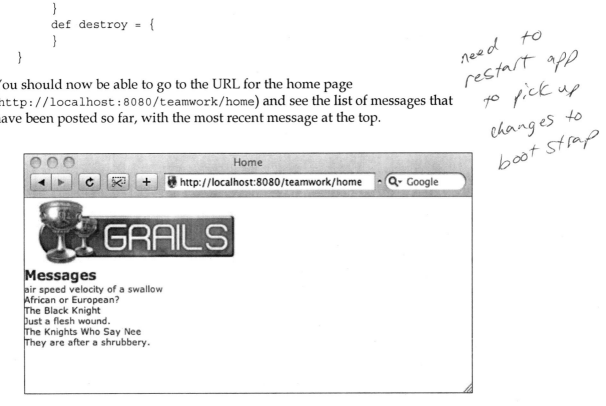

Styles and navigation

In a remarkably short time, you have been able to allow users to create and share messages with other people through the teamwork application. The remaining changes you need to make for now are to:

- Make the **Home Page** the default page for the users
- Allow users to navigate to the **Post Message** page
- Change the stylesheet for the application

Set the default page

As you saw earlier in this chapter, the default mapping for URLs in a Grails application is to use the first path after the application context to match the controller, and the second path to match the action. So `http://localhost:8080/teamwork/message/create` would execute the `create` action on `MessageController`. However, it is possible to override this default behavior. The class `UrlMappings.groovy` in the `grails-app/conf` directory allows you to specify different mapping rules. You will learn about this in more detail later when you create a REST service interface for your application. For now, you are going to create a mapping for the default page of the application to be handled by `HomeController`:

```
class UrlMappings {
    static mappings = {
        "/$controller/$action?/$id?"{
            constraints {
              // apply constraints here
            }
        }
        "/"(controller:'home', action:'index')
        "500"(view:'/error')
    }
}
```

Make the changes highlighted above. You will now be presented with the application home page when you go to `http://localhost:8080/teamwork`.

Update the layout

You need to create some application navigation that will allow users to navigate from the home page to the **Post Message** page and back again. The link to the **Post Message** page will only be available from the home page. But there should be a link to the home page available as a 'global navigation' element, so you will add this to the main layout.

Open `grails-app/view/layouts/main.gsp` and make the following highlighted changes:

```
<html>
<head>
    <title><g:layoutTitle default="Grails"/></title>
    <link rel="stylesheet" href="${createLinkTo(dir: 'css', file:
'teamwork.css')}"/>
    <link rel="shortcut icon" href="${createLinkTo(dir: 'images',
file: 'favicon.ico')}" type="image/x-icon"/>
    <g:layoutHead/>
    <g:javascript library="application"/>
</head>
<body>
<div id="header">
    <h1><g:link controller="home">Teamwork</g:link></h1>
</div>
<div id="navigationcontainer">
    <span id="navigation">
        <g:link controller="home" class="navigationitem">Home</g:link>
    </span>
</div>
<g:layoutBody/>
</body>
</html>
```

You will need to download the `teamwork.css` stylesheet that accompanies this project from `http://www.packtpub.com/files/code/6682_Code.zip` and put it in your `web-app/css` directory. You will also need some images for the navigation, `header_background.png` and `nav_background.png`.

Now, add the link to create new messages to your home page GSP, `views/home/index.gsp`:

```
<%@ page contentType="text/html;charset=UTF-8" %>
<html>
<head> … </head>
<body>
<div class="newactions">
    <span class="newmessage">
        <g:link controller="message" action="create">
            Post Message
        </g:link>
    </span>
</div>
<h2>Messages</h2>
…
</body>
</html>
```

Now you can view the home page, and it should start looking a bit more presentable as shown in the following screenshot:

Using the new stylesheet, the screen for posting messages should be easier to follow, and it will look like this:

Tidying up

Now the application has some basic navigation and is a bit easier to use. Let's take a look at what needs to be finished off before we can move on. You still have the following issues:

- The application is vulnerable to cross-site scripting attacks
- The validation messages could be more meaningful

HTML encoding

You have quite a serious issue at the moment. There is a potential security hole in the application. Message information is not being HTML encoded; so the application is vulnerable to cross-site scripting attacks. To illustrate the issue, create a post with the text: `<script>alert('gotcha');</script>`. Once the post has been created, every time the home page is viewed, the user will see a JavaScript alert box.

This example is going to make life difficult for the users. Bad enough by itself, you could be in serious trouble when exposed to an experienced hacker.

Thankfully, the fix is simple enough. Grails provides a `g:message` tag that is used to look up messages in a message bundle based on a message code. The `g:message` tag also allows you to specify the encoding to be used for the message.

In our `grails-app/views/home/index.gsp` file, you need to make the following highlighted changes:

```
<%@ page contentType="text/html;charset=UTF-8" %>
<html>
<head>
    <meta http-equiv="Content-Type"
            content="text/html; charset=UTF-8"/>
    <meta name="layout" content="main"/>
    <title>Home</title>
</head>
<body>
...
<g:if test="${flash.toUser}">
    <div id="userMessage" class="info">
        <g:message code="posting.new" args="${[flash.toUser]}"
            encodeAs="HTML"/>
    </div>
</g:if>
<g:each in="${messages}" var="message">
    <div class="amessage">
        <div class="messagetitle">
            <g:message code="message.title" args="${[message.title]}"
```

these s/b highlighted!

```
                      encodeAs="HTML"/>
        </div>
        <div class="messagebody">
            <g:message code="message.detail"
                    args="${[message.detail]}" encodeAs="HTML"/>
        </div>
    </div>
</g:each>
</body>
</html>
```

You will also need to add corresponding message codes into your internationalizable message bundle. Grails stores message bundles under the `grails-app/i18n` folder. Open the default `message.properties` file and add the following entries to the bottom of the file:

```
posting.new=You have posted {0}
message.title={0}
message.detail={0}
```

The message tag will look for the message codes supplied and replace the parameters with the values you have passed in the `args` attribute of the message tag. All arguments that are used in a message bundle in this way are encoded as HTML. Refreshing the home page, you will see that the JavaScript alert box is no longer popping up. Instead the JavaScript code is displayed, as it should be.

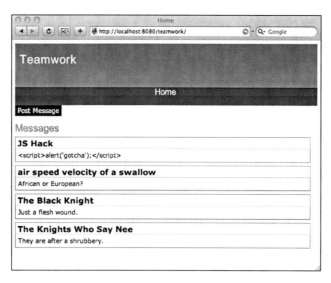

Overriding validation error messages

You saw before that Grails generates default error messages when the validation fails on the user submitting some data. These messages can, and should, be overridden to be more relevant to the application. When a validation error occurs, Grails will look for the related entry in the message bundle. The key that is used is again based on convention. The key is constructed as follows:

```
<classname>.<propertyname>.<constraint>
```

So, if the user doesn't enter a title for the message, the following message key will be used to look up a message:

```
message.title.blank
```

Open up the `messages.properties` file and add the following line at the end:

```
message.title.blank=You must give the message a title!
```

Now, try to create a message without a title and you should see the following:

Now, you need to add messages to the `messages.properties` file for each of the other constraints declared on the `message` class:

```
message.title.size.toobig=The title cannot be longer than 50
characters
message.detail.blank=You must give the message some details
```

Summary

You have now been introduced to most of the basic building blocks of Grails. You have seen how simple it is to create controllers and actions to handle new user requests. You have also seen how to get Grails to bind data from the request to an instance of a domain class and then validate and save it to the database.

GSP provides a very familiar syntax when working with views, and a simple convention is used to look up a default view for a controller and action. The layout mechanism provided by Grails is extremely simple and very powerful, allowing a sitewide structure to be implemented without having to remember to include header and footer files when a new page is created.

You have also seen how Grails supports the use of i18n message bundles. Using message bundles helps you separate the static copy text for your application from the presentation logic and makes it easier to support internationalization, if needed at a later date.

In the next chapter, you will take a whirlwind tour of Groovy that will give you enough understanding to take you through to the end of the book. If you have no previous experience with Groovy, do take the time to go through this chapter, as understanding Groovy will become more important as the application progresses.

4

Introduction to Groovy

The application is at the point now where you need to start getting your hands dirty by writing some of the logic behind it. Before going any further you should take some time to investigate and understand the Groovy language a bit more. A large majority of the code you will write under Grails will be Groovy, so taking the time to understand the contents of this chapter will be well worth it. You will cover the following areas of the Groovy language:

- The similarities to Java
- How to install and run Groovy
- Groovy data structures
- Closures
- Plain old Groovy objects
- Metaprogramming
- Builders

This chapter is not intended to be a complete guide to the Groovy language, but is merely an introduction to what you'll need to complete the example application.

What is Groovy?

Groovy is an object-oriented, dynamic, and functional language for the Java platform. It has a syntax that is very similar to Java and compiles down to Java bytecode; so it can be run in any **JVM(Java Virtual Machine)**.

Object-Oriented

Everything in Groovy is an object. Variables can be defined as a primitive according to Java syntax, but under the hood when Groovy compiles down to bytecode, the variable will become an object.

```
boolean check = null //this is legal in Groovy, but not in Java
```

Because all variables are objects, Groovy is able to implement all operators as method calls. This leads to the following code:

```
1 + 1
```

This code is executed as:

```
1.plus(1)
```

This means you can override operators in Groovy. Here is an example of overriding the plus operator:

```
class Weight {
    int value;
    public Weight plus( Weight other ) {
        return new Weight( value: value + other.value )
    }
}
Weight me = new Weight( value: 100 )
Weight you = new Weight( value: 120 )
Weight total = me + you
assert total.value == 220
```

Dynamic

Groovy leverages a metaprogramming model that allows the structure of defined classes to be altered at runtime. Properties can be injected, and new methods can be defined at runtime.

Groovy uses its dynamic nature to enhance the default JDK at runtime. For example, the JDK contains the class java.lang.String. Groovy provides additional methods, such as toURL(),which can be called from Groovy code. The extensions that Groovy provides to the core JDK classes will be referenced using the abbreviation GDK throughout the rest of this book.

Grails leverages metaprogramming heavily to build a domain-specific language for web development. For example, methods are added to domain objects to allow them to be persisted to (`save`) and retrieved from (`get`) the database. Controllers have methods added at runtime, such as `redirect` and `render`, which allow developers simpler control over the application logic.

Functional

Almost everything is easier to do in Groovy than in Java. A great deal of this is due to the fact that Groovy is able to treat functions (executable blocks of code) as first class objects through its support for closures. At its simplest level, a closure in Groovy is just a block of code that can be passed around as a variable and executed at any point. You will see through the course of this chapter and the rest of the book how powerful this concept is. There is a section later in this chapter dedicated to explaining closures. But for now, here is an example that shows a closure that is assigned to a variable, a closure that is defined inline and a method that receives and executes a closure:

```
//assigning a closure to a variable
def simpleClosure = {
    println 'simple closure called'
}
//declaring a method that will execute a closure
void methodTakingClosure( callback ) {
    callback()
}
//pass the closure into the method to be executed
methodTakingClosure( simpleClosure )
methodTakingClosure {
    println "inline closure called"
}
```

Loosely typed and strongly typed

Groovy takes the best of both worlds by allowing developers to use a mix of strong and loose typing. When declaring a variable in Groovy there is no need to define a type. The following is legal Groovy code:

```
def foo = "some foo"
```

When this is compiled down to Java byte code, it will be equivalent to something like the following in Java:

```
GroovyObject foo = "some foo";
```

Because strong typing is also supported, the following declaration is legal Groovy code:

```
String foo = "some other foo"
```

By being able to define the type, we get the following benefits:

- Transition is easier from Java
- We receive more support from our IDE as it can provide hints like auto-completion from the type
- We can benefit from compile time checking that our code is correct.

Why Groovy?

Groovy is a new language with lots of useful features for making software development simpler, but what about the cost of learning a new language and leaving behind all current investment in learning Java libraries and frameworks? We are going to answer those questions next.

Familiar syntax

Groovy is not Java, but it looks a lot like Java. A good deal of Java **code** can be copied into a Groovy class and run without any modification. This makes **learning** Groovy a fairly simple process, if you come from a Java background.

Direct integration with Java

Groovy classes compile down to Java byte code allowing Java classes to be called from Groovy and vice-versa.

Java class:

```
public class IAmJava {
    public static void main(String[] args) {
        new IAmJava().printSomething();
        new IAmGroovy().printSomething();
    }
    public void printSomething() {
        System.out.println("Something printed from Java");
    }
}
```

Groovy class:

```
class IAmGroovy {
    def printSomething() {
        println "Something printed from Groovy"
    }
}
new IAmJava().printSomething()
new IAmGroovy().printSomething()
```

Running Groovy

To be able to execute the upcoming Groovy examples, you need to look at the options for running Groovy code in a stand-alone environment. This will allow you to experiment with the language features of Groovy in isolation from the Grails framework.

Installing Groovy

The first thing you need to do is install Groovy. Remember that Grails comes bundled with Groovy, so there was no need to install it specifically for our Grails application. If you want to run Groovy code outside of Grails, you will need to install it separately. Here are the installation steps:

- Download the Groovy distributable from http://groovy.codehaus.org/Download
- Extract the archive file to your install location. For example, the tools directory in the root drive
- Create a new environment variable called GROOVY_HOME to reference your Groovy install directory. For example, /tools/groovy-1.5.6
- Modify the PATH environment variable to contain a reference to the GROOVY_HOME/bin directory

So in Windows, your environment variables will now look like this:

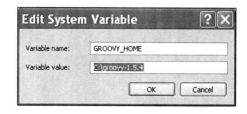

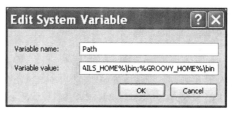

While on a Mac your environment variables would look like:

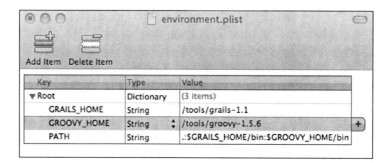

Now, open a command window and run:

`groovy -version`

You should see something like this:

`Groovy Version: 1.5.6 JVM: 1.5.0_13-119`

Some environments may require a restart for the updated environment variables to take effect.

Groovy shell

The Groovy shell is a simple command line program that allows us to quickly spike Groovy code. Running the following from the command line starts the Groovy shell:

```
groovysh
```

You can now enter Groovy code in the shell and have it evaluated immediately. Now enter the following:

```
monkey = 'foo'
```

This will output:

```
foo
```

By evaluating the first line you have created a variable called `monkey` with the value of `foo` that is bound into the context of the Groovy shell. We can now enter:

```
println monkey
```

This will display the following:

```
foo
```

The values bound into the context are retained between the execution of the lines of Groovy code. If you need to remove variables defined in the context of the shell, you can call the `purge` command:

```
purge variables
println monkey
```

This will display the following error, because we have purged all variables declared in the context of the shell:

```
ERROR groovy.lang.MissingPropertyException: No such property: monkey for
class: groovysh_evaluate
        at groovysh_evaluate.run (groovysh_evaluate:2)

    ...
```

The `purge` command is a command specific to the Groovy shell. Run the `help` command to see a full list of the available commands.

Groovy console

The Groovy console is a simple Swing application that allows us to write and execute Groovy scripts. Running the following command from the command line starts the console:

```
groovyconsole
```

Once the console is running, we will see the window as shown in the following screenshot:

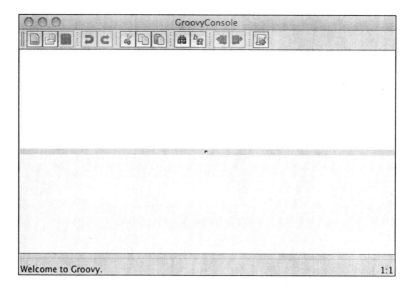

Enter the following code in the console and run it:

```
monkey = 'foo'
println monkey
```

The console should print **foo** at the bottom panel. The console provides some basic syntax highlighting, and also allows us to save and load script files. This makes it a useful starting point for some basic script development and sufficient to run the examples coming later in this chapter.

Execute Groovy scripts

Groovy allows scripts to be executed from the command line.

1. Save the contents of the Groovy console to a file called `firstScript.groovy`,

2. Open a new command line window and go to the directory in which the script has been saved.

3. Now run the following in the command line:

```
groovy firstScript.groovy
```

4. You should see the following output in the command line:

foo

It is possible to precompile Groovy code down to Java byte code, but this is not necessary to follow the examples of this chapter, and Grails manages all compilation of Groovy code for you within the application. You now have enough tools at your disposal to be able to explore the Groovy language in more detail outside the Grails environment.

Groovy classes and scripts

When you create a `.groovy` file, it can be either a class or a script. A class has a very similar structure to a Java class file, with a package declaration at the top, followed by import statements and then the class definition.

```
package example

class ExampleClass {
    def memberVariable
    def static classVariable
    def instanceMethod() {
        return "This is my member variable: ${memberVariable}"
    }
    def static classMethod() {
        return "This is my class variable: ${classVariable}"
    }
}
```

If a `.groovy` file does not contain a class definition, then Groovy will interpret the file as a script rather than a class. Script files are still compiled down to a class in byte code by the Groovy compiler. The advantage of a script is that the overhead of writing and executing a script for a simple Groovy program is much simpler than the Java usage of the `public static void main(String[] args)` signature. Here is an example Groovy script:

```
package example

ExampleClass.classVariable = 'Class 1'
assert ExampleClass.classMethod() == 'This is my class variable: Class
1'

ExampleClass instance1 = new ExampleClass()
```

```
instance1.memberVariable = 'Instance 1'

ExampleClass instance2 = new ExampleClass()
instance2.memberVariable = 'Instance 2'

assert instance1.instanceMethod() == 'This is my member variable:
Instance 1'
assert instance2.instanceMethod() == 'This is my member variable:
Instance 2'

def declaredVariable = 'I am declared'
undeclaredVariable = 'I am undeclared'

assert declaredVariable == 'I am declared'
assert undeclaredVariable == 'I am undeclared'
```

Notice that when you write a script, it is not necessary to explicitly declare a variable. Any variable used will be implicitly declared the first time you assign a value to it.

In the script example above, we are using the **assert** keyword to verify that the results of certain operations adhere to our expectations. In Java, you would need to run your application with asserts turned on. In Groovy, asserts are turned on by default. You will use **assert** frequently throughout this chapter to verify the behavior of Groovy.

Groovy features

You will now embark on a whirlwind tour of some of the language features provided by Groovy. The aim is to give you enough background to continue development of the application.

Semicolons

In Java, the semicolon is used to determine the end of a statement. In Groovy, the use of the semicolon is optional.

```
def knightsSay = 'Ni'
def rabbitsTeeth = 'Fangs';
def name = 'Lancelot'; def favoriteColour = 'blue'

assert knightsSay == 'Ni'
assert rabbitsTeeth == 'Fangs'
assert name == 'Lancelot'
assert favoriteColour == 'blue'
```

We can see that the definition of the first variable does not use a semicolon to end the statement while the second variable definition does. The only real use of semicolons in Groovy is that you can put multiple execution lines of code on the same line in the code:

```
String first, second, third
first = 'one'; second = 'two'; third = 'three'
println first; println second; println third
```

Strings

Groovy provides five separate ways to define a `String`. The first is the basic `Java` `String`. This is defined with single quotes:

```
String myString = 'a basic Java String'
println myString
```

The second way is to use three single quotes, which allows a string to be declared over many lines:

```
String simpleMultiLine = '''
A string that can be split
over many lines
'''
println simpleMultiLine
```

The third is the unfortunately named `GString`, which is declared with double quotes. The power of the `GString` is that it allows you to define placeholders that are executed when the `GString` is declared.

```
String type = 'Groovy'
def gString = "${type} has ${type.size()} characters"
assert gString == 'Groovy has 6 characters'
type = 'Java'
assert gString == 'Groovy has 6 characters'
def otherGString = "${type} has ${type.size()} characters"
assert otherGString == 'Java has 4 characters'
```

As you can see, the `GString` is evaluated when it is declared and subsequent modifications to the variables used as placeholders do not alter it.

The fourth type of String is declared using three double quotes. This allows a String to be defined over a number of lines using placeholders:

```
def to = 'Fred'
def from = 'Tom'
def multiLineString = """
Dear ${to},
This could be a standard letter template.
Yours Sincerely,
${from}
"""

println multiLineString
```

The fifth type of String is known as a `slashy` string. It allows a single backslash character to be interpreted as just a backslash, rather than a marker for some other value.

```
def slashyString = /No need to escape a '\'/
assert slashyString == "No need to escape a '\\'"
```

The benefit of `slashy` strings becomes apparent when performing regular expression matching in Groovy. It is no longer necessary to escape the backslash that is commonly used to define regular expressions. Note that in the following example, Groovy also provides a convenience operator for performing regular expression matching (`==~`).

```
assert 'expectscharacters' ==~ /\w*/
assert !('expectsdigits' ==~ /\d*/)
```

When accessing the contents of a `String`, Groovy provides the convenience of array style subscript operators:

```
def s = 'foo the bar'
assert s[0] == f
assert s[0..<3] == foo
```

Additionally, the GDK adds a number of useful utility methods onto Strings, some of which are demonstrated below:

```
assert 'monkey'.startsWith('mon')
assert 'monkey'.endsWith('key')
assert 'one two'.replace(' ', '_') == 'one_two'
assert 'one two'.tokenize(' ') == ['one', 'two']
assert 'http://www.google.com'.toURL() == new URL('http://www.google.
com')
```

Numbers

Groovy provides the same types for working with numbers that are available in Java. However, it uses two default types if the variable is declared using loose typing. The default for loosely typed numbers is to represent whole numbers as an `Integer` and decimal numbers as a `java.math.BigDecimal`. This default typing can of course be overridden as shown in the following examples:

```
def integer = 1
assert integer.class == Integer

def aLong = 1L
assert aLong.class == Long

def decimal = 1.1
assert decimal.class == BigDecimal

float aFloat = 1.1
assert aFloat.class == Float

def otherFloat = 1.1f
assert otherFloat.class == Float

def aDouble = 1.1d
assert aDouble.class == Double
```

As with Strings, Groovy adds some utility methods to numbers, many of which take closures. In the following examples, all the `times`, `downto`, `upto`, and `step` methods take a closure as a parameter.

Here are some examples of the methods added to the Number interface by Groovy:

```
def result = ''
3.times {
    result += it
}
assert result == '012'

result = ''
3.downto(1) {
    result += it
}
assert result == '321'

result = ''
3.upto(10) {
    result += it
}
assert result == '345678910'

assert 4.next() == 5
assert 4.previous() == 3
assert 2.power(4) == 16

result = ''
0.step(10, 2) {
    result += it
}
assert result == '02468'
```

If any of the above makes you uncomfortable, try to remember that numbers are just objects with methods, the same as anything else.

Lists

Lists in Groovy are based on the Java implementation from the `java.util` package. However, the syntax has been drastically modified to make the declaration much simpler. When defining a list using loose typing, Groovy instantiates the `List` as an `ArrayList` class. Lists are declared with the shortcut notation as shown here:

```
def aList = [1, 2, 3]
assert aList.class == ArrayList

List typed = [1, 2]
assert typed.size() == 2
```

The Java syntax for declaring a `list` is still legal, though a bit more long-winded:

```
List list = new ArrayList()
list.add( 1 )
list.add( 2 )
list.add( 3 )
assert list.size() == 3
```

In the same manner that we saw when accessing the characters of a `String`, Groovy makes the `subscript` operator available to access items in a `List`:

```
def accessList = [1, 2, 3]
assert accessList[1] == 2
accessList[1] = 3
assert accessList == [1, 3, 3]
accessList[1] = 2
```

Groovy allows operator overriding, and a number of convenience operators have been supplied for adding items to a list. The `+=` operator has been overridden to provide an equivalent to `list.addAll()`:

```
def addToList = [1, 2]
addToList += 3
assert addToList == [1, 2, 3]
addToList += [4, 5]
assert addToList == [1, 2, 3, 4, 5]
```

The left shift (`<<`) operator appends an object to the `List` and returns the updated `List`:

```
assert ([1, 2, 3] << 4) == [1, 2, 3, 4]
assert ([1, 2, 3] << [4, 5]) == [1, 2, 3, [4, 5]]
```

The `minus` operator has also been overridden to allow a copy of the list to be created that has the specified elements removed:

```
assert ([1, 2, 3, 4] - 4) == [1, 2, 3]
assert ([1, 2, 3, 4] - [2, 4]) == [1, 3]
assert [1, 2, 3, 4].minus( 3 ) == [1, 2, 4]
assert [1, 2, 3, 4].minus( [4, 2] ) == [1, 3]
```

There are also many other utility methods that have been added onto `java.util.List` by the GDK. A nested list can be flattened:

```
assert [1, 2, 3, [4, 5]].flatten() == [1, 2, 3, 4, 5]
```

The items in a list can be merged together into a `String`:

```
assert '1-2-3-4-5' == [1, 2, 3, 4, 5].join('-')
```

A `list` can be treated as a stack:

```
def stack = [1, 2, 3, 4, 5]
assert stack.pop() == 5
assert stack == [1, 2, 3, 4]
stack.push( 5 )
assert stack == [1, 2, 3, 4, 5]
```

The contents of a list can be reversed:

```
assert [1, 2, 3, 4].reverse() == [ 4, 3, 2, 1]
```

The contents of a list can be sorted:

```
assert [3,1,4,2].sort() == [1,2,3,4]
```

The `collect` method allows a closure to be specified that performs an operation on each item of the specified list and creates a new list from the return value of each closure call.

```
assert [1, 2, 3, 4].collect {it * 2} == [2, 4, 6, 8]
```

The `find` method takes a closure that checks whether each item in the array matches the specified criteria. When the first item of the list is 'found', it is returned and no more items are checked in the list.

```
assert [1, 2, 3, 4].find {it > 2} == 3
```

The `findAll` method is similar to the `find` method. It returns all the items in the original list that match the criteria specified in the closure.

```
assert [1, 2, 3, 4].findAll {it > 2} == [3, 4]
```

Before leaving `Lists`, it is important to mention generics. Groovy doesn't support them. Perhaps a little confusingly, it does allow you to define collections with generic types, but it just ignores the generics definition:

```
List<String> listOfStrings = new ArrayList<String>()
listOfStrings.add( 'a string' )
listOfStrings.add( 123 ) //should not be allowed
assert listOfStrings[0].class == String
assert listOfStrings[1].class == Integer
```

Maps

Maps in Groovy are enhanced in a very similar manner to the `List` class. They can be declared with a much simpler syntax, and provide a number of syntax improvements when putting and retrieving values to and from the `Map`. As with Lists, a number of useful methods are added dynamically by the GDK. The default implementation used when declaring a `Map` is the `LinkedHashMap`:

```
def aMap = ['key1': 'a', 'key2': 'b', 'key3': 'c']
assert aMap.getClass() == LinkedHashMap
```

Commas within the square brackets separate the entries of the map. The key for the map entry is defined to the left of the colon, while the value for the map entry is defined to the right of the colon.

Groovy provides three syntax options when accessing maps. The first is the normal Java syntax, using the `get` method on the `java.util.Map` interface. The second is the subscript notation that is used for arrays. In this case, the value supplied is a key for an entry in the map. The third option is to specify the key as a property on the map object:

```
assert 'c' == aMap.get('key3')
assert 'b' == aMap['key2']
assert 'a' == aMap.key1
```

A number of utility methods are added to maps by the GDK. Here are some familiar examples that appeared in the lists section:

```
def found = aMap.find{ it.key >= 'key2' }
assert found.key == 'key2'
assert found.value == 'b'
assert found.getClass() == LinkedHashMap.Entry

def foundAll = aMap.findAll{ it.key >= 'key2' }
assert foundAll.size() == 2
assert foundAll.getClass() == HashMap
```

In this case, the default argument (`it`) that is passed into our closure by the `find` and `findAll` methods is the `LinkedHashMap.Entry` object. The first entry that matches the criteria defined in the closure is returned by the `find` method, whereas a `HashMap` of entries that match is returned by the `findAll` method.

Ranges

A range is a new data type introduced by Groovy to simplify iteration and work with collections. A range has an upper and a lower bound and represents all values, inclusive, between the upper and lower bounds. A range is defined by separating two numbers by a double dot:

```
assert (1..3).contains(2)
```

The main use of ranges is to simplify iteration and make control structures more meaningful. The output of the two control loops shown here is the same. But the second loop that uses Groovy ranges is much more literate than the old way of looping in Java.

```
def oldResult = ''
for( int i=1; i<=3; i++) {
    oldResult += i
}
assert oldResult == '123'

def result = ''
for(item in 1..3) {
    result += item
}
assert '123' == result
```

A range is a collection that can be accessed in the same way as other collections in Groovy:

```
def aRange = 1..3

assert aRange.size() == 3
assert aRange[0] == 1
assert aRange.contains(2)
```

Ranges can be declared as half exclusive, which means that the contents of the range do not include the upper bound. The notation ..< is used to declare a half exclusive range.

```
def secondResult = ''
(1..<3).each { secondResult += it }
assert '12' == secondResult
```

```
assert (1..3).contains(3)
assert (1..3).size() == 3
assert !(1..<3).contains(3)
assert (1..<3).size() == 2
```

A final note of interest is that ranges are implemented as lists. The underlying object `IntRange` is constructed when a range is defined. This class extends `AbstractList`, so all the operations that are available for lists are also available for ranges.

```
def rangesAreLists = (1..3)
assert rangesAreLists instanceof IntRange
assert rangesAreLists instanceof java.util.List
assert rangesAreLists == [1, 2, 3]
rangesAreLists += 4
assert rangesAreLists == [1, 2, 3, 4]
```

Truth and equality

Groovy handles boolean checks in a manner different from Java. In Java, a boolean check can be performed only against the primitive boolean type. Groovy allows a boolean check to be performed on any object. Given that everything in Groovy is an object, this means that anything can be evaluated to `true` or `false`. Because all objects do not map directly to a boolean value, Groovy defines some rules for boolean comparison.

The Boolean type is as would be expected:

```
assert true
assert !false
```

Strings and GStrings must not be empty:

```
assert 'something'
assert !''
```

Numbers must not be zero:

```
assert 1
assert 1.1
assert !0
assert !0.0
```

Lists must not be empty:

```
assert [1, 2, 3]
assert ![]
```

Maps must not be empty:

```
assert [1: 'one', 2: 'two']
assert ![:]
```

If an object is null, it is always `false`:

```
def nullObject
def instantiated = new Object()

assert instantiated
assert !nullObject
```

There is also a slight difference in Groovy when checking for equality. You saw earlier that operators can be overridden by implementing the corresponding method on the objects representing the operands. In the given example, the `plus` method was overridden. In the same way that the + operator corresponds to the `plus` method, the == operator corresponds to the `equals` method, which allows the == operator to be used in all cases when checking equality. For example, the following code would not work in Java, because the two `String` objects would have a different identity:

```
String s1 = "a string"
String s2 = "" + s1
assert s1 == s2
```

However, in Groovy this code is fine.

Closures

So far, everything we have seen in Groovy can be treated as syntactic sugar on top of Java. Actually everything in Groovy is syntactic sugar over Java as it all compiles down to Java byte code in the end. But, there have been no big language changes. Closures are a little bit different. As mentioned earlier, closures are blocks of code that can be passed around as arguments to a method and executed anywhere. By declaring code in a closure, the code can be used anywhere because it exists as a first class object. A major difference between methods and closures, which at first glance look similar, is that a method cannot be made available to any other part of an application without passing the class that owns it.

To illustrate the benefits of this feature, implement the template design pattern to create a performance monitoring utility.

```
import java.util.concurrent.TimeUnit

//the implementation of the timer
def time( codeToTime ) {
    def start = System.nanoTime()
    codeToTime() //execute the code that needs to be timed
```

```
    def end = System.nanoTime()
    def duration = TimeUnit.NANOSECONDS.toMillis( end - start )

    println "-----"
    println "Your code took ${duration} milliseconds to run"
    println "-----"
}

//example usage of the timer
time {
    (1..10000).each {
        print "${it}, "
    }
    println ""
}
```

In the above example, a method is implemented that takes a closure containing the code to time. Now, any code for which you want to get timing information can be declared as an inline closure to be passed to the `time` method. As an exercise, implement this in Java and compare the solutions.

Closure definitions can also be assigned to variable names to allow them to be reused:

```
def doubleIt = {
    return it * 2
}
(1..3).collect(doubleIt) == [2, 4, 6]
[1, 4, 5].collect(doubleIt) == [2, 8, 10]
```

In the above example, you have defined a closure called `doubleIt`. Notice that this is equivalent to a variable declaration that points to a piece of executable code. We can then pass this variable to methods that take closure arguments, and the closure will be executed when required.

Plain old Groovy objects

Groovy provides language-level support for working with the properties of an object. The following example shows some of the help you receive:

```
//properties are published as getters and setters automatically
class MyPogo {
    def prop1
    String prop2
}

MyPogo pogo = new MyPogo()
```

```
pogo.prop1 = 1..4
pogo.setProp2 ("A String")
assert pogo.getProp1()[0] == 1
assert pogo.prop2 == "A String"
//default constructor uses a Map to populate properties
MyPogo pogo2 = new MyPogo(prop1: [1, 2, 3], prop2: 'Other String')
//simplified reflection
assert pogo2['prop1'] == [1, 2, 3]
assert pogo2.properties['prop2'] == "Other String"
```

You have created a class called MyPogo, which has two properties. Because these properties are defined with default scope, Groovy makes them accessible through getters and setters, as defined by the Java Beans specification. We can see in the example code when we manipulate the pogo instance we are able to call the properties directly, or use the methods defined by the Java Bean specification. This is because Groovy will treat attempts to access a field directly as a call to the relevant getXxx or setXxx method for the property instead.

If you need to bypass the properties and access the field directly, you can use the following notation:

```
assert pogo2.@prop2 == "Other String"
```

Another useful feature Groovy provides when working with plain old Groovy objects is that if no constructor is specified, a default constructor is provided that takes a map. So we can set the values of the properties with a syntax that resembles named arguments.

Groovy also provides some simplified notation for performing reflection on POGOs by allowing the subscript operator to be used to specify the property name to be accessed. Finally, Groovy also exposes all properties on an object as a Map that can be accessed by calling the properties property.

Metaprogramming

The reason why Groovy is able to add so many useful methods to the existing JDK classes is metaprogramming. Through Groovy metaprogramming it is possible to:

- Add new methods and properties to classes and objects at runtime
- Intercept method calls
- Pretend methods exist on objects by handling missing method invocation

As we have demonstrated above, the GDK provides a lot of useful utility methods to the existing JDK classes using metaprogramming. Grails also uses this feature to add persistence methods (save, get, delete, and so on) to our domain objects.

Adding dynamic behavior

Here is an example of how easy it is to add methods and properties to a class at runtime by accessing the `MetaClass` of a class:

```
class Vanilla {
    def whoAmI() {
        return 'Vanilla'
    }
}
//dynamic instance methods can be added
Vanilla.metaClass.save = {
    return 'saved'
}
//dynamic class methods can be added
Vanilla.metaClass.'static'.init = {
    return new Vanilla();
}
//dynamic properties can be added in the same way
Vanilla.metaClass.request = [:]

def vanilla = new Vanilla()
//calling the dynamically added instance method
assert vanilla.save() == 'saved'

//using the dynamically added property
vanilla.request.method = 'GET'
assert vanilla.request.method == 'GET'

//calling the dynamically added class method
def newInstance = Vanilla.init()
assert newInstance.class == Vanilla
```

Note that each method added to the `metaClass` is actually a closure. Because a closure contains a block of code that can be assigned to a variable and executed from anywhere, it is a perfect construct for dynamically adding behavior to classes.

The great pretender

All Groovy classes implement the `GroovyObject` interface; `GroovyClassGenerator` assigns this interface, where a default implementation of the interface is also provided. It is the `GroovyObject` interface that provides the `metaClass` property, which as you saw above, allows methods to be added dynamically to a class. The `GroovyObject` interface also provides a method called `invokeMethod`. This method is called if a method that was requested by client code does not exist. You can pretend that your class supports any method by implementing `invokeMethod`, as shown here:

```
class JustPretend{
    public Object invokeMethod(String name, Object args) {
        println "So you want to call ${name}. OK no problem"
        return null;
    }
}

def pretend = new JustPretend()

pretend.canWeDoThis()
pretend.whatAboutThis()
pretend.surelyThereIsNoWayWeCanDoThis()
pretend.doSomethingWithThese( 'first', 'second', 'third' )
```

Being able to pretend that methods exist on objects is used heavily in the Groovy implementation of builders.

It is worth mentioning that to implement an application in Grails, you will not need to perform any metaprogramming, and it is probably best avoided until you are a little more familiar with Groovy. However, if you are keen to start playing around with metaprogramming, you will get your chance in Chapter 13, where you will learn how to create your own plug-in for Grails!

Builders

The builder design pattern was documented in the famous Gang of Four book, *Object-Oriented Design Patterns*. The aim was to be able to construct a complex object tree in one repeatable manner and swap out the implementation that performs the construction at any point, while leaving the interface to remain the same. Groovy provides a particularly literate syntax for constructing builders through a combination of closures and metaprogramming.

Consider the code below that constructs an object graph to represent the structure of a book:

```
import groovy.xml.MarkupBuilder

def buildBook( builder ) {
    builder.book {
        title( 'Web Application Development' )
        chapters {
            chapter( title: 'Introduction To Grails' )
            chapter( title: 'Manage Users With Scaffolding' )
            chapter( title: 'Post Messages' )
            chapter( title: 'Introduction To Groovy' )
        }
```

```
        author( name: 'Jon Dickinson' )

    }

}

def writer = new StringWriter()
def builder = new MarkupBuilder(writer)

buildBook( builder )

println writer
```

Looking at the `buildBook` method, you can see that it is made up of an easy-to-read nested node structure. This is Groovy builder syntax. Each of the nested code blocks is a closure, and each of the *nodes* is a method call on the builder object. In the above example, an instance of `MarkupBuilder` has been passed into the method. However, the `buildBook` method could just as easily receive a PDF builder or bookstore kiosk builder. Each of these would require special implementation to produce the required output from the defined structure. But the client code in the `buildBook` method that declares the book information would remain unchanged.

`MarkupBuilder` is one of the builders that come already implemented with Groovy. Running this code would produce the following XML:

```
<book>
  <title>Web Application Development</title>
  <chapters>
    <chapter title='Introduction To Grails' />
    <chapter title='Manage Users With Scaffolding' />
    <chapter title='Post Messages' />
    <chapter title='Introduction To Groovy' />
  </chapters>
  <author name='Jon Dickinson' />
</book>
```

Grails makes good use of builders to help provide a domain-specific language for web development. Take a look at the code you have written already, and see if you can spot any builders being used. Pay special attention to the domain objects.

Summary

You have now completed your whirlwind tour of the Groovy language. You have seen the basics of Groovy syntax and the data structures that are core to Groovy. There are some important differences between Java and Groovy, but there are also enough similarities to make you feel at home. Closures are one of the big new ideas introduced by Groovy to the Java platform, and you will continue to make good use of them as the application progresses.

There is a lot more that you can do with Groovy, but hopefully, the topics covered in this chapter will give you enough confidence so that you can continue with the implementation of the application.

Now, let's get back to Grails and building the application.

5

Authentication with JSecurity Plug-in

Now that you have a decent understanding of Groovy, you can carry on building the application. You currently have user administration screens that are being handled by Grails scaffolding, and users can create messages that are visible on the home page. Before adding any new features, you will learn how to leverage Grails plug-ins to add new behavior to your application. You will use a security plug-in to secure the application, so that only the authenticated users can post and view messages, and only the administrators are able to manage users.

Grails provides a plug-in mechanism that makes it easy to integrate other development frameworks and allows them to interact with our application. There are ranges of plug-ins that cover areas such as:

- Security
- Searching
- Rich user interfaces
- Testing
- Performance
- Web services
- Content syndication
- Workflow
- Reporting and so on

The plug-in architecture enables developers to seamlessly integrate external frameworks into Grails. A plug-in can make available a number of artifacts, from domain classes to static resources, as well as taking part in build and runtime events of a Grails application.

The core Grails features are implemented as plug-ins, so the plug-in architecture is at the very heart of Grails. For example, the GORM is a core plug-in that allows Grails applications to persist domain classes via the Hibernate framework. The addition of dynamic behavior to controller classes is implemented through the core controller plug-in.

A large number of optional plug-ins have already been implemented for Grails, and the full list can be found on the Grails web site (http://www.grails.org/Plugins). You will make use of more plug-ins as development of the application continues to integrate feature-rich frameworks with the minimum amount of effort.

In this chapter, you will use the JSecurity plug-in to handle authentication and authorization logic. JSecurity is an open source authentication framework for Java applications. The project site can be found here: http://www.jsecurity.org/.

Where to find plug-ins

A list of the available plug-ins can be found from the Grails web site, or by running the list-plugins script provided with Grails. In your command window run:

```
grails list-plugins
```

This will take a while to run for the first time, as it retrieves the list from a web service and caches the information for future use.

Installing a plug-in

If you go to the plug-ins page on the Grails site, you will see that there are a few that deal with authentication. You are going to use JSecurity as it is fairly easy to integrate with an existing domain model.

As of release 1.1, Grails plug-ins are installed to your user account directories by default. For example, if I were to install the JSecurity plug-in, it would end up in the following location: /Users/jondickinson/.grails/1.1/projects/teamwork/plugins/jsecurity-0.3.

This default location could cause a number of problems such as:

- Other users may not be able to execute the plug-in
- If the name of the project is changed, you must remember to dig around in your user directory to change the installation location of the plug-in

To help avoid these problems, Grails provides a useful mechanism to allow plug-ins to be stored anywhere on a developer's file system. You simply have to specify the desired plug-in location in a Groovy script file called `BuildConfig.groovy`. Create this new file under the `grails-app/conf` directory and add the following to the file:

(handwritten margin note: override the default plug-in loc)

```
grails.project.plugins.dir="/tools/grails-plugins"
```

Now, rather than use a directory structure under your personal user account, Grails will look for plug-ins, and install new plug-ins into this directory.

To install the JSecurity plug-in, make sure that the new directory exists, go to the `teamwork` directory in your command window and run:

```
grails install-plugin jsecurity
```

Once the plug-in has finished installing, open up the **plugins** directory. You can see that a folder called **jsecurity-0.3** has been created with the name and the version number of the plug-in. The version number may be slightly different when you run this script. At the time of writing, the current release version for the plug-in was 0.3. Open the **jsecurity-0.3** folder, and you will see a window as shown in the following screenshot:

(handwritten margin note: Note — IDEA did not pick up the config'd directory; perhaps as last would've h|pd?)

Every Grails plug-in is structured as its very own application, allowing it to include executable application artifacts such as controllers, domain classes, web pages, and so on. This allows plug-in developers to implement and test their plug-ins without needing to import them into a real application. The `grails-app` folder for an installed plug-in contains all the artifacts that are made directly available to your application. The JSecurity plug-in provides a number of tag libraries that allows you to perform logic based on the authenticated status of the current user. You will see how to use these tags towards the end of this chapter.

When a plug-in is installed, it can make scripts available to the application that will allow you to perform set up and build tasks related to the plug-in. The JSecurity plug-in provides the following additional scripts:

- `CreateAuthController` — Creates the authentication controller that allows users to login.

- `CreateDbRealm` — Creates a default set of domain objects to represent users, roles, and permissions. A realm is also generated to perform authentication against the created domain objects.

- `CreateLdapRealm` — Creates a realm to perform authentication against an LDAP server.

- `QuickStart` — Executes the `CreateDbRealm` and the `CreateAuthController` scripts.

The supporting code to integrate the JSecurity framework with Grails is supplied in the `src` folder. This folder also contains a number of template files that are used by the scripts to generate the default artifacts such as domain classes and controllers.

The `application.properties` and `plugin.xml` files are used to define metadata about the plug-in. For example, author, version number, documentation location, included resources, and so on. The Groovy class `JsecurityGrailsPlugin.groovy` is the initialization class for the plug-in. This is where plug-in developers can add objects into the Spring context and add dynamic methods to Grails classes at runtime. You will see how to do this in Chapter 13, when you build your own plug-in.

Configuring JSecurity plug-in

The JSecurity plug-in comes with a quick start script that will let you get up and running with user management very easily. However, the default domain model used by JSecurity is more complicated than your current simple model that contains only a `User` and a `Role` class. You will not use the quick start script, but will implement your own authentication realm and use the `CreateAuthController` script to generate the login action and page.

How does JSecurity work?

JSecurity is a security framework for authentication, access control, cryptography, and session management. It is based on the concepts of roles, permissions, subjects, principles, and realms.

- A role is used to determine whether a particular user has access to a set of resources. In your application, users with the 'Administrator' role will be allowed access to any page. On the other hand, users with the 'User' role will be allowed access to the entire site, apart from the user and role management pages.

- Permissions provide a finer grained level of control over roles. For example, a role may determine whether a user is allowed access to the user management screens, whereas different permissions may be used to determine whether the user can edit, create, or view user details. Your application will not use permissions.

to bad

- A subject is a real person accessing the application, or an instance of User in our domain model.

- A principle is the information we use to uniquely identify a subject. In your application, this is the username property of a user.

- A realm is the glue that performs authentication, to determine if the user is allowed access to the system, and authorization, to determine if the authenticated user is allowed to perform the action they have requested.

You already have the roles (the Role class), subjects (the User class), and principles (the username property) defined for the application. The next step is to implement a realm that will glue all of this together to handle authentication and authorization.

More about realms

Realms are implemented as Groovy classes and must adhere to the following conventions:

- They must be placed in the directory grails-app/realm. If this directory does not exist, you will need to create it.

- The class name must end with 'Realm'. Your realm will be called TeamworkRealm.

While a realm doesn't need to implement an interface or extend a subclass, it should specify the following properties and methods:

- The authTokenClass property is used to define the type of authentication token that should be expected, which is commonly the UsernamePasswordToken. If this property is not specified, then the realm will not be used for authentication.

- The authenticate(authToken) method verifies whether a user has provided the correct authentication details.

- The `hasRole(principal, roleName)` method returns a `boolean` to show whether the user has the specified role.

- The `isPermitted(principle, permission)` method determines whether the user has the specified permission.

Create a simple realm

To create the realm, you will need to make sure that there is a folder called `realms` under the `grails-app` directory of our application. Now create a new file called `TeamworkRealm.groovy` and add the following code into the new file:

```
import org.jsecurity.authc.UnknownAccountException
import org.jsecurity.authc.SimpleAccount
import org.jsecurity.authc.IncorrectCredentialsException
import app.User
class TeamworkRealm {
    static authTokenClass = org.jsecurity.authc.UsernamePasswordToken
    def credentialMatcher
    def authenticate(authToken) {
        return true
    }
    def hasRole(principal, roleName) {
        return true
    }
    def isPermitted(principal, permission) {
        return true;
    }
}
```

The first important element of the code above is the `authTokenClass` property. This tells JSecurity the information that the user will submit to perform authentication. You have specified that a user will submit their username and password when logging in.

The next line defines a property called `credentialMatcher`. By defining this property, you allow the plug-in to inject a JSecurity credential matcher through Spring that will check whether the username and password entered by the user match the username and password stored in the database. The main use of the credential matcher is to encrypt the password that the user has entered, so it can be compared to the encrypted password in the database (more on encrypting passwords will be covered later in this chapter). The plug-in creates a `Sha1CredentialsMatcher` in the Spring context with the name, `credentialMatcher`.

You have also implemented stubs for each of the required methods authenticate, hasRole and isPermitted. If this authentication realm were used as is, by entering any username and password combination, a user would be authenticated with all possible roles and permissions! This is obviously not what we want.

Implement authenticate

To make sure only valid users are allowed to access the application, you must implement the authenticate method.

```
def authenticate(authToken) {
    def user = User.findByUsername(authToken.username)
    if (!user) {
        throw new UnknownAccountException("No account found for user
[${authToken.username}]")
    }

    def account = new SimpleAccount(user.username, user.password,
"TeamworkRealm")
    if (!credentialMatcher.doCredentialsMatch(authToken, account)) {
        throw new IncorrectCredentialsException("Invalid password for
user '${authToken.username}'")
    }
    return account
}
```

This method receives an authToken of the type defined by the authTokenClass property (UsernamePasswordToken for your implementation). Most of the code in this method is concerned with making JSecurity perform the authentication of the username and password submitted by the user.

Pay special attention to the first line of this method. You have already seen that Grails makes it easy to retrieve all objects of a particular type by adding a list method to domain classes. Grails also adds a 'dynamic finder' method to domain classes which makes retrieval of a specific domain object instance trivial.

```
def user = User.findByUsername(authToken.username)
```

With this one line of code, you are querying the database for the user with the supplied username and populating an instance of the User domain class. Here, Grails is using GORM to query the database and populate the object. Impressively, reading a ResultSet and populating a new instance of User class (which would normally also require an SQL query) can be performed in one simple and readable line of code.

Dynamic finders

Although dynamic finder methods are added to our domain classes dynamically at runtime, it is not the reason they are called 'dynamic'. The name comes from the fact that the actual method names can be dynamically constructed. A variety of methods that are available do not actually exist, but the information provided in the name of the method call is enough for Grails to convert the method call into a query against the database.

Dynamic finder methods are available for all properties on a domain class. Here are some examples of dynamic finders that would be valid for our User class.

```
User bob = User.findByFirstNameLike( 'Bob%' )

User yesterdayUser = User.findByDateCreatedGreaterThan( yesterday )

def users = []

users = User.findAllByFirstNameLikeAndDateCreatedGreaterThan( 'Bob%',
yesterday )
```

From the examples above, you can see that dynamic finders:

- Are not limited to simple equality checks
- Can combine two properties as part of a search term
- findBy will return a single result
- findAllBy will return a list of results

The following illustrations show how some of the examples are constructed. The User.findByUsername example is the simplest, and requires a direct match on the username property in the database:

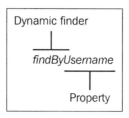

In the next example, User.findByFirstNameLike, a comparison operator (like) is used to match the firstName property rather than equals:

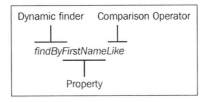

In the final and the most complicated example, you may want to find all the users with a first name like 'Bob' created since yesterday:

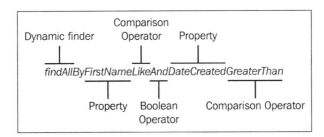

The comparison operators that are available at the time of writing are:

Operator	Description
LessThan	Where the property is less than the value supplied
LessThanEquals	Where the property is less than or equal to the value supplied
GreaterThan	Where the property is greater than the value supplied
GreaterThanEquals	Where the property is greater than or equal to the value supplied
Like	Same as SQL Like operator
Ilike	A case insensitive version of the Like operator
NotEqual	Where the property is not equal to the value supplied
Between	Where the property is between two values
IsNotNull	Where the property is not null
IsNull	Where the property is null
Not	Retrieves objects that are not matched
And	Requires both parts of the finder to be matched
Or	Retrieves objects that match the first, second, or both conditions

does not make clear that the junction operators or and and are limited to two conditions. It is implied however

Implement hasRole

As your security model only includes roles and not permissions, there is no need to implement the `isPermitted` method, other than to always return `true`. The last method to be implemented is `hasRole`. This will determine if an authenticated user is authorized with the given role.

```
def hasRole(principal, roleName) {
    def users = User.withCriteria {
        eq( 'username', principal )
        role {
            eq( 'name', roleName )
        }
    }
    return users.size() > 0
}
```

[handwritten: Using criteria]

The `hasRole` method uses another feature of the GORM, that is, querying by criteria. This approach uses the underlying Hibernate criteria querying capability and allows you to query across object relationships. You will receive a more thorough introduction to querying by criteria in Chapter 8. For now, it is enough to know that you are querying the database for a list of users, where the `username` is equal to the `principal` argument and the user has a role with the `roleName` argument.

Install the authentication controller

Now that you have a realm that allows your application to determine if a user is authenticated and authorized, you need to provide a controller and some actions to receive the users authentication input and send the information to the realm. The JSecurity plug-in comes with a number of scripts to help you set up your application. Now, you can make use of the `CreateAuthController` script. In your terminal window run the following:

```
grails create-auth-controller
```

This script has created a controller (`grails-app/controllers/AuthController. groovy`) and a login page (`grails-app/views/auth/login.gsp`). The controller handles the user authentication actions and the login page allows users to enter their usernames and passwords. The `AuthController` provides the following actions:

- `login` — renders the login page
- `signIn` — receives user input (**Username** and **Password**) and performs authentication against your realm
- `signOut` — logs the user out of the application
- `unauthorized` — renders a view to inform the user that they have requested a resource for which they do not have the required role

If you start up the application and navigate to `http://localhost:8080/teamwork/`
`auth`, you will be presented with the **Login** page, as shown in the following screenshot:

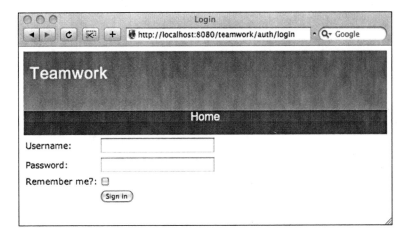

However, users can still click on the **Home** link or navigate directly to the **Create User** page without having to log in.

The authentication filter

It is time to apply the authentication and authorization rules to your application.
JSecurity handles this through a Grails filter. Filters in Grails perform a function
similar to their Java Servlet namesakes. They can be defined for any action on any
controller, and provide three different cut-points for you to hook into. They are:

- `before`: your filter code will be executed before the action, and can stop
  execution of the action if required
- `after`: your filter code will be executed after the action has finished, but
  before the view is rendered
- `afterView`: your filter code will be executed after the view has been rendered
  and just before the response is sent back to the client

The JSecurity filters are concerned with verifying a user's authorization before an
action executes, and so, you must use the `before` cut-point.

Once again, there is no configuration required to create a Grails filter, but a
convention must be followed. The rules for the convention are:

- The filter Groovy class must exist in the `grails-app/conf` directory
- The class name must end in 'Filters'
- The class must have a `filters` closure define

Go to the `grails-app/conf` directory and create the file, `SecurityFilters.groovy`. Add the following code to this file to implement the authorization rules required for our application:

```groovy
class SecurityFilters {
    def filters = {
        auth(controller: "*", action: "*") {
            before = {
                accessControl { true }
            }
        }
        userRoleManagement(controller: "(role|user)", action: "*") {
            before = {
                accessControl {
                    role("Administrator")
                }
            }
        }
    }
}
```

You have defined two filters, `auth` and `userRoleManagement`. The first of these (`auth`) declares that every single action in your application will require authentication. No specific roles are required, but access to every single action will require the user to be authenticated. The `*` notation for the `controller` and `action` attributes represents a wildcard match against the controller and action names. This means that the filter will be applied to all controllers and all actions respectively. The existence of the `accessControl` code block tells JSecurity that it needs to check whether the user is authenticated.

The rules for authorization are defined within the `accessControl` code block. In the `auth` filter, we declare that there are no authorization rules. So, as long as the user is authenticated, it is enough.

 The JSecurity plug-in has added a dynamic method to `FilterContext` called `accessControl`. This method takes a single closure argument. When the method is executed, it first checks whether the user is authenticated and then checks the users roles and permissions against the rules specified in your code block.

The second filter (`userRoleManagement`) implements the first of your authorization rules. This filter will be applied to requests for actions on `RoleController` and `UserController`. The implementation of the `accessControl` code block in this filter declares that the user must have the 'Administrator' role to be authorized to perform these actions.

At this point, you can verify that the security filter is working by restarting the application and trying to access the Home page (`http://localhost:8080/teamwork`) again. Now, when you do this, you are sent to the **Login** page.

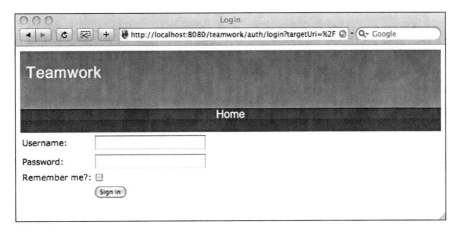

Password encryption

Now that we have the authentication in place, only valid users should be able to access the application. You do have one slight problem as a result of authentication. There are no users in the system, so no one can log in!

Now, revisit the bootstrap data to create one administrator and one user when the application starts up. When you create the new users, you must be sure to encrypt the password. Otherwise, the realm will not be able to match the passwords entered by users from the login page. Our bootstrap class (`grails-app/conf/BootStrap.groovy`) now becomes:

```
import app.Role
import app.Message
import org.jsecurity.crypto.hash.Sha1Hash
import app.User

class BootStrap {

    def init = { servletContext ->
        def user = new Role(name: 'User').save()
        def admin = new Role(name: 'Administrator').save()

        new User(username:'mjones',
                title:'Miss',
                firstName:'Martha',
                lastName:'Jones',
                password: new Sha1Hash("admin").toHex(), role:admin)
                .save()
```

```
        new User(username:'flancelot',
                title:'Mr',
                firstName:'Fred',
                lastName:'Lancelot',
                password: new Sha1Hash("password").toHex(), role:user)
                .save()
        new Message( title:'The Knights Who Say Nee', detail:'They are
after a shrubbery.' ).save()
        new Message( title:'The Black Knight', detail:"Just a flesh
wound." ).save()
        new Message( title:'air speed velocity of a swallow',
                detail:"African or European?" ).save()
    }

    def destroy = {
    }
}
```

In the highlighted code above, you have created two new users: one administrator and one regular user. The passwords for these users have been one-way hashed before being stored in the database.

Before restarting the application, you must make a change to your `User` domain class in which you previously specified that a user's password must be between 6 and 20 characters. Now that passwords are being hashed, it is necessary to store much more than 20 characters for a password. Change the constraint on the password property from:

```
password(blank: false, size:6..20, password:true)
```

To

```
password(blank: false, minSize:6, password:true)
```

Restart the application and try to access the **Home** page by logging in as the new regular user (flancelot/password), you should be able to log in and see the home page. Try to access the **Create User** page (`http://localhost:8080/teamwork/user/create`) as this user, and you will see a *permission denied* message.

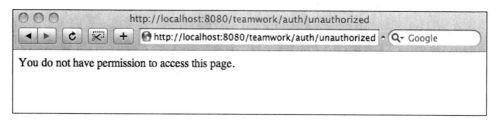

The user has been allowed access to the application because they have entered a valid username and password. However, authorization has been denied when trying to execute the `create` action on `UserController` because they do not have the 'Administrator' role.

Sign out as this user, by going to the URL `http://localhost:8080/teamwork/auth/signOut`, and then sign in again as the administrator user (mjones/admin). You should now be able to access the **Create User** page.

Add the missing pieces

There are three more things that would be worth looking at before we move on from security:

- There is a problem when creating new users in the application, because the password is not being hashed when the user information is submitted through the **Create User** page

- A nicer 'permission denied' page would be better

- You should add a **Sign out** link so that the users don't have to enter the `auth/signOut` URL into the address bar whenever they want to sign out

Encryption of users' passwords

So far, you have been relying on the default behavior of Grails scaffolding to manage users and roles. You have now reached a scenario where it is necessary to add some of your own logic for creating users. However, you want to be able to enhance the existing logic, not replace it entirely. Grails provides another handy script that lets you generate the scaffolding code for a domain class. In your terminal, run:

```
grails generate-all app.User
```

Running this script will re-generate the `UserController` and the view templates necessary for rendering the pages. As this controller already exists (you created it to initialize the dynamic scaffolding) you are prompted to confirm that you want to replace it. Now, enter 'y'.

Open the `UserController` class, and you can see that it has grown substantially. Although, considering the amount of work it does, there doesn't seem to be much code. You need to modify the generated controller in two places to add the encryption of the user's password:

- When the user is created
- When the user is updated

Make the following highlighted changes to the `update` and `save` actions:

```
package app

import org.jsecurity.crypto.hash.Sha1Hash

class UserController {

    def index = { redirect(action:list,params:params) }
    // the delete, save and update actions only accept POST requests
    def allowedMethods = [delete:'POST', save:'POST', update:'POST']

    def list = { … }

    def show = { … }

    def delete = { … }

    def edit = { … }

    def update = {
        def hashPassword = false
        def userInstance = User.get( params.id )
        if(userInstance) {
            if( userInstance.needToHash( params.password) ) {
                hashPassword = true
            }
            userInstance.properties = params
            if(!userInstance.hasErrors() && userInstance.save()) {
                if(hashPassword) {
                    userInstance.password = new Sha1Hash(user.
password).toHex()
                }
                flash.message = "User ${params.id} updated"
                redirect(action:show,id:userInstance.id)
            }
            else {
                render(view:'edit',model:[userInstance:userInstance])
            }
        }
        else {
            flash.message = "User not found with id ${params.id}"
            redirect(action:edit,id:params.id)
        }
    }

    def create = { … }

    def save = {
        def userInstance = new User(params)
        if(!userInstance.hasErrors() && userInstance.save()) {
```

```
        userInstance.password = new Sha1Hash(userInstance.
password).toHex()
            flash.message = "User ${userInstance.id} created"
            redirect(action:show, id:userInstance.id)
        }
        else {
            render(view:'create', model:[userInstance:userInstance])
        }
    }
}
```

For the above code to work, the following method must be added to the User class to determine whether a password has changed, and whether it needs hashing:

```
def needToHash( String password ) {
    return password != this.password
}
```

Hashing the password when the user is created in the save action is simple, as you always need to hash passwords for new users. In the update action however, you need to know if the password has changed before deciding whether to hash the password or not. The interesting point in both of these actions is that you are hashing the password after the hasErrors and save methods have been called on the user object. The reason for performing the password hash after these calls is that if both of them execute correctly, you can be sure that there are no validation errors.

You are able to modify an object after the save method has been called because Grails uses the 'Open Session in View' pattern (http://www.hibernate.org/43.html) for hibernate, which means that the changes to the User object will not actually be persisted to the database until all server-side operations have finished. In this way, you are able to modify the state of your User object any time after the save method has been called, and the data will still be persisted to the database.

Permission denied page

You can very easily create a better experience for users through a custom 'permission denied' page that operates within the context of the application, rather than the default simple text message provided by JSecurity. To do this, you will create a new GSP and modify the unauthorized action in the JSecurity, AuthController.

Create a GSP file under the grails-app/views/auth folder called unauthorized.gsp and then modify the unauthorized action in the AuthController to be empty, as follows:

```
def unauthorized = {}
```

Remember that the rules for looking up the default view for an action are that
Grails looks for a folder matching the controller name (auth) and then for a GSP
file matching the action name (unauthorized). Put the following code in the new
unauthorized.gsp file:

```
<html>
    <head>
        <meta http-equiv="Content-Type" content=
            "text/html; charset=UTF-8"/>
        <meta name="layout" content="main" />
        <title>Permission Denied</title>
    </head>
    <body>
        <div class="nav">
        </div>
        <div class="body">
            <h2>Permission Denied</h2>
            <div class="message">You do not have permission
            to access this page.</div>
        </div>
    </body>
</html>
```

Now try and access the **User List** page and log in as our bootstrapped user
(flancelot/password). You will see the *permission denied* screen, as shown
in the following screenshot:

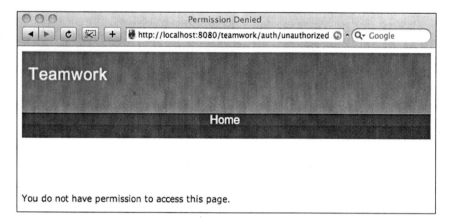

Sign out link

The next change to be made regarding authentication is to add a **Sign out** link, so users don't need to keep entering the auth/signOut action in the address bar. When implementing a **Sign out** link, you need to bear in mind the context in which the sign out action should be performed. Essentially, users who have not logged in should not be able to sign out. Thankfully, JSecurity provides a useful GSP tag that allows you to check if the user is authenticated or not.

To add the **Sign out** link to the site, you need to modify the grails-app/views/layouts/main.gsp layout file to contain the following:

```
<html>
<head> ... </head>
<body>

<div id="header">
    <jsec:isLoggedIn>
        <div id="profileActions">
            <span class="signout">
                <g:link controller="auth" action=
                "signOut">Sign out</g:link>
            </span>
        </div>
    </jsec:isLoggedIn>
    <h1><g:link controller="home">Teamwork</g:link></h1>
</div>

<jsec:isLoggedIn>
    <div id="navigationcontainer">
        <span id="navigation">
            <g:link controller="home" class=
            "navigationitem">Home</g:link>
        </span>
    </div>
</jsec:isLoggedIn>

<g:layoutBody/>
</body>
</html>
```

Now, log in as the user (flancelot/password), and you will see the "**Sign out**" link on the top right corner of the screen, as shown in the following screenshot:

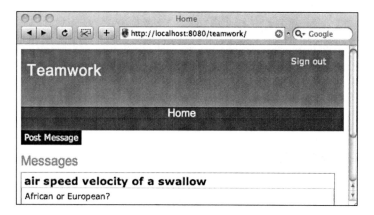

You will notice that the link and the navigation bar disappear once you have signed out.

JSecurity tags

JSecurity provides a number of GSP tags for working with a user's secure state. The available list of tags at the time of writing, in version 0.3, are shown in the following table:

Tag Name	Description
isLoggedIn	Renders the body of the tag if the current user is logged in.
isNotLoggedIn	Renders the body of the tag if the current user is not logged in.
authenticated	Synonym for isLoggedIn
notAuthenticated	Synonym for isNotLoggedIn
user	Renders the body of the tag if the user is either logged in, or has selected the "remember me" checkbox.
principal	Renders the current user's principal. In our application, this will be the username.
hasRole	Renders the body of the tag if the current user has the specified role. Roles are specified either by the name attribute or by the in attribute. If the in attribute is used, a list of roles can be supplied.
lacksRole	Renders the body of the tag if the current user does not have the specified role.
hasPermission	Renders the body of the tag if the current user has the specified permission. Permissions can be specified by type or by permission name, using the permission attribute.
lacksPermission	Renders the body of the tag if the current user does not have the specified permission.

Who posted that?

Now that you have introduced authentication to the application, you will be able to determine which user created a message. This is useful information to be displayed to users of the site, so they know who has posted a particular message.

JSecurity provides a SecurityUtils class that can be used to determine the principle of the user who is logged in. Remember that the principle is the username property on the User class, so you can create a UserService that will encapsulate the logic to get the principal from JSecurity and then load the instance of the User class for the principal.

UserService

Grails also supports the notion of a service layer in your application. Services can be used as utility classes for your application that provide some service to domain or controller classes. For a Groovy class to be recognized as a service, it must live in the `grails-app/services` directory, and the class name must end in "Service". By default, a single instance (singleton) of a service class is created in your application. These services can then be injected into controllers and domain classes by simply declaring a property with the same name as the service. You will learn more about services in Chapter 9, but for now, create your first service to retrieve an instance of `User` from the JSecurity principal.

In your command window, run:

```
grails create-service app.User
```

This will create a class called `UserService.groovy` in your `grails-app/services/app` directory. Add the following code to this class:

```
package app

import org.jsecurity.SecurityUtils

class UserService {

    def getAuthenticatedUser() {
        return User.findByUsername(SecurityUtils.subject.principal)
    }

}
```

Here you are using the `SecurityUtils` class of JSecurity to get access to the principal of the logged-in user, and then using a dynamic finder call on `User` to load the details of the user for the authenticated principal.

Relate messages to users

Now that you can find the `User` instance of the user who is authenticated for a given request, you can associate a new message with a user when it is created. You will need to create a relationship between `Message` and `User`. Modify the `Message` class as follows:

```
package app

class Message {

    String title
    String detail

    Date dateCreated
    Date lastUpdated
```

```
User user
static constraints = {
    title( blank: false, size: 1..50 )
    detail( blank: false )
    user(nullable: false)
    dateCreated( nullable: true )
    lastUpdated( nullable: true )
}
```

[handwritten margin notes: no belongsTo? no hasMany in User?]

Here, you have created a relationship between `Message` and `User` by simply declaring a property of type `User`. In addition, you have used the constraints to specify that the relationship must exist; a message cannot be created without being associated to a user.

Making it happen

There are two places in the application where you can create new messages. The first is in the `save` action on `MessageController`, and the second is in the `BootStrap` class. You need to make sure that both of these places specify the user that created the message, or you will encounter a validation error when trying to save. The message controller must make use of your new user service. Remember, to inject a service into a controller or domain class, you simply have to create a new property with the same name as the service. So for the `MessageController`, make the changes shown below:

```
package app

class MessageController {

    def userService

    def create = { ... }

    def save = {
        def message = new Message(params)
        message.user = userService.getAuthenticatedUser()
        if( !message.hasErrors() && message.save() ) {
            flash.toUser = "Message [${message.title}] has been added."
            redirect(action: 'create')
        } else {
            render(view: 'create', model: [message: message])
        }
    }

}
```

The first change you make is to have the service injected by Spring. The second change uses the service to populate the user relationship on message.

The changes to the `BootStrap` class are equally simple:

```
def init = { servletContext ->
    def user = new Role(name: 'User').save()
    def admin = new Role(name: 'Administrator').save()
    def mjones = new User(username:'mjones',
            title:'Miss',
            firstName:'Martha',
            lastName:'Jones',
            password: new Sha1Hash("admin").toHex(), role:admin)
        .save()
    def flancelot = new User(username:'flancelot',
            title:'Mr',
            firstName:'Fred',
            lastName:'Lancelot',
            password: new Sha1Hash("password").toHex(), role:user)
        .save()
    new Message( title:'The Knights Who Say Nee',
            detail:'They are after a shrubbery.',
            user: mjones ).save()
    new Message( title:'The Black Knight',
            detail:"Just a flesh wound.",
            user: flancelot ).save()
    new Message( title:'air speed velocity of a swallow',
            detail:"African or European?",
            user: flancelot ).save()
}
```

why highlighted? *why highlighted?*

You simply need to assign the users that are created to variables and reuse them when creating the new messages.

Showing the user

The final step, to tie it all together, is to display the name of the user who posted the message when listing messages on the home page of your application. This requires a simple change to the `index.gsp` file under the `grails-app/views/home` directory, a new message key and also a tweak to the `HomeController` to remove a potential performance problem. The change to the `index.gsp` file is as follows:

```
<g:each in="${messages}" var="message">
    <div class="amessage">
```

```
        <div class="messagetitle">
            <g:message code="message.title" args=
            "${[message.title]}" encodeAs="HTML"/>
        </div>
        <div class="messagetitlesupplimentary">
            <g:message code="message.user"
            args="${[message.user.firstName, message.user.lastName]}"/>
        </div>
        <div class="messagebody">
            <g:message code="message.detail" args="${[message.
detail]}" encodeAs="HTML"/>
        </div>
    </div>
</g:each>
```

You have added the details of the user who created the message under the title of the message. You can see that the g:message tag has been used again. This time, you are passing in two arguments: the first name and the last name of the user.

Add the new message key to the message.properties file in the grails-app/i18n folder:

```
message.user={0} {1}
```

The next change is perhaps a little less obvious, depending on how familiar you are with Hibernate.

Hibernate lazy loading

Relationships between domain classes, such as the one you have just created from Message to User, are not always populated by Hibernate when an object is retrieved from the database. Hibernate assigns a proxy to the relationship property, and when this property is accessed, Hibernate will go to the database and populate the object in a just-in-time fashion. This allows Hibernate to load objects without having to populate the entire object graph.

However, you are left with another problem to deal with, known as the n+1 problem. The issue here is that one query to the database will load all the messages to be displayed. But now that the posting user is displayed for each message, as soon as a message is rendered on the home page, your application will make another request to the database to load the user information for that message. If you are only showing a few messages, then it is not too bad. But once the application is being used and you have a few hundred messages, then an additional request to the database for each message is going to start causing problems.

The good news is that there is a solution. It is just something you need to be aware of so you can use the available solution when needed. Hibernate has a notion of fetch strategies that allow you to determine whether certain information should be pre-populated (eager) or fetched just-in-time (lazy). As usual, the GORM provides a very simple syntax for specifying which strategy is to be used.

Eager load users

In the `HomeController`, you should tell the query that loads messages to also fetch the `User` relationship eagerly. This means that when messages are loaded through this query, instead of the `user` property just being a Hibernate proxy, it will be a real instance of the `User` class.

```
package app
class HomeController {
    def index = {
        def messages = Message.list(sort: 'lastUpdated', order:
'desc', fetch: [user: 'eager'])
        return [messages: messages]
    }
}
```

You can also declare that a relationship is always eagerly fetched in domain classes. If you wanted to configure the relationship between `Message` and `User` such that the user was always loaded, you would add a `mapping` property to the `Message` class:

```
package app
class Message {
    String title
    String detail
    Date dateCreated
    Date lastUpdated
    User user
    static mapping = { user lazy:false }
    static constraints = { … }
}
```

Personally, my initial instinct is to leave the relationships lazy by default, and make the query perform eager fetching if required. This approach avoids the risk of loading hundreds of domain objects into memory from the database and allows us to optimize in specific instances where there may be performance problems.

Before running the application again, run the following command from the `teamwork` directory:

`grails clean`

This will make sure that all files get recompiled as needed when you next run the application. This is sometimes necessary when domain classes are modified. If you ever come across an error when running the Grails application that contradicts what your code should be doing, make sure you run this command first to ensure that Grails is executing the correct version of the code. Run the application again and log in. You will see the name of the user who posted the message below the title of the message, as shown in the following screenshot:

Summary

In this chapter, you have been introduced to Grails plug-ins and have used the JSecurity plug-in to implement authentication and authorization for the application. You created a security realm that provides authentication and authorization for the application. You also implemented encryption of user passwords.

Apart from securing the application, you have also been able to associate messages with the user who posted them, so other users will know who the message was from. Through the implementation of this feature, you were introduced to services in Grails, and have also learned more details about how relationships are managed in a Grails application.

In the next chapter, you will see how to create automated tests for your application. You will cover unit testing (verifying the behavior of discrete units of code), integration testing (testing across layers of the application), and functional testing (driving the application as a user would).

6 Testing

does not cover Ted Naleid's Build-test-dont not any BDD (easy6)

We have seen enough of the basics of web development with Grails for now. Before we go any further, we should take a look at automated testing in the Grails world. We will discuss unit testing and some guidelines to write good unit tests. After unit tests we will cover the difference between integration testing and unit testing and how Grails supports both approaches. Finally, we will talk about why automated functional testing can cause so many problems and investigate a plug-in called **Grails Functional Testing** that takes the pain out of functional testing.

Unless you have been building software on Mars for the last few years, you will be aware of the explosion in popularity of automated unit testing and test driven development. A large part of this drive comes from Extreme Programming (http://www.extremeprogramming.org/) and has made a big impact on the community of developers. The original unit testing framework for Java is JUnit. Groovy comes with this framework pre-installed and provides a class called GroovyTestCase that extends and enhances the base TestCase class in the JUnit framework.

A discussion of test-driven development is beyond the scope of this book. However, it is a practice that I personally highly recommend, so I have included some references for the interested reader:

- http://en.wikipedia.org/wiki/Test-driven_development
- http://tech.groups.yahoo.com/group/testdrivendevelopment/
- http://c2.com/cgi/wiki?TestDrivenDevelopment — Ward Cunningham's Wiki

Writing unit tests

Before we get into writing tests for our application, it is useful to review why unit testing is so important and how we can write good unit tests.

Why we write unit tests

Unit tests are written by developers, for developers and test small discreet sections of code, that is, units. This is done:

- To give assurance that the logic of the code is working correctly
- To improve the design of code
- To simplify debugging
- To document the intention of code

Confidence in code

When the application logic is covered by unit tests, we can be confident that the code is going to give the expected results. This is because it is verified every single time the tests are run. This gives us the freedom to refactor the code often as any side effects caused by the refactoring will be caught by the unit tests.

Improve design

Code that is easy to test is generally well designed. However, if it is difficult to test the code, then this signifies that the code would benefit from refactoring. Loosely coupled and highly cohesive code is often easy to test.

Developer productivity

It is easier to debug and verify code that is being executed through unit tests because:

- Running a unit test is faster than starting an application and testing the conditions to exercise code manually.
- Verifying a discreet unit of code is simpler than checking the entire application stack.

Document code

Unit tests also act as documentation for code by describing exactly what the code does and proving the expectations through assertions. As long as tests are run regularly they can never be out of date, unlike comments or Java doc.

How to write unit tests

Now that we have covered why unit testing is required, it is worth looking at what makes a good unit test.

Test discreet units of code

Unit tests should cover discreet modules of code and not rely on external systems or resources such as databases, web services, and so on. Unit tests need to be fast, reliable, and easy to implement.

It is necessary to be able to run the entire suite of unit tests again and again very quickly. If the code being tested makes calls to external systems, the performance of the tests will be affected and the developers will be less likely to run them frequently.

Additionally, if a unit test cannot be repeatedly run and return the same result, then it is pretty much worthless—Outgoes our confidence in the tests! Unit tests that rely on external systems have a greater chance of having something go wrong that is not directly related to the code being tested.

Testing code that relies on external systems makes writing unit tests difficult. As part of our tests we would need to make sure that the external system is set correctly and is ready to be used. If unit tests are hard to write, developers will be less inclined to write tests, or will spend more time setting up complicated tests, rather than implementing the application code.

Trust your libraries

Our tests should make assumptions that third-party libraries are working, because we only want to test our code or we will be writing tests forever! For example, it is not necessary to test the methods on the String object from the JDK, but it is critical to test the application code that uses methods on the String to retrieve a filename.

Test your production code

Unit tests should run against the code that will go into production, and should not be replications of the code.

This sounds obvious, but it is amazing how often people who are new to unit testing do not make tests execute against their application code. Here is an example of one of these tests:

```
package app
class UserUnitTests extends GroovyTestCase {
    void testBadCanDetermineIfAPasswordNeedsHashing() {
        def user = new User( password: 'oldpassword' )
        assertTrue( 'newpassword' != user.password )
    }
}
```

[handwritten: why not show the right way.]

[handwritten: GroovyTestCase circled]

[handwritten: s/b assertTrue user.needToHash('newpassword')]

Here, we have duplicated the logic from our `User` class that determines if a password needs to be hashed. Now imagine that we want to change the logic within the `needToHash` method on the `user`. Once this change is made, the test continues to pass without any modification, despite the change to the implementation of the code that should be under test. It no longer represents the state of the application code. We no longer have the confidence in our code that it is working correctly, and the test is regarded as out-of-date.

Descriptive test names

[handwritten: documentation ability is better w/ e.g.'s]

To help in our quest to make unit tests useful as documentation for code, we need to make the names of test methods as descriptive and as readable as possible. A test method that verifies the full name of a user is constructed from the first and last name and should look like:

```
testUserFullNameCombinesFirstAndLastName
```

This gives us a readable description of what is being tested. It also allows the tests to read almost like a functional specification of the class being tested. Moreover, this document doesn't get out-of-date!

Test one thing at a time

Following on from descriptive test names is the rule to only test one thing at a time. There are two reasons for this. Firstly, if the test is checking lots of different pieces of logic, then it becomes very difficult to write a descriptive name for the test. The second issue is how easy the test is to understand. A test that checks all the validation rules for the `User` class is going to get extremely large and complex. However, one test per validation rule, or one test per property, is much simpler to comprehend. For example, a test that checked all of the validations in one go for a user would have a name like:

```
void testUserValidation()
```

Whereas we should be writing tests like this:

```
void testUsernameMustHaveBetween4And20CharactersAndMustBeUnique()
void testTitleCannotBeBlankAndMustBeOneOfTheAvailableOptions()
void testFirstNameMustHaveBetween1And20Characters()
...
```

JUnit refresher

Unit testing in Groovy, and therefore Grails, is based on the JUnit (http://www.junit.org) test framework. We will quickly review how to use this framework before getting into unit testing in Grails. JUnit allows developers to write tests that validate their code, by exercising the code, and performing assertions on the state of the code at a given point. Tests are implemented as methods in a class, and each test method equates to a distinct test.

Since JUnit 4, there are two ways to declare tests and test classes. Groovy and Grails use the original convention based approach that was used before annotations were made available in Java. Pre JUnit 4 tests are defined as follows:

- A test class must extend the `TestCase` class
- Test methods within a test class must:
  - be declared as public
  - have a return type of `void`
  - accept no arguments
  - the name of the method must begin with the word `test`

Here is a simple Java example that performs a test on the `String` class.

```java
package example;
import junit.framework.TestCase;
public class JUnitPre4Test extends TestCase {
    public void testString() {
        String foo = "foo";
        assertTrue( foo.endsWith( "oo" ) );
    }
}
```

You will notice that the `class` and `test` method in the example meet the requirements that were defined above.

SetUp and TearDown

The JUnit `TestCase` class contains two test life cycle management methods. They are the `setUp` and the `teardown` methods. These methods are executed before and after each test method is executed. By overriding these methods, we can prepare common data for each test in a `test` class.

Asserting expectations

The whole point of writing tests is to verify the state of our code at certain points during execution. JUnit provides a set of `assertXxx` methods to help us. The following methods are made available when we extend `TestCase`:

Assert Method	Description	Example
assertTrue	Checks that a value is true.	`assertTrue( user.enabled )`
assertFalse	Checks that a value is false.	`assertFalse( user.enabled )`
assertEquals	Checks that a value is equal to the supplied expectation. This method is overloaded for each primitive type and Object.	`assertEquals( "foo", myString )`
assertNotNull	Checks that a value is *not* **null**.	`assertNotNull( myObject )`

Assert Method	Description	Example
assertNull	Checks that a value *is* **null**	`assertNull( myObject )`
assertSame	Checks that two objects are actually the same object, uses ==	`assertSame( firstObj, secondObj )`
assertNotSame	Checks that two objects do not reference the same instance	`assertNotSame( firstObj, secondObj )`

Unit tests in Grails

Grails leverages the built-in testing support provided by Groovy to implement its testing environment. Groovy bundles the JUnit JAR file and also extends it with some useful methods.

Groovy test extensions

In addition to the assert methods provided by JUnit, `GroovyTestCase` provides a few more options:

Assert Method	Description	Example
assertArrayEquals	Checks that the contents of an array is the same as the supplied expectation.	`assertArrayEquals([1,2,3], myArray)`
assertLength	Checks that an array is a certain size.	`assertLength([1,2,3], 3)`
assertContains	Checks that an array contains a given value.	`assertContains([1,2,3], 3)`
assertToString	Verifies that the `toString` method on an object returns the correct value.	`assertToString(myObject, "contents of my object are:" )`
assertScript	Verifies that the supplied script executes without throwing an exception.	`assertScript( "4+3" )`
shouldFail	Allows us to wrap some test code with a closure that expects an exception.	`See below`
shouldFailWithCause	Allows us to specify the expected type of exception.	`See below`

Additional assert methods provided by Groovy Test Case

Of the additional assert methods supplied by GroovyTestCase, only the shouldFail methods really require further explanation. The shouldFail method takes a closure. When the method executes this closure, it expects an exception to be thrown by the code within the closure. If no exception is thrown then the test fails. This is a very neat way of testing for error cases.

Imagine you have a method that throws an IllegalArgumentException if you pass **null** to it. To test this in a Groovy test you would do the following:

```
package app

class ShouldFailTest extends GroovyTestCase {

    void testExceptionTesting() {
        shouldFail {
            noNullsPlease( null )
        }
    }

    void noNullsPlease( arg ) {
        if(!arg) {
            throw new IllegalArgumentException('You can not pass null
in here!')
        }
    }
}
```

In the example above, the test will pass if an exception is thrown when we call the noNullsPlease method, and fail if no exception is thrown. We can make the test even more explicit by using the shouldFailWithCause method:

```
package app

class ShouldFailTest extends GroovyTestCase {

    void testExceptionTesting() {
        shouldFailWithCause( IllegalArgumentException ) {
            noNullsPlease( null )
        }
    }

    void noNullsPlease( arg ) {
        if(!arg) {
            throw new IllegalArgumentException('You can not pass null
in here!')
        }
    }
}
```

Create a grails test

As with everything else, Grails implements a convention that determines where unit test classes should live. This is in the test/unit folder under our project folder.

You may not have realized it, but you have already created a number of Grails unit test classes. Every time one of the Grails 'create' commands is executed, an appropriate unit test class is also created. For example, when we created the User domain class, the test class UserTests was created in the test/unit/app folder.

Let's go ahead and create a test for our User domain class that verifies that we can determine if a password needs to be hashed. Put the following code in the new test class:

[handwritten: Missing import grails.test.GrailsUnitTestCase]

[handwritten: why not use the already geared test case?]

```
package app

class UserUnitTests extends GrailsUnitTestCase {

    void testCanDetermineIfAPasswordNeedsHashing() {
        def user = new User( password: 'oldpassword' )
        assertTrue( user.needToHash( 'newpassword' ) )
        assertFalse( user.needToHash( 'oldpassword' ) )
    }
}
```

With this test, we are simply confirming that the needToHash method on User can tell if the password supplied is different to the user's current password.

Our test class extends GrailsUnitTestCase. This enables them to be recognized as test classes because GrailsUnitTestCase extends GroovyTestCase, which in turn extends the JUnit TestCase. Also, our test method:

- returns void
- has the prefix test
- and takes no arguments

Finally, we set up the user data and perform the JUnit assertions to verify that the code can determine whether a password should be hashed or not.

Running our tests

We now have a test class to verify the behavior of the User domain class—UserTests. Now, it is time to see how Grails executes tests. Open the terminal in the project folder and run:

```
grails test-app
```

This will execute all of the tests. We will see output similar to that shown below in the terminal:

```
Running 1 Unit Test...
Running test app.UserTests...
                testCanDetermineIfAPasswordNeedsHashing...SUCCESS
Unit Tests Completed in 366ms ...
```

Besides showing the results in the terminal, Grails generates an HTML report of the results of the tests, which can be found in the folder `grails-app/test/reports/html/index.html`.

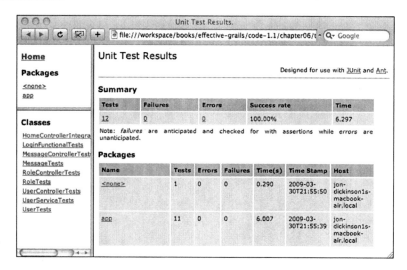

Grails testing plug-in

When executing unit tests in Grails, it is important to understand that the tests do not run within the Grails container. This means that the dynamic methods and properties that are supplied by the Grails framework are not available when running unit tests. As a result, at first glance, the only options that are available when testing code that uses the dynamic behavior of Grails, are to either mock the dynamic behavior, or to use integration tests that will run within the Grails container.

Mocking all of the behavior of the Grails framework requires a lot of in-depth knowledge of Groovy meta-programming, and can lead to your mocked behavior leaking into other tests and causing unexpected results.

Running tests that should really be unit tests as integration tests can slow down the execution speed of the tests, as they will be communicating with the database. This can lead to unreliable results, as you will always have to think about the state that exists in the database from one test to the next.

Grails 1.1 has added a testing plug-in as a core plug-in to provide a standard approach for mocking the behavior of Grails dynamic methods. Therefore, code that doesn't need to integrate with other systems can run as a unit test.

The grails testing plug-in provides support for mocking `domain` and `controller` classes.

Mock Method	Description
mockDomain	Mocks the standard dynamic methods on a `domain` class. Also takes a list of `domain` class instances to be used as the source of data for database operations.
mockForConstraintsTests	Adds the `validate` method to the supplied class, which will operate against the defined constraints for the class. This makes it possible to test the constraints for a `domain` class.
mockController	Mocks the standard dynamic methods and properties for a `controller` class.
mockTagLib	Mocks the dynamic methods and properties that are added to a tag library.
mockLogging	Mocks the logging behavior for a class. Log calls are written to standard out.
mockFor	Mock a class and specify dynamic behavior for it.
registerMetaClass	Registers a `meta` class so you can use metaprogramming within a test to define your own mock behavior. The advantage of registering a `meta` class is that the dynamic behavior that is added to the `meta` class is cleaned up when the `tearDown` method is called on the test. Now you can be sure that any behavior you define will not leak into another test.

great!!

Testing Metacontroller

Let's take a look at how to use some of these mocking methods in practice. The goal is to test the behavior of the `save` action on `MessageController`. This action relies on a number of collaborators:

see p. 107

- `UserService` — to retrieve the authenticated user
- `Message` — the domain class to be validated and persisted
- Dynamic behavior — the `params` property and the `redirect` and `render` methods

Create a test class in the `test/unit/app` folder called `MessageControllerTests`. `groovy`. This class will contain two tests; one for each branch in the code for the save action:

auto genned
code is
Controller Unit
Test Case

```groovy
package app

import grails.test.GrailsUnitTestCase

class MessageControllerTests extends GrailsUnitTestCase {
    def savedMessages
    def serviceControl

    void setUp() {
        super.setUp()
        savedMessages = []
        mockDomain(Message, savedMessages)
        mockController(MessageController)
        serviceControl = mockFor(UserService)
        serviceControl.demand.getAuthenticatedUser() {-> return new
User() }
    }

    void tearDown() {
        super.tearDown()
        serviceControl.verify()
    }

    void testCreateViewIsRenderedIfTheMessageDoesNotValidate() {
        def messageController = messageController {
            params.title = 'no detail'
            params.detail = ''
        }

        messageController.save()

        assertEquals('create', messageController.renderArgs.view)
        def message = messageController.renderArgs.model.message
        assertEquals('no detail', message.title)
        assertEquals('', message.detail)
        assertNull(messageController.flash.toUser)
        assertEquals(0, savedMessages.size())
    }

    void testMessageCanBeCreated() {
        def messageController = messageController {
            params.title = 'detail'
            params.detail = 'some detail'
        }

        messageController.save()
```

```
        assertEquals('create', messageController.redirectArgs.action)
        assertEquals('Message [detail] has been added.',
messageController.flash.toUser)
        assertEquals(1, savedMessages.size())
    }

    def messageController = { fn ->
        fn.delegate = new MessageController()
        fn.delegate.userService = serviceControl.createMock()
        fn()
        return fn.delegate
    }
}
```

All the mocking methods for unit testing are made available through extending
GrailsUnitTestCase, which in turn extends GroovyTestCase, so we still have the
additional support provided by Groovy. The mocking necessary to run the tests is
performed in the setUp method. This keeps the tests clean and concise, while making
sure the mocked environments are available within the tests. It is important that the
super class setUp method is still called, as this prepares all the metaprogramming
help that is needed to support mocking.

The dynamic behavior that is added by Grails to the Message domain class is mocked
by calling the mockDomain method, passing the class to mock. It is then followed by
a list that will be used as the in-memory persistent storage when "saving" messages.
Once the mockDomain method has been called, all basic GORM methods such as list,
save, findBy* and so on, will be available on the Message class.

When mocking a controller class with the mockController method, all dynamic
properties (for example, params, request, flash and so on) and methods (render,
redirect) will be made available for new instances of the controller class that is
defined. The mock also makes two new read only properties available (renderArgs
and redirectArgs) that allow us to verify the arguments that have been passed to
render and redirect.

The next and final bit of mocking we need to perform in this test is the behavior
of the UserService class that we expect to be injected to the MessageController.
In this case, a general mock control is created for the service class on which
we can declare the expected behavior. In the above example, we are telling the
serviceControl that the getAuthenticatedUser method should be called and it
will return a new User object, when it is called.

Each of the tests then uses the `messageController` method, defined at the bottom of the class, to inject the necessary data and behavior into a new controller instance that can then be tested. This `messageController` method uses some interesting Groovy tricks to allow the tests to use a nice syntax to set up values on the `MessageController` class. The `messageController` method takes one argument, which is a closure. It then sets the delegate of this closure to be a new instance of the `MessageController` class. The mocked `UserService` is then set on the `MessageController` instance. The closure that was passed is executed, and then the `MessageController` instance is returned. It is important to understand what the delegate property on a closure is used for.

When a closure is executed, any variable that is accessed within the closure that cannot be found within the scope of the closure is then looked for in the `delegate` property of the closure. By making an instance of `MessageController` the delegate of the closure, we are saying that any variables or methods accessed in the closure should be executed against the new `MessageController` instance.

This allows us to set the values in the `params` object on a `MessageController` using the following syntax in our tests:

```
def messageController = messageController {
    params.title = 'no detail'
    params.detail = ''
}
```

Here we have created a new instance of `MessageController` that has a `title` parameter with the value 'no detail', and a `detail` parameter with the value of an empty string. Without using this Groovy trick, we would have to use the following syntax to set up a new instance of the controller:

```
def messageController = new MessageController()
messageController.userService = serviceControl.createMock()
messageController.params.title = 'no detail'
messageController.params.detail = ''
```

This is a much more verbose syntax. Given that tests must be as simple to create and read as possible, the first syntax is more preferable.

The first test verifies the behavior of the action if the message data that is supplied by the user is not valid. The assertions here are:

- The create view must be rendered again.
- The message with the original data must be passed in the model to the view.
- There must not be a success message put onto flash scope for the user.
- The in-memory store of messages must not have any entries, as this will indicate that the message has been saved.

The second test checks the behavior of the action if the message data is valid. The assertions are:

- A redirect must have been issued to the create action
- The user must receive a success message
- There must be a message saved in the underlying message list

Testing validation

Despite the fact that validation rules for domain classes are so trivial to write, it is still possible to get them wrong. Validation rules are key to the integrity of your data and your application. If you don't test them, you are putting your application at risk! Fortunately, the Grails testing plug-in makes the unit testing of these rules trivial.

Create a unit test class for the Message domain class under test/unit/ MessageTests.groovy, and add the following code:

[handwritten: Again, not using the auto-generated class - why?]

```
package app

import grails.test.GrailsUnitTestCase

class MessageUnitTests extends GrailsUnitTestCase {
    void testMessageMustHaveATitle() {
        def message = new Message( title: '', detail: 'some details',
user: new User() )
        mockForConstraintsTests( Message, [ message ] )

        message.validate()
        assertTrue( message.hasErrors() )
    }
    void testMessageTitleCanBe50Chars() {
        def fiftyCharTitle = generateTitle(50)
        def message = new Message( title: fiftyCharTitle.toString(),
detail: 'some details', user: new User() )
        mockForConstraintsTests( Message, [ message ] )

        message.validate()
        assertFalse( message.hasErrors() )
    }
    void testMessageTitleCannotBeLongerThan50Chars() {
        def fiftyOneCharTitle = generateTitle(51)
        def message = new Message( title: fiftyOneCharTitle.
toString(), detail: 'some details', user: new User() )
        mockForConstraintsTests( Message, [ message ] )

        message.validate()
        assertTrue( message.hasErrors() )
```

[handwritten right margin: shouldn't we test for specific msg. this could pass on some other error. ironic after comments on p. 116 in 'Test Your Production' Code' section]

[handwritten: also, should test length]

```
    }
    def generateTitle( length ) {
        def title = new StringBuilder()
        (1..length).each{title.append('a')}
        return title
    }
}
```

In this class, there are three tests to check that:

- A title cannot be empty
- A title can be up to fifty characters
- A title cannot be more than fifty characters

Each of these tests constructs an instance of a `Message` in the relevant state, and then calls the `mockForConstraintsTests` method, which passes in the class to be mocked and also the instances of the class that will be mocked. The tests can then call the `validate` method and assert that the result of calling `hasErrors` is correct.

Limitations of Grails in unit tests

Earlier, in the guidelines for writing unit tests, we saw that unit tests should test discreet units of code. Specifically, we should not be relying on external systems such as databases. Grails actually supports this approach at the framework level. In the earlier chapters, we saw that Grails dynamically adds methods onto the domain classes to allow them to be persisted to the database. When we run unit tests, the Grails environment is not loaded, so these methods are not available. Therefore, it is impossible for us to persist data to the database when writing unit tests in Grails. Fortunately, we are able to test that an application interacts with the Grails framework correctly in unit tests, by mocking the environment with the testing plug-in.

If we want to test that our data can be persisted to the database correctly then we need to write integration tests.

Integration testing

While unit tests confirm that discreet units of code are performing as expected, there are areas of the code that we can't be entirely sure are working unless we integrate with some external system or resource. We would like to be sure that our objects are being persisted to, and can be read from the database, or that we have integrated a particular framework correctly. To cover these scenarios, we need to use integration tests.

Writing integration tests is often a more complicated and fraught process than unit testing. When writing integration tests, we face the following challenges:

- Dependencies can be complicated to set up.
- Making tests repeatable can be tricky.

External dependencies

With unit testing, we have the advantage of having no external dependencies, so any problems or test failures should be limited to the scope of our code. When running integration tests, we need to prepare databases, transaction managers, and other environment configuration. An error in any of these areas can cause the tests to fail.

Repeatable tests

Automated tests that do not have a repeatable outcome are worthless and generate a lot of maintenance work. Taking the example of integration tests that persist data to a database, we have to be careful that our tests do not rely on states created by other tests in the test suite. Relying on side effects of other tests will lead to errors caused by data issues, rather than our code or configuration.

Integration tests in Grails

The `HomeController` class performs a query against the database to list all of the messages in the system. The messages that are returned from this class must be ordered by the date they were last updated in descending order. No other logic is performed in the action, because the database handles the ordering. Therefore, there is little point writing a unit test. This sounds like a good example for performing an integration test.

Writing integration tests in Grails is similar to writing unit tests, apart from two important differences:

- Integration tests must be in the folder `test/integration`
- Integration tests run in the full Grails environment. For example, domain classes *do* have the `save` method added to them, and calling this method will persist the object to the database.

Now, let us create an integration test for the `HomeController` by creating the file `tests/integration/app/HomeControllerIntegrationTests.groovy`. Add the following code to the test class:

```
package app
class HomeControllerIntegrationTests extends GroovyTestCase {
    void testMessagesAreReturnedInDescendingDateOrder() {
        def flancelot = User.findByUsername( 'flancelot' )
        new Message( title: 'first message', detail: 'first detail',
                user: flancelot ).save( flush: true )
        Thread.currentThread().sleep( 1000 )
        new Message( title: 'second message', detail: 'second detail',
                user: flancelot ).save( flush: true )
        def messages = new HomeController().index().messages
        assertEquals( 'second message', messages[0].title )
        assertEquals( 'first message', messages[1].title )
    }
}
```

In this test, we look up the same user that we used when manually testing the application. Two new messages are created and persisted to the database. Notice that there is a slight hack put in place to ensure that the first message and the second message have distinct persistence times, so we can guarantee the order they will be retrieved in. We then execute the `index` action on `HomeController` to get the model containing messages that are shown to the user on the home page. Once the action has been executed, we can assert that the first message in the model is the second message that was created and the second message is the first one that was created. Remember that the `lastUpdated` property is populated when the `Message` instance is saved to the database.

When we run the `grails test-app` command in our terminal window, Grails will execute both, unit tests and integration tests. Although the HTML report will, somewhat confusingly, have the title of **Unit Test Results**.

BootStrap for environments

You may be surprised to see the above integration test fail! If you open the HTML test report, you will see that the messages created as part of the `BootStrap` class are interfering with our test data. This is because the database is being cleared and the `BootStrap` data is loaded into the database for integration tests, the same as it does when running the application for development. However, it is not all bad news. We are able to look up the `'flancelot'` user, because this user is being created by the bootstrap, so there is no need to worry about creating new users and roles specifically for the integration tests.

We will discuss some more about the environments that are available in Chapter 13 when we cover deployment. For now it is enough to be aware that there are three default environments that the application can be run under:

- Development—used when the application is run with the `grails run-app` command
- Testing—used when the integration test runs
- Production—used when the application is packaged and deployed to a server

As part of the API, Grails provides access to the environment that the application is running under at any given point. We need to make sure that the users are still populated in the database for development and test modes. But we need to stop the `BootStrap` messages from being loaded when we run the integration tests. Make the following change to `BootStrap.groovy file`:

```
import app.Role
import org.jsecurity.crypto.hash.Sha1Hash
import app.User
import app.Message
import grails.util.Environment

class BootStrap {

    def init = { servletContext ->
        def user = new Role(name: 'User').save()
        def admin = new Role(name: 'Administrator').save()

        def mjones = new User(username:'mjones',
                title:'Miss',
                firstName:'Martha',
                lastName:'Jones',
                password: new Sha1Hash("admin").toHex(), role:admin)
                .save()

        def flancelot = new User(username:'flancelot',
                title:'Mr',
                firstName:'Fred',
                lastName:'Lancelot',
                password: new Sha1Hash("password").toHex(), role:
user)
                .save()

        if( Environment.current == Environment.DEVELOPMENT ) {
            new Message( title:'The Knights Who Say Nee',
                    detail:'They are after a shrubbery.',
                    user: mjones ).save()
            new Message( title:'The Black Knight',
                    detail:"Just a flesh wound.",
```

Could & probably
Should use
deletes &
inserts in
tests.
use environs
for data
in dev
& set up
of initial
default
values.

```
                        user: flancelot ).save()
              new Message( title:'air speed velocity of a swallow',
                    detail:"African or European?",
                    user: flancelot ).save()
        }
      }
      def destroy = {
      }
    }
```

This conditional check will only allow the messages to be created when the application is started up, under the development environment. Run the tests again and they should all pass now.

Functional testing

Functional tests allow us to verify that an entire vertical slice of the application is working, that is, from the user action, down through the layers of our code, and back up again to verify the response sent to the user. This means that we must exercise the entire application, rather than discrete units of code. A common approach to this in web development is to run the application on a server and execute tests that are able to act as a very simple web browser. These tests make HTTP requests to the server and parse the HTML responses.

As with integration tests, there are a number of common issues inherent when writing automated functional tests, and they are as follows:

- Environment setup
- Making tests repeatable
- Performance of tests
- Fragility of tests
- Making the tests comprehensible

Environment setup

Functional tests must test the application running, in the way a user would experience it. For Java web development, this means a web application that is deployed to a servlet container. We also need to be able to run these tests against potentially different environments. Each of the developers must be able to run the tests on their machine, as well as configure an environment that the build server can execute the tests against.

This can lead to lots of configuring, just to keep it up-to-date.

Repeatable tests

As with integration tests, we need to make sure that our functional tests can be run in a repeatable manner. They should be executable on their own, or as part of a larger suite of tests.

Test performance

Functional tests are tests that are executed over the full implementation stack of our application. In addition, they will make HTTP requests to drive the application and parse the HTML response that comes back. All of this takes time. There is always a trade off to be made between having a large set of tests that give a high level of coverage, but take a long time to execute, and a small set of tests that check some key areas of an application and execute quickly, but don't give full coverage.

Fragility of tests

As mentioned before, functional tests in web development often work by sending HTTP requests to a server and parsing the HTML response allowing us to verify the state of the application. Unfortunately, this approach can make functional tests very brittle, as a change in the layout of the HTML can lead to the test no longer being able to understand the response being received by the server.

We must strike a balance when writing our functional tests between verifying every element of the page, and simply checking a few key parts. The first approach will give us extremely comprehensive, but brittle tests, while the second will give us a greater return on our test-investment and more robust tests, but at the risk of missing important regressions.

Making tests understandable

Having readable tests is an important goal in all areas of testing, but quite often the target audience of functional tests is different from unit and integration tests. In an ideal world we would like to be able to work with the product owner and professional testers to write functional tests. If this is to happen, then the tests need to be written in a structure or language that is comprehensible to non-developers.

Functional testing In Grails

There are a few plug-ins for Grails that allow you to write functional tests. These plug-ins will drive the user interface of an application and verify the information that is displayed to the user. The one we will look at is called **Grails Functional Testing**. It provides a builder DSL over the HtmlUnit (`http://htmlunit.sourceforge. net/`) framework.

Benefits of functional testing in Grails

As you will see shortly, getting started with functional testing in Grails is incredibly easy. Environment setup is taken care of when the plug-in starts up the Grails container before executing the tests and then shuts it down subsequently. This means any data defined in `BootStrap.groovy` is made available to the tests, so as with manual testing, common test data can be preloaded. We also get the benefit of not having to worry about separate configuration for different environments as Grails comes ready to run with its own Servlet container and database.

Functional tests implemented with the functional testing plug-in are also easy to read. The Groovy builder syntax that is provided for testing makes for very literate tests.

Installing the functional testing plug-in

Install the plug-in from the command line by entering the following:

```
grails install-plugin functional-test
```

This will install the plug-in and create a new folder named `functional` under the `test` folder.

Next we will create a test to verify that the authentication mechanism is working. Run the following code in your command line:

```
grails create-functional-test Login
```

This will create a test class called `LoginFunctionalTests.groovy` under the new `test/functional` folder.

Open the file that has been generated and add the following code:

```
class LoginFunctionalTests extends functionaltestplugin.
FunctionalTestCase {

    void testAccessToHomePageRequiresAuthentication() {
        get( '/home' )
        assertTitle( 'Login' )
```

```
form( 'login' ) {
    username = 'flancelot'
    password = 'password'
    click 'submit'
}
assertTitle( 'Home' )
    }
}
```

The test above will go to the home page of the application and assert that the login page was loaded, thereby verifying that the initial authentication is in place. We then access the form with the name `login` and set the `username` and `password` fields on the form before submitting it. The result of this should be that we have logged in and can view the home page.

The test above is simply a JUnit test, so the usual conventions must be followed to have methods recognized as tests. The other important point to note is the simplicity of the language used to execute the tests. There is no clutter and the intent of the test is very easy to read and understand. This is the key to writing successful and maintainable functional tests.

Before the test can be run, we need to add two hooks into the login page. This is so we can be sure that the tests will be able to pick up the required elements. Open up `grails-app/views/auth/login.gsp` and make the following changes:

```
<g:form action="signIn" name="login">
    <input type="hidden" name="targetUri" value="${targetUri}"/>
    <table>
        <tbody>
            <tr>
                <td>Username:</td>
                <td><input type="text" name="username"
value="${username}"/></td>
            </tr>
            <tr>
                <td>Password:</td>
                <td><input type="password" name="password"
value=""/></td>
            </tr>
            <tr>
                <td>Remember me?:</td>
                <td><g:checkBox name="rememberMe"
value="${rememberMe}"/></td>
            </tr>
            <tr>
```

```
            <td/>
            <td><input type="submit" name="submit" value="Sign
in"/></td>
        </tr>
     </tbody>
   </table>
</g:form>
```

This change is just a case of adding the `name` attribute to the `form` and `submit` buttons, so that they can be called by the script. Now execute the test and it should pass:

```
grails functional-tests
```

This will start up the application, and then execute the steps in the test against the application. The result of running the test will be the output in the console as well as in the `test/reports` folder.

Testing guidance

Unit tests are easier to write, easier to maintain, faster to run, and are far less likely to have complicated side effects than either integration or functional tests. For this reason, it generally makes more sense to think of having high unit test coverage as your initial testing goal.

Integration tests are useful when verifying that a particular database query is performing correctly. These sorts of checks simply cannot be performed by unit tests, and relying on functional tests is even more difficult, as you do not have direct access to the data that is returned from the query.

Functional tests are great for performing end-to-end tests by making sure that all layers of the application are interacting with each other. We can also benefit from implementing automated functional tests for each new piece of functionality in order to help find regressions further on down the development road. When creating functional tests, there is always a balance to be struck between the length of time the tests take to run and the level of test coverage. This must often be worked out on a project-by-project basis, but you will generally find starting from a position of writing more tests is easier to adjust, than a position of writing no tests.

Summary

Now, we have covered all the testing approaches that are needed to verify the code and the rest of the application. We have covered what unit testing is, why it is so important and how to create good tests.

We have discussed the difference between unit tests and integration tests, and some of the issues associated with integration testing. We must remember the differences between the execution contexts when running unit tests and integration tests in Grails:

- Unit tests do not run under the full Grails environment, and so do not have any of the dynamic methods or properties available that Grails provides
- Integration tests do run under the full Grails environment, so we are able to test how our code integrates with the Grails framework and the database

Finally, we discussed the minefield that can be functional testing and installed a plug-in that allows us to get started with functional testing in a matter of minutes.

In the next chapter, we will allow users to share files with other team members and show them how Grails supports file upload, as well as giving us a chance to investigate some advanced GORM querying techniques using criteria.

7
File Sharing

Besides posting messages, our users also want to be able to upload files to share with other members of their team. Sounds good! But wait a minute, isn't file uploading a bit of a pain? First of all, we need to read the binary file data off the request, and then we need to figure out where to put the file. Do we store it on the file system, or in a database? Well, let's take a look.

In this chapter, we will see how easy it is to manage file uploads and downloads in a Grails application.

File domain object

The first step, as usual, is to create a domain object to represent a file. We want to store the following information:

- Name
- The data of the file
- A description of the file
- The file size
- Who uploaded the file
- The date the file was created and last modified

Create the `File` domain class as follows:

```
package app
class File {
    private static final int TEN_MEG_IN_BYTES = 1024*1024*10
    byte[] data
    String name
    String description
    int size
    String extension
    User user

    Date dateCreated
    Date lastUpdated

    static constraints = {
        data( nullable: false, minSize: 1, maxSize: TEN_MEG_IN_BYTES )
        name( nullable: false, blank: false )
        description( nullable: false, blank: false )
        size( nullable: false )
        extension( nullable: false )
        user( nullable: false )
    }
}
```

There should be nothing unfamiliar here. You have created a new domain class to represent a file. The file data will be stored in the data property. The other properties of the file are all metadata. Defining the `user` property creates the association to a `user` object. The constraints are then defined to make sure that all of the information that is needed for a file has been supplied.

There is one important side effect of setting the `maxSize` constraint on the data property. GORM will use this value as a hint when generating the database schema for the domain objects. For example, if this value is not specified, the underlying database may end up choosing a data type to store the binary file data that is too small for the size of files that you wish to persist.

FileController

Now, we will need a controller. Let's name it `FileController`. Our controller will allow users to perform the following actions:

- Go to a page that allows users to select a file
- Submit a file to the server
- Download the file

Create the `FileController` groovy class, alongside our existing `MessageController`, by following the actions shown below:

```
package app

class FileController {

    def create = {
        return [ file: new File() ]
    }

    def save = {
    }

    def download = {
    }
}
```

In the `create` action, we are simply constructing a new file instance that can be used as the backing object when rendering the file-upload form. We will fill in the implementation details of the `save` and `download` actions as and when we will need them.

File Upload GSP

The next step is to create a GSP to render the form that allows users to upload a file to the application. Create the file `grails-app/views/file/create.gsp` and enter the following markup:

```
<%@ page contentType="text/html;charset=UTF-8" %>
<html>
<head>
    <meta http-equiv="Content-Type" content=
        "text/html; charset=UTF-8"/>
    <meta name="layout" content="main"/>
    <title>Post File</title>
</head>
<body>
<g:hasErrors bean="${file}">
    <div class="validationerror">
        <g:renderErrors bean="${file}" as="list"/>
    </div>
</g:hasErrors>
<g:form action="save" method="post" enctype="multipart/form-data"
class="inputform">
    <fieldset>
        <dl>
```

```
          <dt>Title <span class="requiredfield">required</span></dt>
          <dd><g:textField name="name" value="${file.name}"
size="35" class="largeinput"/></dd>
          <dt>File <span class="requiredfield">required</span></dt>
          <dd><input type="file" name="data"/></dd>
          <dt>File description <span class="requiredfield">required
</span></dt>
          <dd><g:textArea name="description" value="${file.
description}" cols="40" rows="10"/></dd>
        </dl>
    </fieldset>
    <g:submitButton name="Save" value="Save"/> |
    <g:link controller="home">Cancel</g:link>
</g:form>
</body>
</html>
```

This GSP looks very similar to the `create.gsp` file for messages. Obviously, it has different fields that correspond to fields on the `File` domain class. The important difference is that this form tells the browser it will be submitting the file data:

```
<g:form action="save" method="post" enctype="multipart/form-data">
```

Run the application, go to `http://localhost:8080/teamwork/file/create` and sign in with the username *flancelot* and the password *password*. You should see the window as shown in the following screenshot:

Saving the file

Now that our users can select files to upload, we need to implement the save action so that these files can be persisted and can be viewed by other users.

Grails file upload

Grails provides two methods of handling file upload. We are going to use both of them. The two approaches are:

- Using data binding
- Using the Spring MultipartFile interface

Data binding makes receiving the data of the file very simple, but is quite limited if used on its own. There is no way of binding anything other than the data of the file, such as the filename or the size of the file, to our domain object.

By also providing access to the Spring MultipartFile interface, Grails allows us to programmatically access any other information we might want from the file.

The save action

Update the FileController class and implement the save action as follows:

```
package app

import org.springframework.web.multipart.MultipartFile

class FileController {

    def userService
    def create = {
        return [ file: new File() ]
    }

    def save = {
        def file = new File( params )
        file.user = userService.getAuthenticatedUser()
        MultipartFile f = request.getFile( 'data' )
        file.size = f.getSize() / 1024
        file.extension = extractExtension( f )

        if(file.save()) {
        flash.userMessage = "File [${file.name}] has been uploaded."
            redirect(controller: 'home')
        } else {
            render(view: 'create', model: [file: file])
```

```
            }
        }
    def extractExtension( MultipartFile file ) {
        String filename = file.getOriginalFilename()
        return filename.substring(filename.lastIndexOf( "." ) + 1 )
    }
    def download = {
    }
}
```

Apart from the implementation of the save action, we have had to import Spring MultipartFile and also inject the userService.

The first highlighted line within the save action performs the binding of request parameters to the File domain object. The usual binding will take place, that is, the name and the description properties of the File object will be populated from the request. In addition, since we have a property on our domain object that is an array of bytes, the contents of the file object in the request will also be bound into our File object.

A quick review of our code shows that we have the following property on the File class:

```
byte[] data
```

Also the create.gsp defines the file input field with the same name:

```
<dd><input type="file" name="data" /></dd>
```

 Grails is also capable of binding the contents of a file to a String property. In this case, we could just declare the data property in our File class as a String, and Grails would bind the file contents as a String.

The next line of interest occurs when we fetch the MultipartFile off the request by using the getFile method. We simply specify the request parameter that contains the file data and Grails does the rest. With an instance of MultipartFile we can access the file size and the original file name to extract the file extension.

Once we have finished populating our File object, we can call the save method and GORM will manage the persistence of the file object and the file data to the database.

Validation messages

The last thing we need to remember to add is the validation messages that will be displayed if the users don't enter all the data that is needed to save a file. Add the following to `grails-app/i18n/messages.properties`:

```
file.name.blank=You must give the file a name
file.description.blank=The file must have a description
file.data.minSize.notmet=No file has been uploaded
file.data.maxSize.exceeded=The file is too large. The maximum file
size is 10MB
```

Viewing files

The next step is to show the uploaded files to the other team members using the application. We will display files on the home page next to messages. So we must:

- Update the home page controller
- Update the home page GSP
- Add new message entries

The `HomeController` changes to:

```
package app
class HomeController {
    def index = {
        def messages = Message.list( sort: 'lastUpdated', order:
'desc', fetch: [ user: 'eager' ] )
        def files = File.list( sort:'lastUpdated', order:'desc',
fetch:[user:'eager'] )
        return [messages: messages, files: files]
    }
}
```

A list of files is retrieved in exactly the same way as a list of messages. We then need to add the files to the model that is to be rendered.

In order to render the files, the home page GSP at `grails-app/views/home/index.gsp` must be updated. Add the following code after the message `div`:

```
<div class="panel">
<h2>Files</h2>
<g:each in="${files}" var="file">
    <div class="afile">
        <div class="filename">
```

[handwritten: there is NO message div]

[handwritten: the layout in book source is different than what we've coded thus far]

```
                <a href="${g.createLink(controller: 'file', action:
'download', id: file.id)}">
                    <g:message code="${file.name}" encodeAs="HTML"/>
                </a> -
                    <g:message code="file.size" args="${[file.size]}"/>
                <div class="filenamesupplimentary">
                    <g:message code="message.user"
                            args="${[file.user.firstName, file.user.
lastName]}"/>
                </div>
            </div>
            <div class="filebody">
                    <g:message code="${file.description}"
encodeAs="HTML"/>
            </div>
        </div>
    </g:each>
</div>
```

The code above should look almost the same as the message list. The main difference is that the file name is wrapped by a link, which will allow a user to download the file by calling the `download` action on the `file` controller with the `id` of the current file. The implementation of the download action will follow shortly.

Add the following message to the message bundle (`grails-app/i18n/` `messages.properties`):

```
file.size={0} KB
```

Before running the application we also need to add a link to the home page that will allow our users to create new files. We can't have them enter the URL into the address bar all the time, can we? Update the `newactions` div on the `grails-app/home/index.gsp` file to be:

```
<div class="newactions">
    <span>
        <g:link controller="message" action="create">Post Message</g:link>
    </span>
    <span>
        <g:link controller="file" action="create">Post File</g:link>
    </span>
</div>
```

Now, run the application again, add a new file, and you should see a window that looks like the following screenshot:

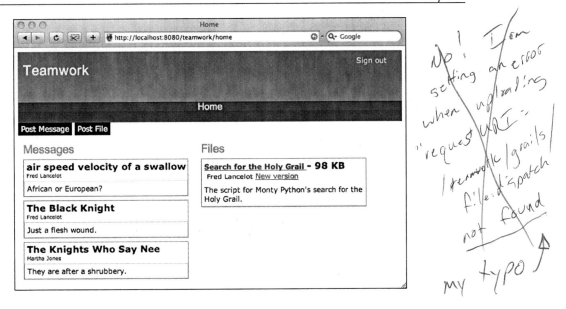

Modeling for efficiency

The implementation we have for file upload works fine and is easy to understand, but it is also quite naive in terms of efficiency. The problem is that every time a user views the information about a file, all the binary data for the file will be loaded into the memory. By altering our domain model slightly, we can easily improve the performance. We will need a domain class to represent the data as a one-to-one relationship with the `File` object. We saw in Chapter 5 that relationships between domain objects are lazy by default. This means that, by extracting the data out into its own object, retrieving a list of files will not load the binary data of the file, unless we request it specifically.

Create a new domain class named `FileData` in the same package as the `File` domain class:

```
package app
class FileData {
    private static final int TEN_MEG_IN_BYTES = 1024*1024*10
    static belongsTo = [file:File]
    byte[] data
    static constraints = {
        data( nullable: false, minSize: 1, maxSize: TEN_MEG_IN_BYTES )
    }
}
```

The `FileData` class is defined as belonging to `File` because it is not possible for an instance of `FileData` to exist without an instance of `File`. By specifying that `FileData` *belongs to* `File`, we are saying that all persistence operations on file will cascade to `FileData` automatically. This means that when a file is saved the data object is saved. Similarly, when a file is deleted the data object will be deleted.

The `File` domain class must also be updated to replace the old `byte[]` `data` property with a reference to the new `FileData` class:

```
package app
class File {
    String name
    String description
    int size
    String extension
    User user
    FileData fileData
    Date dateCreated
    Date lastUpdated
    static constraints = {
        name( nullable: false, blank: false )
        description( nullable: false, blank: false )
        size( nullable: false )
        extension( nullable: false )
        user( nullable: false )
        fileData( nullable: false )
    }
}
```

We now need to change the `save` action on `FileController` and the file input field on the `create.gsp` file. The `save` action must be changed in the following manner:

```
def save = {
    def file = new File( params )
    file.user = userService.getAuthenticatedUser()
    MultipartFile f = request.getFile( 'fileData.data' )
    file.size = f.getSize() / 1024
    file.extension = extractExtension( f )
    if(file.save()) {
        flash.userMessage = "File [${file.name}] has been uploaded."
        redirect(controller: 'home')
    } else {
        render(view: 'create', model: [file: file])
    }
}
```

While the file input element for `create.gsp` changes to:

```
<dd><input type="file" name="fileData.data"/></dd>
```

It is necessary to change the name of the input field to allow automatic binding of the submitted data to a new file instance. Supplying data on the request using dot notation allows Grails to bind request data into nested objects on the domain classes. For example, the `File` class has a property called `fileData`, which is a `FileData` instance. `FileData` has a property called `data`, which is an array of **byte**. By giving the file input field a name of `fileData.data`, we can be sure that the contents of the submitted file will bound to the `data` property of the object, which is assigned to the `fileData` property of our new `File` instance. All of this is handled through Grails data binding:

nice.

```
def file = new File( params )
```

Downloading files

The final piece of the puzzle is to allow users to download files that their teammates have posted on the site. We already have the link on the home page:

```
<a href="${g.createLink(controller:'file', action:'download', id:file.
id)}">
    <g:message code="${file.name}" encodeAs="HTML"/>
</a>
```

The `File` class needs to be given a `downloadName` property, which can be used for the filename when downloading. This is simply derived from the name given to the file and the file extension:

```
def getDownloadName() {
    return "${name}.${extension}"
}
```

The `download` action already exists in the `FileController`; we just need to implement it, which is surprisingly simple:

```
def download = {
    def file = File.get(params.id)
    response.setContentType( "application-xdownload")
    response.setHeader("Content-Disposition", "attachment;
filename=${file.downloadName}")
    response.getOutputStream() << new ByteArrayInputStream( file.
fileData.data )
}
```

an issue for files w/ embedded spaces.

The first line uses the `get` method on `File`. This method is dynamically injected by the GORM to retrieve the instance of the class from the database with the specified ID. The next two lines set the necessary headers on the `HttpServletResponse` to tell the client that we are downloading a file with a given name. Finally, we create a `ByteArrayInputStream` from the data of our file and copy the file data to the response using the GDKs overloaded left shift operator (`<<`) on `OutputStream`.

As of Grails 1.1, it is possible to fetch instances of domain classes in read-only state by using the `read` method that is dynamically added to each domain class. This new operation would be appropriate for our `download` action as there should be no need to modify the file while downloading. If we used the `read` method instead of the `get` method, the first line of our download action would look like:
`def file = File.read(params.id).`

If we were implementing file download in Java, we would need to either programmatically copy the data from our `ByteArrayInputStream` to the response `OutputStream` or find a utility class to do this for us.

Start up the application again and check that files can be downloaded now.

Summary

We have added support for file sharing to the teamwork application. This was incredibly easy due to the support that is built-in to Grails for handling file upload. We then used our knowledge of the default GORM behavior for the relationships to enable lazy loading of file binary data to reduce the memory footprint of the application.

In the next chapter, we will allow users to keep a version history of files in the application. While adding version history for files, we will learn about some more advanced techniques for querying the database through GORM.

8

More GORM and Criteria

After successfully implementing file upload (as done in Chapter 7), we decide to get some feedback on the application from our users. It all starts well, our test-users post some messages and upload a few files. They start uploading different versions of a sales pitch. Suddenly someone pipes up: "How about if we could group the different versions of this document? We go through a number of revisions and it would be useful to be able to see the changes all together."

Being the pragmatic user-centered people that we are, and given how simple it was to get basic file upload working, we decide to get right on it! The first step is… You guessed it—domain modeling.

More GORM relationships

We are going to extract all the file details that are currently on the File class to a FileVersion class. The File class will become a file version aggregation, containing links to the current version and a list of FileVersion instances that represents the version history of the file. This version history must be sorted so that we can display the history of the file in a descending order, according to its date.

First of all, extract the existing responsibilities from the File class into the FileVersion class:

```
package app

class FileVersion implements Comparable {

    static belongsTo = File

    String name
    String description
    int size
    String extension
    User user
```

```
        FileData fileData
        Date dateCreated
        Date lastUpdated
        static constraints = {
            name( nullable: false, blank: false )
            description( nullable: false, blank: false )
            size( nullable: false )
            extension( nullable: false )
            user( nullable: false )
            fileData( nullable: false )
        }
        def getDownloadName() {
            return "${name}.${extension}"
        }
        public int compareTo(obj) {
            return obj.dateCreated.compareTo( dateCreated )
        }
    }
```

Notice that we have implemented the `java.lang.Comparable` interface in `FileVersion` to allow instances of `FileVersion` to have a natural sort order.

Don't forget that we also need to update the `FileData` class so that it *belongs to* `FileVersion` instead of `File`:

```
    package app;
    class FileData {
        private static final int TEN_MEG_IN_BYTES = 1024*1024*10
        static belongsTo = [fileVersion:FileVersion]
        byte[] data
        static constraints = {
            data( nullable: false, minSize: 1, maxSize: TEN_MEG_IN_BYTES )
        }
    }
```

Now the `File` class simply becomes a container:

```
    package app
    class File {
        static hasMany = [ versions: FileVersion ]
        SortedSet versions
        FileVersion currentVersion
    }
```

A `File` instance refers to the latest version of the file in the `currentVersion` property and stores the rest of the file version history in the `versions` property.

Sort order of relationships

We have seen before how to use the `hasMany` property to tell Grails to construct a one-to-many relationship. This will create a `versions` property on the `File` class on its own. The explicit declaration of the `version` property as a `SortedSet` tells Grails that the items contained in this relationship must be ordered. This is why we had to implement the `Comparable` interface on the `FileVersion` class, to allow the items in the set to be compared for ordering.

Update validation messages

Before continuing, since we have moved the constraints for uploading a file to the `FileVersion` class, we need to update our validation message keys in `grails-app/i18n/messages.properties`:

```
fileVersion.name.blank=You must give the file a name
fileVersion.description.blank=The file must have a description
fileData.data.minSize.notmet=No file has been uploaded
fileData.data.maxSize.exceeded=The file is too large. The maximum file
size is 10MB
```

Querying with criteria

We will deal with the changes necessary to save a file and add new versions with our new domain structure shortly. While the new structure is fresh in our minds, let's look at how to query the new structure and the changes that must be made to the `HomeController` in order to allow the files to be returned in the correct order.

Remember that our current action for the home page is:

```
def index = {
    def messages = Message.list( sort: 'lastUpdated', order: 'desc',
        fetch: [ user: 'eager' ] )
    def files = File.list( sort: 'dateCreated', order: 'desc',
        fetch: [ user: 'eager' ] )
    return [messages: messages, files: files]
}
```

File no longer has a dateCreated property, as it is now just an aggregation of FileVersion instances. We need to be able to fetch files in the order specified by the date that the currentVersion file was created. To be able to do this we need to construct a slightly more complicated query. In fact, something that might look like the following in SQL:

```
select file.*
from file file, file_version fileversion
where file.version_id = fileversion.id
order by fileversion.date_created desc
```

Wouldn't it be nice if Grails provided us with a programmatic mechanism for constructing more complex queries for Hibernate? Enter Criteria.

Comparing criteria and dynamic finders

Grails provides a Groovy HibernateCriteriaBuilder, which allows us to create complex queries using the Groovy builder syntax in code. The criteria builder is built on top of the Hibernate criteria API. As a quick introduction, we will revisit the examples that were used in Chapter 5 for dynamic finders.

```
User bob = User.findByFirstNameLike( 'Bob%' )

User yesterdayUser = User.findByDateCreatedGreaterThan( yesterday )

def users = []
users = User.findAllByFirstNameLikeAndDateCreatedGreaterThan('Bob%',
yesterday )
```

The equivalent queries using criteria would be:

```
User.withCriteria {
    like( 'firstName', 'Bob%' )
}
User.withCriteria {
    gt( 'dateCreated', yesterday )
}
def users = []
users = User.withCriteria {
    like( 'firstName', 'Bob%' )
    gt( 'dateCreated', yesterday )
}
```

For the simplest example, we can see that using a dynamic finder might be preferable to the criteria. As the examples become more complicated the clarity and flexibility of criteria becomes obvious.

Using logical operators

In the previous examples, each node of the builder is used to define a criterion that must be met when searching for users. We can also declare nodes that act as logical combinations of criteria:

```
User.withCriteria {
    or {
        like( 'firstName', 'Bob%' )
        gt( 'dateCreated', yesterday )
    }
}
```

In this example, all the users whose first name starts with Bob *or* were created since yesterday are returned.

Querying across relationships

In addition to combining criteria with logical operators using nesting, we can use a similar approach for querying across associations. Nodes in our criteria can be used to specify object relationships that we wish to join across. So, to address our retrieval issue with the new domain structure, we can use the dateCreated date on the currentVersion association as shown below:

```
def index = {
    def messages = Message.list( sort: 'lastUpdated', order: 'desc',
        fetch: [ user: 'eager' ] )
    def files = File.withCriteria {
        currentVersion {
            order('dateCreated', 'desc')
        }
    }
    return [messages: messages, files: files]
}
```

Here we perform a criteria query on the File domain class. We specify the currentVersion property as a node, which allows any nested criteria to be applied against the FileVersion object at the end of the currentVersion relationship. In this case, the nested criteria specifies the order for retrieval.

Specifying a fetch mode for relationships

We are not quite finished yet. By using the previous code, we have lost the Hibernate EAGER fetch strategy on the user relationship. To restore this we must simply specify a `fetchMode` node under the `currentVersion` node. The code of the `HomeController` now looks like:

```
package app

import org.hibernate.FetchMode
class HomeController {

    def index = {
        def messages = Message.list(sort: 'lastUpdated',
            order: 'desc', fetch: [user: 'eager'])
        def files = File.withCriteria {
            currentVersion {
                order('dateCreated', 'desc')
                fetchMode( 'user', FetchMode.EAGER )
            }
        }
        return [messages: messages, files: files]
    }
}
```

Criteria reference

The full list of available criteria for querying at the time of writing is:

Criteria	Description	Example
between	Check if a property is between two values.	between('age', 16, 70)
eq	Check if a property is equal to a value.	eq('start', today)
eqProperty	Check if a property is equal to another property.	eqProperty('start', 'begin')
gt	Check if a property is greater than a value.	gt('start', yesterday)
gtProperty	Check if a property is greater than another property.	gtProperty('start', 'end')
ge	Check if a property is greater than or equal to a value.	Ge('start', yesterday)
geProperty	Check if a property is greater than or equal to another property.	geProperty('totalPayed', 'bill')
idEq	Check if an objects id equals the value.	idEq(101)

Criteria	Description	Example
ilike	Perform a case-insensitive `like` check on a property.	`ilike('name', 'lance%')`
isEmpty	Check if a collection property is empty.	`isEmpty('messages')`
isNotEmpty	Check if a collection property is not empty.	`isNotEmpty('roles')`
isNull	Check if a property is **null**.	`isNull('title')`
isNotNull	Check if a property is not **null**.	`isNotNull('name')`
lt	Check if a property is less than a value.	`lt('age', 16)`
ltProperty	Check if a property is less than another property.	ltProperty('end', 'start')
le	Check if a property is less than or equal to a value.	`le('age', 70)`
leProperty	Check if a property is less than or equal to another property.	`leProperty('age', 'maxAge')`
like	Perform a `like` check against a property.	`like('name', 'Lance%')`
ne	Check if a property does not equal a value.	`ne('paid', today)`
neProperty	Check if a property does not equal another property.	`neProperty('name', 'updatedName')`
order	Use a property to order the results.	`order('lastModified', 'desc')`
sizeEq	Check if a collection property has a size equal to a value.	`sizeEq('messages', 10)`
sizeGt	Check if a collections size is greater than a value. (Only for Grails 1.1).	`sizeGt('failedAttempts', 2)`
sizeGe	Check if a collections size is greater than or equal to a value. (Only for Grails 1.1).	`sizeGe('failedAttempts', 3)`
sizeLt	Check if a collections size is less than a value. (Only for Grails 1.1).	`sizeLt('failedAttempts', 3)`
sizeLe	Check if a collection's size is less than or equals to a value. (Only for Grails 1.1).	`sizeLe('failedAttempts', 2)`
sizeNe	Check if a collection's size is not equal to a value. (Only for Grails 1.1).	`sizeNe('failedAttempts', 3)`

Logical criteria

Remember, we can also combine criteria using logical nodes. The logical nodes that are available are:

Criteria	Description	Example

and	Perform a logical AND on the criteria contained in the code block.	`and {`
		`    ge('age', 16)`
		`    notNull('niNumber')`
		`}`

or	Perform a logical OR on the criteria contained in the code block.	`or {`
		`    eq('status', HAS_VISA)`
		`    notNull('niNumber')`
		`}`

not	Perform a logical NOT on the criteria contained in the code block.	`not {`
		`    inList('age',`
		`[16..70])`
		`}`

> Nodes at the same level, without any logical nodes specified, will automatically be used as if contained in an and block.

Setting criteria properties

We saw in the finished `HomeController` that we could determine the Hibernate fetch strategy through a node in the criteria builder. We are able to set any property on the Hibernate `Criteria` object by specifying the property name as a node in our criteria builder. In the following example, we will limit our search to ten results:

```
def files = File.withCriteria {
    currentVersion {
        order( 'dateCreated', 'desc' )
        fetchMode( 'user', FetchMode.EAGER )
    }
    maxResults( 10 )
}
```

For a complete list of the available properties, look at the Hibernate `Criteria` Javadoc (http://www.hibernate.org/hib_docs/v3/api/org/hibernate/Criteria.html).

Projections & scrollable Results

> The Grails `HibernateCriteriaBuilder` also supports using Projections (http://www.hibernate.org/hib_docs/v3/api/org/hibernate/criterion/Projections.html) and Scrollable Results (http://www.hibernate.org/hib_docs/v3/api/org/hibernate/ScrollableResults.html).

Updating FileController

After our brief detour into the rich world of Grails support for Hibernate Criteria querying, it is time to get back to the application. To recap, we have modified our domain model to handle version history for uploaded files, and have updated the `HomeController` to use Criteria to retrieve the list of files, given the new domain structure.

We now have two scenarios for file upload:

- Posting a new file
- Posting a new version of an existing file

Updating the create file view

To handle the new case, posting a new version of an existing file, we need a new action to load the **Post File** page. Add the following action to the `FileController`:

```
def newVersion = {
    def model = [file: new FileVersion(), fileId: params.id]
    render( view: 'create', model: model )
}
```

By specifying the `create` view for the `newVersion` action, we are able to reuse the `create.gsp` file to render the **Post File** page for both scenarios. Notice that we have added a new parameter to the view model: `fileId`. This contains the id of the `File` that we want to add the new version to.

We also need to handle the scenario where we are creating a file for the first time, rather than adding a new version to an existing file. Previously the `create` action returned a new instance of `File`, now it must be changed to return a new instance of `FileVersion`:

```
def create = {
    return [ file: new FileVersion() ]
}
```

We now have to update the `create.gsp` file to use the new `fileId` parameter.

```
<g:hiddenField name="fileId" value="${fileId}"/>
```

We do this by adding a hidden input field to the form. Nothing else should be changed on this form as we have kept the interface of the `VersionFile` class the same as the `File` class that it was previously working with.

Handling save

The last part of being able to save a new version of a file is to enhance the save action:

```
def save = {
    def currentVersion = new FileVersion(params)
    currentVersion.user = userService.getAuthenticatedUser()
    MultipartFile f = request.getFile('fileData.data')
    currentVersion.size = f.getSize() / 1024
    currentVersion.extension = extractExtension(f)

    File file
    if(params.fileId) {
        file = File.get( params.fileId )
        file.versions << file.currentVersion
        file.currentVersion = currentVersion
    } else {
        file = new File( currentVersion: currentVersion )
    }
    if (file.save()) {
        flash.userMessage = "file [${currentVersion.name}]"
        redirect(controller: 'home')
    } else {
        render(view: 'post', model: [file: currentVersion])
    }
}
```

(handwritten margin notes:) or fix w/ change to create.gsp has Errors loop

(handwritten note near render line:) added   currentVersion.errors = file.errors

(handwritten note:) ↑ no such view

(handwritten note at left:) Source code is different

There are two main changes that have been made to the logic of the save action:

- We create and bind the file data to a `FileVersion` object, rather than a `File` object
- We determine whether to add the `FileVersion` to an existing `File` object, or create a new one.

Looking at the `save` action, we should be starting to get nervous about the amount of work it is doing. It is no longer simply persisting data and handling validation. It is starting to handle some of our application logic and is becoming very difficult to test. For example, to test the logic that determines whether to add the file version to a new file or an existing file would require us to:

- Set up security details.
- Put a real file into the request object.
- Check the state of the database to see what had been persisted.

That is an awful lot of work to test a simple if/else statement. We will see how to extract this logic out into a service in the next chapter. For now, we will leave it as it is and move on to rendering file versions on the home page.

Render file versions

Almost everything is in place now. The only change left is to render file versions on the home page.

The code that looks the most complex, which is due to the nature of templates, out of all the changes we have made, is the view logic. We need to modify the **Files** panel on the home page to show the version information for files:

```
<div class="panel">
    <h2>Files</h2>
    <g:each in="${files}" var="file">
        <g:set var="currentVersion" value="${file.currentVersion}"/>
        <div class="afile">
            <div class="filename">
                <a href="${g.createLink(controller: 'file', action:
                    'download', id: currentVersion.id)}">
                    <g:message code="${currentVersion.name}"
                        encodeAs="HTML"/>
                </a> -
        <g:message code="file.size"
            args="${[currentVersion.size]}"/>
            <div class="filenamesupplimentary">
                <g:message code="message.user"
                        args="${[currentVersion.user.firstName,
                        currentVersion.user.lastName]}"/>
            <span>
                <a class="newversion" href="${g.createLink
                    (controller: 'file', action: 'newVersion',
                    id: file.id)}">
                        <g:message code="file.newversion"/>
```

```
                    </a>
                  </span>
                </div>
              </div>
              <div class="filebody">
                <g:message code="${currentVersion.description}"
                    encodeAs="HTML"/>
              </div>
              <g:if test="${file.versions}">
              <div class="versions">
                <span class="versionsheader">
                    <g:message code="file.oldversions"/></span>
                <ul>
                    <g:each var="fileVersion"
                        in="${ file.versions }">
                        <li>
                            <a title="${fileVersion.description}"
                                href="${g.createLink(controller:
                                    'file', action: 'download',
                                    id: fileVersion.id) }">
                                ...${fileVersion.name}
                            </a>
                        </li>
                    </g:each>
                </ul>
              </div>
              </g:if>
            </div>
        </g:each>
    </div>
```

The GSP code above iterates over the files that are returned by HomeController. Each file is given a link to upload a new version. If a file has a version, then the version files are shown within the context of the file with a link to download each of them. We can no longer use the file object to display information directly, as the metadata for the main file is on the currentVersion property rather than the file object. We have used the g:set tag to make the currentVersion property directly accessible as a local variable in the page. This avoids the need to reach inside the file to get the current version every time we want to display some file metadata.

You will need to add the following message keys before running the application to test file versions:

```
file.newversion=New version
file.oldversions=Previous versions:
```

After making these changes, run the application and add a new file. You should see a home page that looks like the following screenshot:

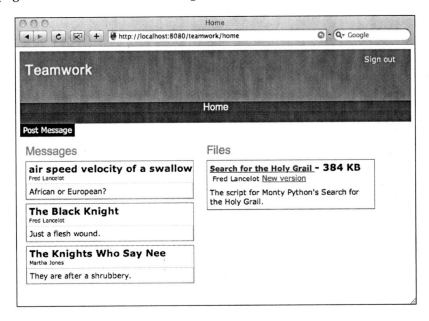

Click on the **New version** link and load a new file. You should see a new file on the home page with its previous version shown in-line below:

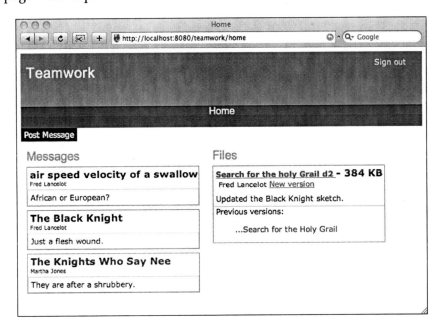

Fix file download

The very last change that we have to make is to fix the download action on FileController so that it is used with FileVersion rather than File:

```
def download = {
    def fileVersion = FileVersion.get(params.id)
    response.setContentType( "application-xdownload")
    response.setHeader("Content-Disposition",
        "attachment; filename=${fileVersion.downloadName}")
    response.getOutputStream() <<
        new ByteArrayInputStream( fileVersion.fileData.data )
}
```

Summary

In this chapter, we have added version history to files that are posted in the application. Adding this functionality allowed us to learn more about managing relationships between entities in Grails. We also investigated creating more complicated queries that cross relationships using Grails HibernateCriteriaBuilder. This provides a nice way to execute some complex queries.

In the next chapter, we are going to look at how we can use services to encapsulate application logic and reduce the burden on controllers.

9
Services

In the last two chapters, we allowed our users to post new files while using the application and also keep a version history of files. Unfortunately, as a result of these changes, we have accrued a certain amount of technical debt in the `FileController` class. This class is no longer handling just the flow of the application, but it is now responsible for managing the logic to enable the version history for files. We need to remove this logic from the controller, so that it can get back to controlling the flow of our application.

Introducing services

Grails supports a service layer that allows us to extract the logic of our application from controllers into reusable and testable services. This means that controllers can focus on controlling the application flow, rather than becoming cluttered with business logic.

Service classes are defined by another convention:

- They must exist under the `grails-app/services` folder.
- The class name must end in `Service`.

As with controllers and domain classes, Grails provides a command-line tool to generate service classes. In the terminal window run:

```
grails create-service app.File
```

This will create the Groovy class `grails-app/service/app/FileService.groovy` with the following code:

```
package app

class FileService {

    boolean transactional = true

    def serviceMethod() {
    }
}
```

Grails uses Spring's support for declarative transactions to allow all service methods to be transactional. If we decide that we don't want a service to be transactional, then we must declare the `transactional` property as **false**:

```
boolean transactional = false
```

When transactions are enabled, all method calls are wrapped within one transaction, and a rollback will take place if any one of the methods called throws an exception.

Dependency injection

Grails uses Spring's dependency injection mechanism to inject services into domain classes, controllers or other services as and when needed.

Dependency injection is a design pattern to remove creational coupling from our code. When using dependency injection, the normal practice is to *wire up* objects through configuration files. This is so that classes that depend on other classes only need to understand how to use the interface of the class and not how to construct it.

Grails uses Spring to handle dependency injection and provides a layer of convention over the top, so there is no need to maintain configuration files to wire classes together. The following rules define the convention for dependency injection and services:

- All services are bound into the Spring context
- Services are injected into properties on controller, service, and domain classes that have the same name as the service class
- Properties for injection that are loosely typed can be reloaded when code changes without restarting the application, though in development mode only
- Properties for injection that are strongly typed require the application to be restarted to pick up code changes to their services

For example, now that we have our `FileService`, **suppose** we add a property to our `FileController` such as:

```
def fileService
```

An instance of `FileService` will be created when **the application** starts up and this instance will be injected into the `fileService` **property on the** controller whenever a new instance of the controller is instantiated. **Changes to** the file service will be available when we refresh a page, without needing **to restart** the application, because the type of the service is not declared.

However, if we strongly type our `fileService` property:

```
FileService fileService
```

The service will still be injected, but will not reload without an application restart.

 By default, services are stored in the Spring context as singletons, which means that they are not thread-safe. Hence, we need to avoid storing any state in a service unless we are willing to change the scope of the service.

Service scope

The scope of a service defines the rules regarding the lifetime of an instance of a service and when new instances are constructed. Defining the scope of a service is handled through the `static scope` property, for example:

```
static scope = 'prototype'
```

The available scopes are:

Scope	Description
prototype	A new service is created each time it is injected into a class.
request	A new service is created each time a HTTP request is made.
flash	The service is created for this request and the next request. Same as flash scope in the controller and view layers.
conversation	When using web flows, the service will be created at the beginning of a new conversation and thrown away at the end of the conversation.
session	A service exists for the length of a user session.
singleton	Only one instance of the service is ever created. This is the default behavior.

Implementing FileService

To keep the logic in our controllers down to handling nothing but the flow of the application, we need to extract as much logic as possible from `FileController` into a service. The responsibilities we are going to move to the service are:

- Constructing the new `FileVersion` object
- Managing the `File` object and its version history
- Persisting the changes to the database

Take a look at the full listing of the `FileService`. We will discuss each method individually after the listing.

```
package app

class FileService {

    public static final Integer KB_DIVIDER = 1024;

    boolean transactional = true

    def userService

    def saveNewVersion( params, multipartFile ) {
        def version = createVersionFile( params, multipartFile )
        def file = applyNewVersion( params.fileId, version )
        file.save()
        return file;
    }

    def applyNewVersion( fileId, version ) {
        if( fileId ) {
            File file = File.get( fileId )
            if( file ) {
                file.newVersion( version )
                return file
            }
        }
        return new File( currentVersion: version )
    }

    def createVersionFile( params, multipartFile ) {
        def currentVersion = new FileVersion(params)
        currentVersion.user = userService.getAuthenticatedUser()
        currentVersion.size = multipartFile.size / KB_DIVIDER
        currentVersion.extension = extractExtension(multipartFile)
        return currentVersion
    }

    def extractExtension( file ) {
```

```
        String filename = file.originalFilename
        return filename.substring(filename.lastIndexOf(".") + 1)
    }
}
```

There is a fair bit of code here, so let's look at it one method at a time. First, the createVersionFile method:

```
def createVersionFile( params, multipartFile ) {
    def currentVersion = new FileVersion(params)
    currentVersion.user = userService.getAuthenticatedUser()
    currentVersion.size = multipartFile.size / KB_DIVIDER
    currentVersion.extension = extractExtension(multipartFile)
    return currentVersion
}
```

The method receives the request parameters and a MultipartFile. Note that the request parameters are stored in a Map, so our service has no dependency on the HttpServletRequest interface from the Servlet specification. Apart from the use of the UserService to find the current authenticated user, this method is almost a direct cut and paste of the FileController code. Because the logic to populate the VersionFile object depends on a number of collaborators (userService, params, and multiPartFile), we have decided to keep this logic out of the file domain class and put it into the service.

Next we extract the logic that looks up a file instance and manages the version history for the file:

```
def applyNewVersion( fileId, version ) {
    if( fileId ) {
        File file = File.get( fileId )
        if( file ) {
            file.newVersion( version )
            return file
        }
    }
    return new File( currentVersion: version )
}
```

This method is responsible for finding the File instance specified by fileId and, if the file exists, applying a new version to the file. If the file does not exist, a new file is created with the supplied version. Notice that we are calling a method on File that does not exist yet:

```
file.newVersion( version )
```

We have decided to put this method in the `File` class because a file is an aggregation of `FileVersion` instances and so should be responsible for managing its versions. Add the following method to the `File` class:

```
def newVersion( version ) {
    versions = (versions)?:new TreeSet()
    versions << currentVersion
    currentVersion = version
}
```

If there are no versions yet, the `versions` property is instantiated. Then the `currentVersion` is added to the `versions` `SortedSet`, and the new `version` argument is assigned as the `currentVersion`.

Now, back to the `FileService` class. We finally create the `saveNewVersion` method to link the usage of the `createNewVersion` and `applyNewVersion` methods. This is the method that will be called from the controller:

```
def saveNewVersion( params, multipartFile ) {
    def version = createVersionFile( params, multipartFile )
    def file = applyNewVersion( params.fileId, version )
    file.save()
    return file;
}
```

We have also moved the GORM `save()` call into the service, so the controller can remain completely free of persistence code.

> You might be tempted to replace the last three lines in the `saveNewVersion` method with:
>
> ```
> return applyNewVersion( params.fileId, version
> ).save()
> ```
>
> This will not work! If there is a validation error, the save method will populate the `errors` property, then return **null**. We need to be able to return a `File` object with the `errors` property populated.

By updating our save action in `FileController` to use the new `FileService`, we end up with:

```
package app

class FileController {

    def fileService
    def save = {
        def multipartFile = request.getFile('fileData.data')
```

```
def file = fileService.saveNewVersion(
    params, multipartFile )
if ( file.hasErrors() ) {
    file.currentVersion.errors = file.errors
    render(view: 'post', model: [file: file.currentVersion])
} else {
    flash.userMessage = "file [${file.currentVersion.name}]"
    redirect(controller: 'home')
}
}
def create = {…}
def download = {…}
def newVersion = {…}
}
```

these changes render the corrections made in previous chapter irrelevant

This is much simpler and allows us to focus on how the application should react to the user, rather than getting lost in the logic of the application.

The simplified version of the controller declares a fileService member variable. This tells Grails to inject an instance of the FileService class whenever a controller is constructed.

We then call the saveNewVersion method on fileService, passing the request parameters and a MultipartFile. The retrieval of the MultipartFile instance has been kept in the controller because we need to have access to the request object for this operation.

The service is now responsible for persisting changes in the File object to the database. Remember that the save operation populates the errors property on a domain object if there are validation errors when persisting the object. All we need to do in the controller is to check if calling hasErrors on the file returns **true**.

Finally, because we persist a File instance and allow the saved changes to cascade down to the FileVersion instances, all of the validation errors will be on the File instance, even if saving a FileVersion instance was the cause of the errors. For this reason, we need to put the contents of the errors object on the File object onto the currentVersion property that we return to the view.

Now re-run the application to verify the changes we have made. There should be no change to the behavior of the application, only the underlying implementation is now easier to maintain.

never discusses moving method extract Extension from controller to service

Summary

In this chapter, we have seen the Grails service layer in action. We have also seen the options that are available to control the lifecycle of a service. We now also understand how Grails makes services available to the rest of the application through dependency injection. Services are useful for encapsulating the logic of our application in the following scenarios:

- Where the complexity becomes too much for controllers
- Where the logic does not fit naturally into a domain class

In the next chapter, we are going to look at including tagging in the application so that files and messages can be tagged, which will allow users to limit the amount of data that is displayed on their home page. *te*

not told to remove userService from fileController? - see note at least, not clearly

10
Managing Content through Tagging

Over the last few chapters, we added the ability for our users to upload and share files with their teammates. As with messages, files are displayed on the home page in the order they are added to the system. Currently all messages and files are displayed on the home page. Over time, our home page is going to become rather large and unwieldy. We need a user's home page to show only the files and messages that they are interested in. To do this, users need to be able to tag their content.

We will implement a simple tagging solution, restructure the home page and then add some new pages to the application for viewing all of the messages and files.

The new Grails concepts that will be introduced in this chapter are:

- Working with inheritance in the domain classes, and looking at which strategies GORM supports for persistence
- Using polymorphic queries over a domain inheritance hierarchy
- Encapsulating view-rendering logic in GSP templates
- Manipulating collections with the Groovy `collect` and `sort` methods

Add basic tagging

Tagging is a loose, community-based way of categorizing content. It allows a group of people to categorize by consensus. Anyone is able to tag a piece of content. The more a tag is used, the more meaning it takes on and the more widely used it becomes. This categorization by consensus has been dubbed as *folksonomy* (`http://en.wikipedia.org/wiki/Folksonomy`) in recent times.

So let's get started by building our tagging support.

Tagging domain model

When implementing tagging in our system, we need to consider the following:

- We must be able to have many tags in our system
- We must be able to associate a single tag with many different files and messages
- We need to make sure that new domain objects can be easily tagged without having to change the tagging logic
- We want to know when a domain object was tagged

To satisfy these requirements, we need to create the following new domain classes:

- Tag—to store the name of the tag. There is one instance of this class per unique tag name in the application.
- Tagger—to store the relationship from domain objects to a tag. This allows us to store the date a tag was added to a domain object.

Let's create these domain classes and then write a test to prove that we can tag a message using this tagging structure.

The Tag class

We are going to separate the tagging classes out from our application domain classes. Create a folder under `grails-app/domain` called `tagging`. This is where we will put the domain model to implement tagging.

Our `Tag` class is extremely simple and holds only a `name` property:

```
package tagging
class Tag {
    String name
    static constrains = {
        name( blank: false )
    }
}
```

The Tagger class

The next class that we are going to create is the `Tagger` class. In relational terms, this object represents a link table between a `Tag` and any other domain class. It is important that the relationship between tagged domain classes and the `Tagger` relationship class is unidirectional. By this, we mean the domain classes are allowed to know that they can be tagged, but tags do not know which domain classes can be tagged, otherwise every tagged domain class would need a special relationship class.

Create the `Tagger` class as a domain class in the `tagging` package as follows:

```
package tagging
class Tagger {
    Tag tag
    static constraints = {
        tag( nullable: false )
    }
}
```

The basics of our tagging model are complete! We now need some logic to allow tags to be created. Create a new service class called `TagService` under `grails-app/services/tagging`, as shown below:

```
package tagging
class TagService {
    boolean transactional = true
    def createTagRelationships(String spaceDelimitedTags) {
        return spaceDelimitedTags?.split(' ')?.collect { tagName ->
            createTagRelationship( tagName )
        }
    }
    def createTagRelationship(String tagName) {
        def tag = Tag.findByName(tagName)?:
                new Tag(name: tagName).save()
        return new Tagger( tag: tag )
    }
}
```

This service provides two utility methods to create new relationships by tag name or by a space delimited string of tag names. The important behavior of these two methods is that they do not allow duplicate tags to be created in the application. If a tag name already exists, the tag will be retrieved from the database and used as the tag in the relationship.

Notice that the `createTagRelationships` method is using the `collect` method to simplify what would normally take a few more lines of code to achieve. We did briefly cover the `collect` method back in our introduction to Groovy in Chapter 4, but to reiterate: the `collect` method is dynamically added to any object that can be iterated over. For example, collections, arrays, strings and so on. It takes a closure as its argument and executes this closure for each item in the collection. The return value from each execution of the closure is added to a new collection that the `collect` method builds up and then returns once it has finished iterating the original collection.

In `createTagRelationship`, we are using another neat language feature of Groovy called the "Elvis operator". It is named so, as it looks like Elvis' hair style. This is a shorter version of the normal Java ternary operator. If the operand being checked is true then the checked operand will be returned as the default, otherwise the alternative operand will be used. So in our example:

```
def tag = Tag.findByName(tagName) ?: new Tag(name: tagName).save()
```

If a tag can be found from the database then it is used, otherwise a new tag is created.

Tagging a message

The next step is to allow a message to be tagged. Write some integration tests to make sure the relationships are working before using tagging in the application.

In the folder `test/integration/app`, create the file `TaggableIntegrationTests.groovy` and add the following code:

```
package app
import tagging.Tag
class TaggableIntegrationTest extends GroovyTestCase {
    User flancelot
    protected void setUp() {
        flancelot = User.findByUsername('flancelot')
        Tag.list().each { it.delete() }
        Message.list().each { it.delete() }
    }
}
```

The code above sets up the test data needed to create messages and associate tags to messages. Remember that the *flancelot* user already exists because it was created by the `BootStrap` class.

The first test will determine that we can add tags to a message and then retrieve messages by tag. Add the following test method to your test class:

```
void testCanRetrieveMessagesByTags() {
    Message message = new Message(user: flancelot, title: 'tagged',
            detail: "I've been tagged.").save(flush: true)
    Message secondMessage = new Message(user: flancelot,
            title: 'other tagged',
            detail: "I've been tagged.").save(flush: true)
    message.addTag('urgent')
    message.addTag('late')
    secondMessage.addTag('urgent')
```

```
def taggedMessages = Message.withTag( 'urgent' )
assertEquals(2, taggedMessages.size())
assertEquals(2, Tag.list().size())
def secondMessages = Message.withTag( 'late' )
assertEquals(1, secondMessages.size())
assertEquals(2, Tag.list().size())
}
```

The test above does the following:

- Creates two new messages
- Adds the `urgent` tag to both messages
- Adds the `late` tag to one message
- Checks if we can retrieve both messages by using the `urgent` tag
- Checks if only one message is returned for the `late` tag

Notice that the highlighted lines of code have not been implemented yet. To allow this test to pass, we need to add the following methods to the `Message` domain class:

- `addTag`—instance method to allow a message to be tagged
- `withTag`—class method to retrieve all messages with a particular tag

Add the following method to the `Message` class (don't forget to import `tagging.Tagger`):

```
def addTag(String tagName) {
    tags = (tags)?:[]
    tags << tagService.createTagRelationship( tagName )
}
```

This method simply delegates the creation of the tag relationship off to the `TagService` class, and then stores the relationship in the `tags` list.

Add the following method to the `Message` class that retrieves all messages with a given tag name:

```
def static withTag(String tagName) {
    return Message.withCriteria {
        tags {
            tag {
                eq('name', tagName )
            }
        }
    }
}
```

This method must be static on the Message class, as it is used to load message instances for a given tag. We do not want to have to instantiate a message before we can perform the search.

Before running the test, you will notice both of these new methods assume that there is a property on the Message class called tags. This has not yet been created. We need to create a one-to-many relationship from Message to Tagger that will allow messages to be tagged. We also need to inject the TagService into new instances of the Message class so the work for creating a new tag relationship can be delegated. Add the relationship to the Message class and inject TagService as shown below:

```
class Message {
    def tagService
    static hasMany = [tags:Tagger]
    ...
}
```

Now we can run our tests by entering the following on the command line:

```
grails test-app
```

We should see some output in the command line similar to:

```
Running test app.TaggableTest...
                    testCanRetrieveMessagesByTags...SUCCESS
```

Tagging a file

Now that we have implemented tagging for messages, we need to make tagging available for files.

Currently the logic for creating and fetching tags is in the Message domain class. We need to extract this logic so the File domain class can reuse it. It's time to look at how GORM supports inheritance.

GORM inheritance

The GORM supports inheritance of domain classes by default through the underlying Hibernate framework. Hibernate has a number of strategies for handling inheritance and Grails supports the following two:

- Table-per-hierarchy—this strategy creates one database table per inheritance hierarchy. This is the default strategy in Grails.

- Table-per-subclass—this strategy creates a database table for each subclass in an inheritance hierarchy and treats the inheritance (*is a*) relationship as a foreign key (*has a*) relationship.

Taking our domain as an example, we have two classes. They are `Message` and `File`. We are going to make them both extend a super class `Taggable`, which will handle all of our tagging logic and state.

Table-per-hierarchy

If we were to choose the table-per-hierarchy strategy, we would end up with one table called `Taggable` that contained the data for both `Message` and `File`. The database structure would look something like:

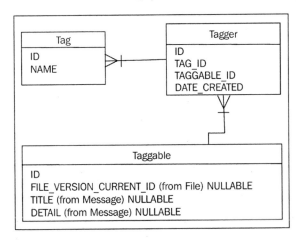

The interesting side-effect of this approach is that all of the fields to be persisted must be `nullable`. If a `File` is created and persisted, it is obviously not possible for the fields from `Message` to be populated.

Table-per-subclass

By using the table-per-subclass strategy, we would keep two separate tables called `Message` and `File`, and both would have the tags relationship inherited from `Taggable`. So the `Message` table will look like:

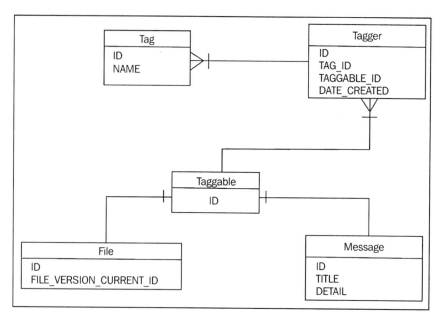

We can see in the diagram above that the `Message` and `File` tables have remained separate and a table representing the superclass `Taggable` has been created, which the subclass tables have foreign key relationships to. In the table-per-subclass strategy, a table must exist to represent the inheritance (*is a*) relationship.

We are going to follow the table-per-subclass strategy so that we can retain database level data integrity. The default behavior for GORM is to use the table-per-hierarchy strategy. To override this we must use the `mapping` property:

```
static mapping = {
    tablePerHierarchy false
}
```

Taggable superclass

Now that we have discussed how GORM handles domain class inheritance, it is time to implement our `Taggable` superclass that will allow `Message` and `File` to handle tagging. Create a domain class in the `tagging` package that:

- Contains a set of `Tagger` instances
- Defines the hibernate inheritance mapping strategy to use
- Implements the `addTag` method from `Message`
- Implements the `withTag` method from `Message`

The implementation for the base class looks like:

```
package tagging
class Taggable {
    def tagService
    static hasMany = [tags: Tagger]
    static mapping = {
        tablePerHierarchy false
    }
    def addTag(String tagName) {
        tags = (tags)?:[]
        tags << tagService.createTagRelationship( tagName )
    }
    def static withTag(String tagName) {
        return Taggable.withCriteria {
            tags {
                tag {
                    eq('name', tagName )
                }
            }
        }
    }
}
```

Now that we have the tag-specific logic implemented in a base class, we need to remove the `addTag` and `withTag` methods from the `Message` class, as well as the `tags` relationship and the `tagService` property, and make the `File` and `Message` classes extend `Taggable`. `Message`, as shown below:

```
import tagging.Taggable
class Message extends Taggable {
    ...
}
```

Make the following changes to the `File` class:

```
import tagging.Taggable
class File extends Taggable {
    ...
}
```

Run the tests again and we can see that `TaggableIntegrationTests` still passes. Now add a test to verify that `File` objects can be tagged:

```
void testFileCanBeTagged() {
    def fileData = new FileData(data: [0])
    def aVersion = new FileVersion(name: name, fileData: fileData,
            description: 'foo', extension: 'pdf', user: fred)
    def firstFile = new File( currentVersion: aVersion )
            .save(flush: true)
    def secondFile = new File( currentVersion: aVersion )
            .save(flush: true)

    firstFile.addTag('draft')
    secondFile.addTag('draft')
    secondFile.addTag('released')

    def draftFiles = File.withTag('draft')
    assertEquals(2, draftFiles.size())
    assertEquals(2, Tag.list().size())

    def releasedFiles = File.withTag('released')
    assertEquals(1, releasedFiles.size())
    assertEquals(2, Tag.list().size())
}
```

(handwritten note: ? not in book. source doesn't make sense.)

This test verifies that `File` instances can be tagged in exactly the same way as `Message` instances.

Polymorphic queries

So far so good, however, there is an additional implication to inheritance with domain classes that we need to investigate, that is, the introduction of polymorphic queries. When we query a domain superclass, we are performing a polymorphic query, which means the query will actually run over the subclasses and return all matching instances from all of the subclasses.

In more practical terms, when we call the `withTag` method on `File` or `Message`, we are actually going to receive all `File` and `Message` instances with the specified tag. This is because the `withTag` implementation exists on the `Taggable` class, so we are performing the query against the `Taggable` class:

```
def static withTag(String tagName) {
    return Taggable.withCriteria {
        tags {
            tag {
                eq('name', tagName )
            }
        }
    }
}
```

Let's write a test to prove this:

```
void testTaggedObjectsCanBeRetrievedByType() {
    def fileData = new FileData( data: [0] )
    def aVersion = new FileVersion( name: 'v1', fileData: fileData,
            description: 'foo', size: 101, extension: 'pdf',
            user: fred )
    def firstFile = new File( currentVersion: aVersion )
            .save(flush: true)
    def message = new Message(user: fred, title: 'tagged',
            detail: "I've been tagged.").save(flush: true)

    firstFile.addTag('draft')
    message.addTag('draft')

    assertEquals(1, Message.withTag('draft').size())
    assertEquals(1, File.withTag('draft').size())
}
```

Here we are creating a file and a message, and tagging each of them as draft. If we didn't know about polymorphic queries, we would expect to be able to retrieve one message with the 'draft' tag and one file with the 'draft' tag.

Running the tests now, we will see the following failed test in the output:

```
Running test app.TaggableTest...

                testCanRetrieveMessagesByTags...SUCCESS

                testFileCanBeTagged...SUCCESS

                testTaggedObjectsCanBeRetrievedByType...FAILURE
```

Open the tests HTML report (`test/reports/html/index.html`) to get more detail on the reason for the failure as shown in the following screenshot:

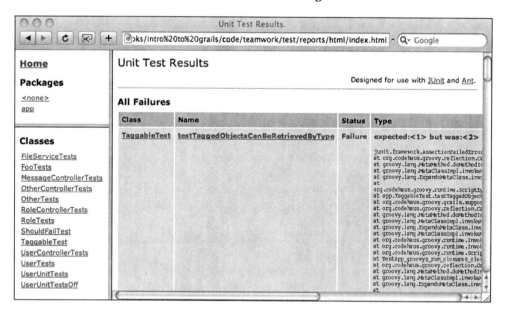

Our expectation was that there should be one item in the returned results; instead two items were returned—the tagged message and the tagged file.

This functionality may be useful to us in the future, but for now, we need to be able to search by a specific type. To solve this problem, we can create another `withTag` method that also takes a type. We end up with the following methods in `Taggable`:

```
def static withTag(String tagName) {
    return withTag(tagName, Taggable)
}

def static withTag(String tagName, Class type) {
    return type.withCriteria {
        tags {
            tag {
                eq('name', tagName )
            }
        }
    }
}
```

Now we can optionally specify a type that we wish to query. The default behavior, if no type is specified, is to perform a polymorphic query against `Taggable`. We can now add a `withTag` method onto the `Message` and `File` classes that will override the default behavior of the `Taggable` class so that our test passes. Add the following method to `Message`:

```
def static withTag(String tagName) {
    return Taggable.withTag(tagName, Message)
}
```

And add the following method to `File`:

```
def static withTag(String tagName) {
    return Taggable.withTag(tagName, File)
}
```

Now run the tests again and all should pass.

Exposing tagging to the users

The domain model is up and running so we can move on to allowing users to tag messages and files. In the first instance, we will allow users to tag messages and files when they are created. To do this, we need to make the following changes:

- The GSPs that render the forms to submit messages and files must allow users to enter tags
- The `Taggable` class needs to handle adding many tags in one go
- The controllers must handle tags entered by the user
- The `FileService` class must populate user tags on the `File`
- The home page needs to render the tags that were added to each message and file

Add the Tags input field

We are going to allow users to input tags in free text and make them delimited by spaces. So we simply need to add a new text input field to each of the **Post Message** and **Post File** screens. The `fieldset` element in the message `create.gsp` becomes:

```
<fieldset>
    <dl>
        <dt>Title</dt>
        <dd><g:textField name="title" value="${message.title}"
size="35"/>
        </dd>
```

```
        <dt>Message detail</dt>
        <dd><g:textArea name="detail" value="${message.detail}"/></dd>
        <dt>Tags</dt>
        <dd><g:textField name="userTags" value="${userTags}"
                size="35"/></dd>
    </dl>
</fieldset>
```

While the `fieldset` for the file `create.gsp` becomes:

```
<fieldset>
    <dl>
        <dt>Title</dt>
        <dd><g:textField name="name" value="${file.name}"
                        size="35"/></dd>
        <dt>File</dt>
        <dd><input type="file" name="data"/></dd>
        <dt>Message detail</dt>
        <dd><g:textArea name="description"
                value="${file.description}"/></dd>
        <dt>Tags</dt>
        <dd><g:textField name="userTags" value="${userTags}"
                size="35"/></dd>
    </dl>
</fieldset>
```

Add multiple tags to Taggable

We can already store a list of tags against a `Taggable` class, but currently they must be added one at a time. For our users convenience, we really need to be able to handle adding multiple tags in one go. Let's create the `addTags` method on `Taggable`:

```
def addTags(String spaceDelimitedTags) {
    tags = (tags)?:[]
    tags.addAll(tagService.createTagRelationships(spaceDelimitedTags))
}
```

Once again, here we just delegate the logic to the `TagService` class.

Saving the users tags

The next step is to handle the new user input so that the tags will be persisted. The `save` action on `MessageController` is updated as shown below:

```
def save = {
    def message = new Message(params)
    message.addTags( params.userTags )
    message.user = userService.getAuthenticatedUser()
```

```
if( !message.hasErrors() && message.save() ) {
    flash.toUser = "Message [${message.title}] has been added."
    redirect(action: 'create')
} else {
    render(view: 'create',
        model: [message: message, userTags: params.userTags])
}
}
```

We need to convert the user input, a space delimited list of tags, into our structured tagging model. This means we are not able to take advantage of the Grails data binding support and must add the tags manually through the addTags method that we created earlier. When there are validation errors, we must also make sure the tags entered by the user are made available on the page model so the tags are not lost when rendering the error messages.

In FileController, we must also make the users tags are available on the model when rendering validation errors. Change the current line in the save action from:

```
render(view: 'post', model: [file: file.currentVersion])
```

to:

```
render(view: 'post', model: [file: file.currentVersion,

        userTags: params.userTags])
```

The call to addTags takes place in the saveNewVersion method in FileService:

```
def saveNewVersion( params, multipartFile ) {
    def version = createVersionFile( params, multipartFile )
    def file = applyNewVersion( params.fileId, version )
    file.addTags( params.userTags )
    file.save()
    return file
}
```

Displaying tags

The last step for our basic tag handling is to display the tags to the users. To accomplish this we need to be able to get a list of tags as a string and then render the string representation on the home page. Add a read-only property implementation to Taggable:

```
def getTagsAsString() {
    return ((tags)?:[]).join(' ')
}
```

unnecessary

We also need to override the `toString` implementation on `Tagger`:

```
public String toString() {
    return tag.name
}
```

Open up the `index.gsp` file under `views/home` and add the following under the `messagetitle` div:

```
<div class="tagcontainer">
    <g:message code="tags.display" args="${[message.tagsAsString]}" />
</div>
```

Then add the following under the `filename` panel:

```
<div class="tagcontainer">
    <g:message code="tags.display" args="${[file.tagsAsString]}" />
</div>
```

Create the entry for `tags.display` in the message bundle file under `i18n/messages.properties`:

```
tags.display=tags: {0}
```

Now if we run the application, we should see that users are able to add tags to their messages and files:

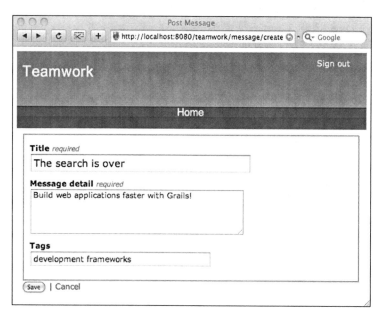

These tags can be displayed on the home page as shown in the following screenshot:

Customize the home page

With tagging in place, we can enhance the application to allow users to create their own home page. The aim is to allow users to specify the tags they are interested in, so any content with these tags will be displayed on their home page. This will allow us to break the home page up into two sections:

- A **Most Recent** section, containing the last five file uploads and messages
- A **Your Data section**, containing all the files and messages that are tagged according to the user's preferences

Introducing templates

Taking this approach means that files and messages will be displayed in many different places on the site, instead of just the home page. By the end of this chapter, messages and files will be rendered in the context of:

- A **Most Recent** section
- A **Your Data** section

In the future, we will probably render messages and files in the following contexts as well:

- Show all files and messages
- Show files and messages by tags
- Show files and messages by search results

Ideally we want to encapsulate the rendering of a file and a message so they look the same all over the site, and we don't need to duplicate our presentation logic. Grails provides a mechanism to handle this, through GSP, called **templates**.

A template is a GSP file, just the same as our view GSP files, but is differentiated from a view by prefixing the file name with an underscore. We are going to create two templates—one template for messages, which will be called `_message.gsp` and the other for files, which will be called `_file.gsp`.

The templates will be responsible for rendering a single message and a single file.

Templates can be created anywhere under the `views` folder. The location that they are created in affects the way they are executed. To execute a template we use the grails `render` tag. Assume that we create our message template under the `views/ message` folder. To render this template from a view in the same folder, we would call the following:

```
<g:render template="message" />
```

However, if we need to render a message from another controller view, say the home page, which exists under `views/home`, we would need to call it like so:

```
<g:render template="/message/message" />
```

Passing data to a template

The two examples of executing a template above would only be capable of rendering static information. We have not supplied any data to the template to render. There are three ways of passing data into a template:

- Send a map of the data into the template to be rendered
- Provide an object for the template to render
- Provide a collection of objects for the template to render

Render a map

This mechanism is the same as when a controller provides a model for a view to render. The keys of the map will be the variable names that the values of the map are bound to within the template. Calling the render tag given below:

```
<g:render template="message" model="[message: myMessage]" />
```

would bind the `myMessage` object into a `message` variable in the template scope and the template could perform the following:

```
<div class="messagetitle">
    <g:message code="${message.title}" encodeAs="HTML"/>
</div>
```

Render an object

A single object can be rendered by using the `bean` attribute:

```
<g:render template="message" bean="${message}" />
```

The `bean` is bound into the template scope with the default variable named `it`:

```
<div class="messagetitle">
    <g:message code="${it.title}" encodeAs="HTML"/>
</div>
```

Render a collection

A collection of objects can be rendered by using the `collection` and `var` attributes:

```
<g:render template="message" var="message" collection="${messages}" />
```

When using a collection, the `render` tag will iterate over the items in the collection and execute the template for each item, binding the current item into the variable name supplied by the `var` attribute.

```
<div class="messagetitle">
    <g:message code="${message.title}" encodeAs="HTML"/>
</div>
```

Be careful to pass in the actual collection by using `${}`. If just the name of the variable is passed through, then the characters in the `collection` variable name provided will be iterated over, rather than the items in the `collection`. For example, if we use the following code, the `messages collection` will be iterated over:

```
<g:render template="message" var="message" collection="${messages}" />
```

However, if we forget to reference the messages object and just pass through the name of the object, we will end up iterating over the string `"messages"`:

```
<g:render template="message" var="message" collection="messages" />
```

Template namespace

Grails 1.1 has introduced a template namespace to make rendering of templates even easier. This option only works if the GSP file that renders the template is in the same folder as the template itself. Consider the first example we saw when rendering a template and passing a Map of parameters to be rendered:

```
<g:render template="message" model="[message: myMessage]" />
```

Using the template namespace, this code would be simplified as follows:

```
<tmpl:message message="${myMessage}"/>
```

As we can see, this is a much simpler syntax. Do remember though that this option is only available when the GSP is in the same folder as the template.

Create the message and file templates

Now, we must extract the presentation logic on the home page, `views/home/index.gsp`, to a message and file template. This will make the home page much simpler and allow us to easily create other views that can render messages and files.

Create two new template files:

- `/views/message/_message.gsp`
- `/views/file/_file.gsp`

Taking the code from the index page, we can fill in `_message.gsp` as follows:

```
<div class="amessage">
    <div class="messagetitle">
        <g:message code="message.title"
                args="${[message.title]}" encodeAs="HTML"/>
    </div>
    <div class="tagcontainer">
        <g:message code="tags.display"
                args="${[message.tagsAsString]}" />
    </div>
    <div class="messagetitlesupplimentary">
        <g:message code="message.user"
                args="${[message.user.firstName, message.user.
```

```
lastName]}"/>
    </div>
    <div class="messagebody">
        <g:message code="message.detail"
                args="${[message.detail]}" encodeAs="HTML"/>
    </div>
</div>
```

Likewise, the `<div>` that contains a file panel should be moved over to the new _
`file.gsp`. This means the main content of our home page (`views/home/index.gsp`)
becomes much simpler:

```
<div class="panel">
    <h2>Messages</h2>
    <g:render template="/message/message"
            collection="${messages}" var="message"/>
</div>
<div class="panel">
    <h2>Files</h2>
    <g:render template="/file/file" collection="${files}" var="file"/>
</div>
```

User tags

The next step is to allow users to register their interest in tags. Once we have
captured this information then we can start to personalize the home page. This is
going to be surprisingly simple, although it sounds like a lot! We just need to:

- Create a relationship between `Users` and `Tags`
- Create a controller to handle user profiles
- Create a form that will allow users to specify the tags in which they
  are interested

User to tag relationship

Creating a relationship between users and tags is very simple. Users will select a
number of tags that they want to watch, but users themselves are not 'tagged', so the
`User` class cannot extend the `Taggable` class. Otherwise users would be returned
when performing a polymorphic query on `Taggable` for all objects with a certain tag.

Besides allowing a user to have a number of tags, it is also necessary to be able to add
tags to a user by specifying a space delimited string. We must also be able to return
the list of tags as a space delimited string.

The updates to the user class are:

```
package app

import tagging.Tagger

class User {
    def tagService
    static hasMany = [watchedTags: Tagger]

    ...

    def overrideTags( String tags ) {
        watchedTags?.each { tag -> tag.delete() }
        watchedTags = []
        watchedTags.addAll( tagService.createTagRelationships( tags ))
    }
    def getTagsAsString() {
        return ((watchedTags)?:[]).join(' ')
    }
}
```

User ProfileController

The `ProfileController` is responsible for loading the current user for the **My Tags** form, and then saving the tags that have been entered about the user. Create a new controller class called `ProfileController.groovy` under the `grails-app/controller/app` folder, and add the following code to it:

```
package app

class ProfileController {
    def userService
    def myTags = {
        return ['user': userService.getAuthenticatedUser() ]
    }
    def saveTags = {
        User.get(params.id)?.overrideTags( params.tags )
        redirect( controller:'home' )
    }
}
```

The `myTags` action uses `userService` to retrieve the details of the user making the request and returns this to the `myTags` view. Remember, if no view is specified, Grails will default to the view with the same name of the action.

The `saveTags` action overrides the existing `user` tags with the newly submitted tags.

The myTags form

The last step is to create the form view that will allow users to specify the tags they would like to watch. We will create a GSP view to match the myTags action in ProfileController. Create the folder grails-app/views/profile and then create a new file myTags.gsp and give it the following markup:

```
<%@ page contentType="text/html;charset=UTF-8" %>
<html>
<head>
    <meta http-equiv="Content-Type" content="text/html; charset=UTF-
8"/>
    <meta name="layout" content="main"/>
    <title>My Tags</title>
</head>
<body>
<g:form action="saveTags">
    <g:hiddenField name="id" value="${user.id}"/>
    <fieldset>
        <dl>
            <dt>My Tags</dt>
            <dd><g:textField name="tags" value="${user.tagsAsString}"
                        size="35" class="bigfield"/></dd>
        </dl>
    </fieldset>
    <g:submitButton name="Save" value="Save"/>
    |
    <g:link controller="home">Cancel</g:link>
</g:form>
</body>
</html>
```

This view will be rendered by the myTags action on the ProfileController and is provided with a User instance. The form submits the tags to the saveTags action on the ProfileController. The user id is put in a hidden field so we know which user to add the tags to when the form is submitted, and any existing tags for the user are rendered in the text field via the tagsAsString property.

Add a link to the myTags action in the header navigation from our layout in main.gsp:

```
<div id="header">
    <jsec:isLoggedIn>
        <div id="profileActions">
            <span class="signout">
    <g:link controller="profile" action="myTags">My Tags</g:link> |
```

```
        <g:link controller="auth" action="signOut">Sign out</g:link>
            </span>
        </div>
    </jsec:isLoggedIn>

    <h1><g:link controller="home">Teamwork</g:link></h1>
</div>
```

Now restart the application, log in as the default user and you will be able to specify which tags you are interested in.

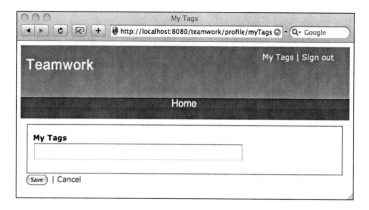

Personalizing the home page

Now that we have a way of allowing users to register interest in specific tags, we can update the home page to have a more personal feel. We are going to modify the homepage to display only the five most recent posts and files, as well as all of the tagged content that the user is interested in.

Content service

To help retrieve this information, we are going to introduce a `ContentService` class that can handle the necessary logic and call this from the `HomeController`. Under `services/app`, create a new class `ContentService.groovy`. First of all, we will implement the code to retrieve all the items tagged with one of the tags that the current user is interested in:

```
package app

import tagging.Taggable
import org.hibernate.FetchMode

class ContentService {

    def userService
```

```
def allWatchedItems() {
    def watchedTags = userService.authenticatedUser.tags
    return watchedTags ?
        Taggable.withTags( watchedTags, lastUpdatedSort ) : []
}
private lastUpdatedSort = {one, other ->
    one.lastUpdated < other.lastUpdated? 1 :
        (one.lastUpdated == other.lastUpdated) ? 0 : -1
}
}
```

The `allWatchedItems` method gets all of the instances of Tag that the user is interested in and then performs a polymorphic query on `Taggable` to get all of the items with one or more of these tags. When querying for the items, we also pass in a reference to a closure that can be used as a comparator on Groovy List objects for sorting. The return value from this closure is an integer that determines if the first object is less than, equal to or greater than the second object.

To allow the `lastUpdatedSort` closure to work, we need to add the `lastUpdated` property to the `File` domain class.

So the code for the `File` domain class is as shown below:

```
package app

import tagging.Taggable

class File extends Taggable {
    static hasMany = [versions: FileVersion]
    SortedSet versions
    FileVersion currentVersion
    Date lastUpdated
    def newVersion(version) {
        versions = (versions) ?: new TreeSet()
        versions << currentVersion
        currentVersion = version
    }
    def static withTag(String tagName) {
        return Taggable.withTag(tagName, File)
    }
}
```

We need to add a method to the User class to retrieve a list of Tag instances that the user is watching. At the moment the User class can only return a list of Tagger instances. Add the following method to the User class:

```
def getTags() {
    return watchedTags.collect{ it.tag }
}
```

We have also not implemented the withTags method on Taggable, so let's take a look at it now:

```
def static withTags( checkTags, sorter ) {
    return Taggable.withCriteria {
        tags {
            'in'('tag', checkTags)
        }
    }.sort( sorter )
}
```

This method performs a polymorphic query against Taggable to find all subclass instances that have a relationship to a Tag instance that is in the supplied list of tags to check. The results are then sorted using the sorter closure, which in our case, happens to be the lastUpatedSort closure from ContentService.

The next responsibility of the ContentService is to return the five most recent items posted to the application. It can be implemented by using the following code:

```
def fiveMostRecentItems() {
    def messages = Message.list(sort: 'lastUpdated', order: 'desc',
            fetch: [user: 'eager'], max: 5)
    def files = File.createCriteria().listDistinct {
        currentVersion {
            order('dateCreated', 'desc')
            fetchMode('user', FetchMode.EAGER)
        }
        fetchMode('tags', FetchMode.EAGER)
        maxResults(5)
    }
    return mergeAndSortListsToSize(messages, files, lastUpdatedSort,
5)
}
private mergeAndSortListsToSize(list1, list2, sorter, size) {
    def merged = list1
    merged.addAll( list2 )
    merged = merged.sort( sorter )
```

```
    if ( merged.size() >= size ) {
        merged = merged[0..<size]
    }
    return merged
}
```

First, the five most recent messages are retrieved, followed by the five files where the latest version was updated most recently. Both of these results are then merged together into one list, ordered and then limited to five results by the `mergeAndSortListsToSize` method. Notice how we have been able to reuse the `lastUpdatedSort` closure here.

Update the HomeController

Now that the `ContentService` is implemented, we can use this code from the `HomeController` to display the required information:

```
package app

class HomeController {
    def contentService
    def index = {
        return [
        latestContent: contentService.fiveMostRecentItems(),
            myContent: contentService.allWatchedItems()]
    }
}
```

We can see that the five most recent items are made available to the home page via the `latestContent` variable, and the user's watched items are available in the `myContent` variable.

Update the home page

We now have the situation where we are returning collections of mixed types; messages and files instances are stored side-by-side in the same collection. We will implement a template to handle this so we can continue to reuse the individual file and message templates and keep the implementation of the home page clean. Create the following folder: `grails-app/views/shared`. Now create a new template GSP called `_item.gsp`. This will determine which template to use, based on the type of a particular object:

```
<%@ page import="app.Message" contentType="text/html;charset=UTF-8" %>
<%@ page import="app.File" contentType="text/html;charset=UTF-8" %>
<g:each in="${data}" var="item">
    <g:if test="${item.class == File}">
```

```
        <g:render template="/file/file" bean="${item}" var="file"/>
    </g:if>
    <g:if test="${item.class == Message}">
        <g:render template="/message/message" bean="${item}"
var="message"/>
    </g:if>
</g:each>
```

We can use this template from our home page. Replace the main content div in views/home/index.gsp with the following:

```
<div id="mostrecent" class="panel">
    <h2>Most Recent Updates</h2>
    <g:render template="/shared/item" bean="${latestContent}"
var="data"/>
</div>
<div id="yourdata" class="panel">
    <h2>Items of Interest</h2>
    <g:render template="/shared/item" bean="${myContent}" var="data"/>
</div>
```

Everything is in place for our personalized home page! Run the application and create some messages and files. Make sure to tag the files and then create some tags for our user as shown in the following screenshot.

All Messages and Files

Our home page is starting to feel really useful now! It provides an initial overview for the users to quickly see what new information has been posted by their teammates and keep an eye on things that interest them. The only problem is that as more and more messages and files are posted, the old content can't be viewed any more. We need a couple of new pages to list all messages and files. Hopefully, by now, we are starting to see how trivial this is going to be. In fact, we can add the new pages without even restarting our application!

In `MessageController`, create a new action called `list`:

```
def list = {
    def messages = Message.list(sort: 'lastUpdated', order: 'desc',
              fetch: [user: 'eager'])
    return [messages: messages]
}
```

In `FileController` create a new action called `list`:

```
def list = {
    def files = File.withCriteria {
        currentVersion {
            order('dateCreated', 'desc')
            fetchMode('user', FetchMode.EAGER)
        }
    }
    return [files: files]
}
```

We will also need to import the Hibernate fetch mode for `FileController`:

```
import org.hibernate.FetchMode
```

Create a new view under `views/message` called `list.gsp` and give it the following markup:

```
<html>
<head>
    <meta http-equiv="Content-Type" content="text/html; charset=UTF-
8"/>
    <meta name="layout" content="main"/>
    <title>Messages</title>
</head>
<body>
<div class="singlepanel">
```

```
    <h2>View All Message</h2>
    <g:render template="message" collection="${messages}"
var="message"/>
</div>
</body>
</html>
```

Then create a new view under `views/file` called `list.gsp` and give it the following markup:

```
<html>
<head>
    <meta http-equiv="Content-Type" content="text/html; charset=UTF-
8"/>
    <meta name="layout" content="main"/>
    <title>Files</title>
</head>
<body>
<div class="singlepanel">
    <h2>View All Files</h2>
    <g:render template="file" collection="${files}" var="file"/>
</div>
</body>
</html>
```

Update the layout (`views/layouts/main.gsp`) to link to the two new pages in the navigation:

```
<g:link controller="message" action="list" class="navigationitem">All
Messages</g:link> |
<g:link controller="file" action="list" class="navigationitem">All
Files</g:link>
```

Without restarting the application, go back to your web browser and you should be able to see two new links on the primary navigation: **All Messages** and **All Files**. This is what you should see on the **All Messages** screen as shown in the following screenshot:

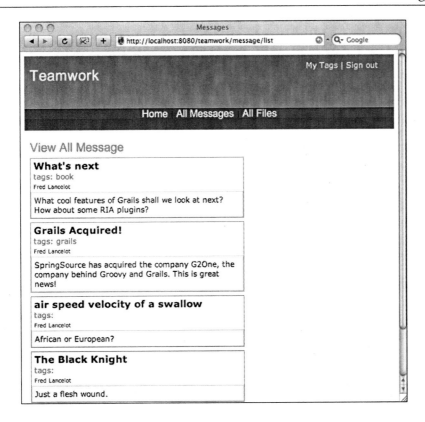

This is what the **All Files** screen should look like:

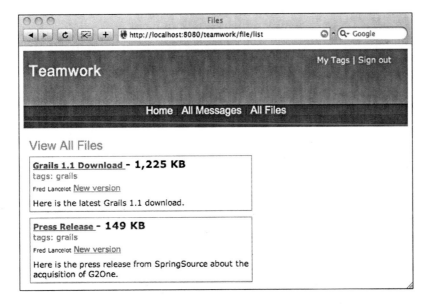

Summary

In this chapter, we have seen how to construct a domain model to allow files and messages to be tagged. We used inheritance to enable tagging for the `Message` and `File` domain classes and saw how GORM supports persistence of inheritance structures to the database. Creating an inheritance structure in our domain classes allowed us to make use of polymorphic queries.

Our home page started to become a bit complicated, but Grails templates came to the rescue allowing us to extract repeatable and reusable presentation logic into templates for rendering messages and files.

Once the tagging structure was set up and the templates were in place, we moved on to allow users to customize their home page by specifying tags that they are interested in. Finally, while creating the pages to view **All Messages** and **All Files**, once again, we saw how trivial it is to create new pages and rework an applications structure in Grails.

In the next chapter, we will see how Grails supports AJAX and look at some of the **Rich Internet Application (RIA)** plug-ins that are available.

11

AJAX and RIA Frameworks

We are going to enhance the user experience of our application by using AJAX and **Rich Internet Application (RIA)** frameworks. We will see how Grails provides built-in support for AJAX, and then introduce a plug-in that provides a number of components based on popular user interface design patterns. The enhancements we will implement in this chapter are:

- To allow tags to be updated through AJAX
- To automatically suggest existing tags when a user is tagging content
- To use a tag cloud to filter content by tags

Edit tags inline

Our users have expressed a desire to be able to change the tags for files and messages once they have been posted. There is no need to update the contents of messages, and we can already upload new versions of files. There should be no need to send users off to another page just to update the tags for a message or a file. We can use the built-in Grails support for AJAX to allow our users to edit their tags inline.

Grails uses the Prototype framework (`http://www.prototypejs.org`) to provide built-in AJAX support. The `remoteLink` and `formRemote` Grails tags provide all the AJAX support we need to start editing tags inline.

The remoteLink tag

The remoteLink tag allows us to:

- Call an action asynchronously
- Update a given HTML element on success or failure
- Register JavaScript functions to be called before or after the action has been executed
- Register JavaScript functions to be called when certain events are fired

For our basic example, we only need to use the first two features — calling actions asynchronously and updating an HTML element on success.

Basic usage of the remoteLink tag is very similar to the link tag, which we have seen already. The following table shows the attributes that are available:

Attribute	Description
action	The name of the action to execute.
controller	The name of the controller that contains the action.
id	The id of the domain object to be used.
update	Can be a Map or a String. If a Map is used, then the success and failure keys should be specified; the values must be the HTML id of the element to be updated on success and failure respectively. If a String is used, then this gives the HTML id of the element to be updated, whatever the response state.
before	The JavaScript function to be called before the remote call is made.
after	The JavaScript function to be called after the remote call is made.
asynchronous	Whether the call is asynchronous, default to true.
method	The HTTP request method to be used.
onSuccess	A JavaScript function to be called on success.
onFailure	A JavaScript function to be called on failure.
on<ErrorCode>	A JavaScript function to be called for a given HTTP response code, for example, on500="alert('There was an error!');".
onUninitialized	A JavaScript function to be called when the underlying AJAX framework is not initialized correctly.
onLoading	A JavaScript function to be called when the remote call is executing.
onLoaded	A JavaScript function to be called once the remote call has finished loading the response.
onComplete	A JavaScript function to be called once the response has finished loading and all updates have finished executing.

From the table above, we can see that there is a lot that can be done with the `remoteLink` tag. It will allow us to create a robust user experience where the majority of the issues that can take place with remote calls can be handled. Working with AJAX and handling all the potential error cases in a graceful manner is not a trivial task. It is certainly a more complicated issue than can be covered in any great depth here. However, you'll be glad to know that we can get some mileage from basic usage of the `remoteLink` tag. We'll go into this in more detail later, but for now, rest assured that our example will be as simple as the following:

```
<g:remoteLink controller="taggable" action="editTags"
    id="${taggable.id}"
 update="tags${taggable.id}">edit
</g:remoteLink>
```

The formRemote tag

The `formRemote` tag works in a very similar manner to the `remoteLink` tag. All the same attributes are available when specifying which action to submit to and also for handling AJAX events. The differences from the `remoteLink` tag are:

- A `name` attribute is required.
- The action and controller to submit to is handled through a `url` attribute that takes a map containing an action key and a controller key. For example, `url="[controller:'taggable', action:'saveTags']"`.
- The `formRemote` tag can have nested input elements, as a normal HTML form element would.

As with the `remoteLink` tag, a lot of flexibility is provided for handling AJAX events. However, we will be able to meet our basic requirements by using the `formRemote` tag in the simplest way. Here's a sneak preview of our intended usage:

```
<g:formRemote name="tagForm"
        url="[controller:'taggable',action:'saveTags']"
        update="tags${taggable.id}" class="inlineedit">
    // form input fields here.
</g:formRemote>
```

Taggable controller

After that brief introduction to the `remoteLink` and `formRemote` tags, we have all the tools we need to implement inline editing of tags in our application. As we are limiting the inline editing to tags only, and we have abstracted the domain logic for tags into the `Taggable` class, we should be able to add this new feature without modifying the application domain classes `Message` and `File`. There is currently no controller in our application for dealing with tags directly. Therefore, this is something we will need to introduce.

Before we create the new controller, we need to think about the different user actions that will be introduced to get inline editing to work. Users need to be able to:

- Ask for an inline form to allow them to change the tags
- Save the tags they have entered
- Cancel any edits they might have made by mistake
- View the changes they have made inline

We can handle these actions as three controller actions:

- `editTags` — to load the tags for the current object and render them in an inline form
- `saveTags` — to save the tags that have been entered, then render the pdated tags
- `showTags` — to render the current tags, when a user decides to cancel an edit

Each of these controllers will render only a small snippet of HTML that will be used to change the contents of the `div` where the tags are displayed. Now, there will be two states that tags can be rendered as: viewable and editable. We will encapsulate these two views into two templates:

- `_editTagsForm.gsp` — to render tags in an editable state
- `_showTags.gsp` — to render tags in a viewable state

By thinking about the user actions and the visible states of the application, we can decompose what could be quite a complex set of user interactions into very simple and clean code.

Under the `grails-app/controllers` folder, create a new folder `taggable` and a new Groovy class under that folder, `TaggablController.groovy`. The following code implements the three actions we identified earlier:

```
package tagging
class TaggableController {
    def editTags = {
```

```
        def taggable = Taggable.get( params.id )
        render( template: "editTagsForm",
                model: [taggable: taggable] )
    }
    def saveTags = {
        def taggable = Taggable.get( params.id )
        taggable.clearTags()
        taggable.addTags( params.tags )
        render( template: 'showTags', model: [taggable: taggable] )
    }
    def showTags = {
        def taggable = Taggable.get( params.id )
        render( template: 'showTags', model: [taggable: taggable] )
    }
}
```

We can see that each of these actions renders a template, only a small snippet of HTML, to display the tags in the necessary state. As these actions are called by AJAX requests from the client, we only need to render a small part of the page to be updated. Note that we are calling templates from a controller in the previous example. Previously we had only executed templates from GSP files.

Tag views

Let's take a look at the two new view templates we need to render the different states that tags can be viewed in.

We will need to create a `taggable` folder, to match the `TaggableController`, under `grails-app/views`. Under this folder, create the GSP file `_editTagsForm.gsp` and add the following code:

```
<g:formRemote name="tagForm" url="[controller:'taggable',action:'save
Tags']"
        update="tags${taggable.id}" class="inlineedit">
    <input type="hidden" name="id" value="${taggable.id}"/>
    <fieldset>
        <dl>
            <dt>Tags</dt>
            <dd><g:textField name="tags" value="${taggable.
tagsAsString}" size="35"/></dd>
        </dl>
    </fieldset>
    <input type="submit" value="Save"/> |
    <g:remoteLink controller="taggable" action="showTags"
            id="${taggable.id}"
 update="tags${taggable.id}">Cancel
    </g:remoteLink>
</g:formRemote>
```

Now, we can see the real usage of the `formRemote` tag in our application. We specify the `saveTags` action on the `TaggableController` as the destination for our form submission. All the input elements within the form are exactly the same, as if this were a normal HTML form. Apart from the form declaration, the item of note is the **cancel** link.

Previously, we had been able to specify the **cancel** link as just an HTML link that took us back to the home page. Now, because we are performing asynchronous requests to change a small section of the page, we need to be able to cancel without reloading the entire page. In the template above, we use the `remoteLink` tag to handle our cancel action and replace the current form with the read only view of tags.

Now, we need the template that renders the read only view of tags. Create the GSP file _showTags.gsp under the new `taggable` views folder and add the following:

```
<span class="tags">${taggable.tagsAsString}</span>

<g:remoteLink controller="taggable" action="editTags"
    id="${taggable.id}"
 update="tags${taggable.id}">edit
</g:remoteLink>
```

This template is extremely simple. We render the tags from the `taggable` object as a string, and then use the `remoteLink` tag to create a link that will swap the read only view of tags for the editable view.

Notice that the `remoteLink` and the `formRemote` tags all specify the same HTML id in their update attributes, `tags${taggable.id}`. Currently this id does not exist in any of our pages. We need to find all the places where we are rendering tags and make sure that tags are rendered within an element that specifies this id. Thankfully, we have already encapsulated the rendering of tags for messages and files into the templates _message.gsp and _file.gsp, so allowing tags to be edited from anywhere on the site is a simple case of modifying these two templates.

Modify the _message.gsp file so that the current markup for rendering tags changes to:

```
<div class="tagcontainer" id="tags${message.id}">
    <g:render template="/taggable/showTags"
            model="[taggable: message]"/>
</div>
```

We add the necessary id to the `div` containing tags, and pass off the responsibility of rendering tags to the read only view that we created earlier.

Modify the `_file.gsp` template in the same way:

```
<div class="tagcontainer" id="tags${file.id}">
    <g:render template="/taggable/showTags"
            model="[taggable: file]"/>
</div>
```

Tagging domain changes

We are very nearly there! You will have noticed that we are calling the `clearTags` method in the `saveTags` action on `TaggableController`. This method does not exist yet. However, the implementation of this method is very simple. All we have to do is add the following method to the `Taggable` domain class:

```
def clearTags() {
    tags.each {it.delete()}
    tags = []
}
```

The `clearTags` method simply deletes all of the relationships to existing tags of this object, and then sets the tags relationship to an empty list.

Include the Prototype library

The application is almost ready to allow users to perform inline editing of tags. The last change we need to make is to tell the application to use the Prototype JavaScript framework so that AJAX actions can be performed. Open the main layout `views/layouts/main.gsp` and update the `head` element as shown below:

```
<head>
    <title><g:layoutTitle default="Grails"/></title>
    <link rel="stylesheet" href="${createLinkTo(dir: 'css',
            file: 'teamwork.css')}"/>
    <link rel="shortcut icon" href="${createLinkTo(dir: 'images',
            file: 'favicon.ico')}" type="image/x-icon"/>
    <g:layoutHead/>
    <g:javascript library="application"/>
    <g:javascript library="prototype"/>
</head>
```

This tells Grails to include the Prototype framework on each page.

Try it out

Everything should be ready for us to check out the application now. Before we do it, let's just recap the work required to get inline editing of tags up and running.

- We created a new controller for the `Taggable` class. This controller performs three very simple actions: render the tags in editable state, save the updated tags, and render the tags in read-only state.
- We created two new templates to render tags in the read-only state and editable state.
- We added a `clearTags` method to the `Taggable` domain class.

Run the application, log in, add a message, add a file, and you should see a home page similar to the following:

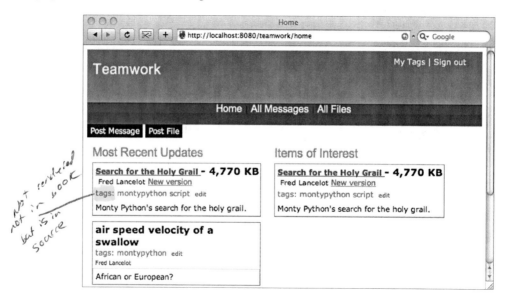

Notice that there is a link rendered next to the tags for messages and files. Clicking this link will allow the user to edit the tags for an item inline.

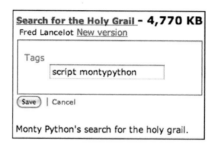

Auto-complete tags

The next step, which will continue to improve tagging in our system, is to automatically suggest some tags that already exist when a user starts entering their tags. This will allow the users to avoid duplicating tags and create a more meaningful *folksonomy* for their content. Here are the details that we will need to implement in order to get auto-complete to work:

- Write some JavaScript to check for changes in the input box for tags
- Implement an AJAX call when we receive changes to check for tags matching the users' input so far
- Implement the action on the server that will find all tags matching the users' input
- Parse the data that comes back from the server
- Render the list of matching tags in a pop up box
- Make a rendered list of selectable tags so that the users can choose to auto-complete with the tag they want to use.

That sounds like a lot of work! Surely someone else has done all of this before? If we take a look at the Grails plug-ins page (http://www.grails.org/Plugins), there is a whole section of plug-ins devoted to creating rich user interfaces. A quick look at the documentation shows that there are two plug-ins that provide solutions for the auto-suggest design pattern. These are:

- GrailsUI
- RichUI

We are going to use the RichUI plug-in as it has more features than GrailsUI plug-in and the default styling of the auto suggest feature in RichUI works better in our application than the GrailsUI version. Interestingly, both plug-ins wrap the YUI auto-complete widget (http://developer.yahoo.com/yui/autocomplete).

Installing the RichUI

As with all Grails plug-ins, this is simply a case of running the following command in our command line:

```
grails install-plugin richui
```

Implement the auto-complete

Now that we have the RichUI plug-in installed, there are a few simple changes that we need to make to get the auto-complete to work:

- Implement an action that will return matching tags, given some partial tag input.

- Replace the input field we use to capture tag names with the RichUI auto-complete widget.

Suggest tags action

We will add an action to `TaggableController` that will expect a partial tag name, and then return a list of matching tags as XML.

```
def suggestTags = {
    def tags = Tag.findAllByNameLike("%${params.query}%")
    renderAsXml(tags)
}
def renderAsXml(tags) {
    render(contentType: "text/xml") {
        results {
            tags.each {tag ->
                result {
                    name(tag.name)
                    id(tag.id)
                }
            }
        }
    }
}
```

We can use a simple dynamic finder to retrieve the tags that match a partial tag name. Notice that the name of the request parameter that we expect the partial tag name to come in on is `query`. The interesting part comes when we need to convert our list of matching tags into XML.

The `renderAsXml` method uses the usual `render` method, but instead of specifying a view or a template, we specify a closure. The `render` method will execute this closure against the Groovy `MarkupBuilder`, and an XML element for each node in the closure will be rendered.

To give a concrete example, let us assume that the tags list contains two tags:

```
tags = [new Tag('one'), new Tag('oneother')]
```

When this list of tags is passed to the `renderAsXml` method, the following XML will be the output:

```
<results>
    <result>
        <name>one</name>
        <id>1</id>
    </result>
    <result>
        <name>oneother</name>
        <id>2</id>
    </result>
</results>
```

For more details on using `MarkupBulider`, see the following page on the Groovy site: `http://groovy.codehaus.org/Creating+XML+using+Groovy's+MarkupBuilder`.

RichUI autoComplete widget

The `autoComplete` widget should be used within a form and is declared as follows:

```
<resource:autoComplete skin="default" />
...
<g:form>
...
<richui:autoComplete name="tags"
    action="${createLinkTo('dir': 'taggable/suggestTags')}"
    delimChar=" " value="${user.tagsAsString}"
    forceSelection="false"/>
...
</form>
```

The first line manages importing all of the dependencies that are required for using the `autoComplete` widget. The `autoComplete` declaration in the code above creates an auto complete input field that:

- Has the `name` and `id` attributes of `tags`
- Submits its data to the `suggestTags` action on `TaggableController`
- Uses space as a delimiting character. Otherwise the entire contents of the input field will be sent to the `suggestTags` action
- Is pre-populated with the tags on the user object
- Does not require one of the suggestions to be selected.

The example above was taken from the `myTags.gsp`, where users are able to specify the tags they want to watch.

The full list of attributes that are available for the `autoComplete` tag are:

Attribute	Description	Required
name	The name of the input field, also used for id if not specified separately.	yes
action	The action to return the matching data for auto completion.	yes
id	The id of the input field.	no
class	A CSS class to be applied to the input field.	no
style	Inline CSS styling for the input field.	no
shadow	Whether to use a shadow for the auto complete box (true|false).	no
minQueryLength	Length of the data in the input field before the query is sent to the server, default = 0.	no
queryDelay	Delay in seconds before the query is sent to the server, default = 0.	no
delimChar	Character to specify delimiter for multiple entries.	no
value	The initial value of the input field.	no
forceSelection	Whether to force the selection of a suggested item (true|false).	no
typeAhead	Determines whether the type ahead feature should be used (true|false).	no
onItemSelect	Specify a JavaScript function that can be called when an item is selected.	no

The last change we need to make in order to get our auto-complete feature working is to use the widget provided by the RichUI plug-in. The users will need auto-complete in the following scenarios:

- When a user creates a message
- When a user creates a file
- When a user updates tags for a message
- When a user updates tags for a file
- When a user sets the tags they are interested in watching

In the `create.gsp` files under `views/file` and `views/message` folders respectively, replace the existing tags input field with the following:

```
<richui:autoComplete name="userTags"
    action="${createLinkTo('dir': 'taggable/suggestTags')}"
    delimChar=" " value="${userTags}" forceSelection="false"/>
```

In the template `views/taggable/_editTagsForm.gsp`, replace the current tags input field with:

```
<richui:autoComplete name="tags"
    action="${createLinkTo('dir': 'taggable/suggestTags')}"
    delimChar=" " value="${taggable.tagsAsString}"

    forceSelection="false"/>
```

In the `views/profile/myTags.gsp`, replace the text input field with the following:

```
<richui:autoComplete name="tags"
    action="${createLinkTo('dir': 'taggable/suggestTags')}"
    delimChar=" " value="${user.tagsAsString}"

    forceSelection="false"/>
```

The changes above will provide the option of auto-complete for tagging wherever the user needs to update tags.

Finally, update the `head` element of the main layout again (`views/layouts/main.gsp`) in order to allow the application to load the resources required for the RichUI plug-in. This is as follows:

```
<head>
    <title><g:layoutTitle default="Grails"/></title>
    <link rel="stylesheet" href="${createLinkTo(dir: 'css',
        file: 'teamwork.css')}"/>
    <link rel="shortcut icon" href="${createLinkTo(dir: 'images',
        file: 'favicon.ico')}" type="image/x-icon"/>
    <g:layoutHead/>
    <g:javascript library="application"/>
    <g:javascript library="prototype"/>
    <resource:autoComplete skin="default" />
</head>
```

Run the application and log in to see the auto-complete feature in action when editing tags on the home page:

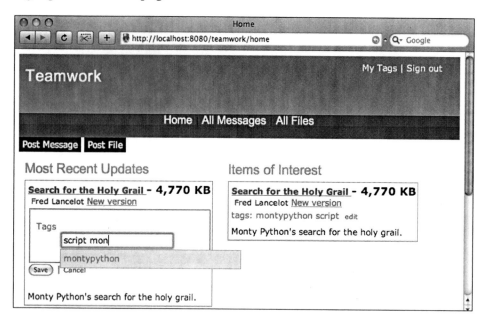

Auto-complete will also be available when a user selects the tags he/she is interested in, as shown in the following screenshot:

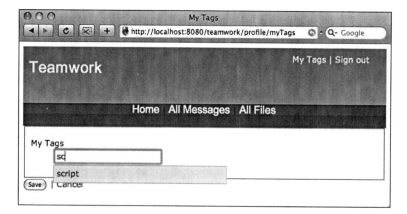

Introducing tag clouds

One interesting user interface design pattern that has come out of tagging is the tag cloud. This is a visual representation of the popularity of tags within the context of a system. Each of the tags is displayed and given a size determined by the number of times it is used in the system, relative to the popularity of the other tags. The following screenshot shows an example tag cloud of the contents of this chapter, where each word will be counted as a tag. This cloud was produced by Wordle (http://www.wordle.net/).

We are going to use tag clouds to allow users to filter messages and files on the **Show All** pages for messages and files. There are two reasons for using a tag cloud here:

- The tag cloud gives the user early feedback of how many results they are likely to get when they decide to filter by a tag.
- Tag clouds help to enforce a meaningful *folksonomy*, as the more popular a tag becomes, the more obviously it stands out. This registers the tags in the users' mind and leads to them being used more in the future, rather than each user sticking to their own disparate set of tags.

RichUI tag cloud component

Once again, the good news is that the RichUI plug-in provides a component that will handle all the client-side presentation work for us. Here is a simple static example of using this component from the plug-in online documentation:

```
<richui:tagCloud values="['Java': 5, 'Grails': 16, 'Groovy': 12]" />
```

This will render a tag cloud with Java in very small text, Groovy in quite large text, and Grails in really big text. The data that we need to pass into the `tagCloud` tag is a map, where each key is the text to be rendered and each value is the relative weight, or amount of usages, of the tag.

Drop the code above into your **All Files** page to see an example of what is rendered.

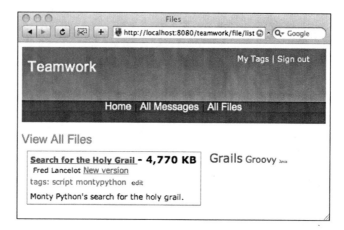

The attributes that are available for the `tagCloud` tag are:

Attribute	Description	Required
values	The map containing the tags and the weight of each tag.	yes
class	CSS class to be used for the tag cloud container.	no
style	Inline CSS style for the tag cloud container.	no
linkClass	CSS class for the links in the tag cloud.	no
linkStyle	Inline CSS style for the links in the tag cloud.	no
controller	The controller to submit link selection to.	no
action	The action to submit link selection to.	no
sortField	Whether the tags should be sorted by key or value (key|value). Defaults to key.	no
sortOrder	Whether to sort the tags ascending or descending (asc|desc). Defaults to asc.	no
minSize	The minimum size for a tag's font. Defaults to 0.	no
maxSize	The maximum size for a tag's font. Defaults to 50.	no
showNumber	Whether the weight of the tag should be displayed or not (true|false). Defaults to false.	no

Fetch the tag cloud map

We know that in order to render a tag cloud for our tags, we need to produce a map that holds each tag as a key and the number of occurrences as the value. Let's put a new method on the `TagService` class to handle this:

```
def cloudData( type ) {
    def data = [:]
    Tag.list().each { tag ->
        def count = type.withCriteria {
            tags {
                eq( 'tag', tag )
            }
        }.size()
        if( count ) {
            data.put( tag.name, count )
        }
    }
    return data
}
```

We have decided to show a tag cloud on the message and file list pages only. For this reason, it is probably best if we only retrieve tags that are used by messages on the message list page and by files on the file list page. This is why we take a type parameter in this method, it allows us to perform a query on the particular type and avoid performing a polymorphic query. Then if there are no results for a particular tag, we simply don't add it to the data map.

The alternative would be to return all possible tags in the system, whether they were applicable or not. By filtering out the tags that are not being used, we help to enforce an effective *folksonomy* of tags for our users.

Filter by tags

The `file` and `message` controllers need to be updated now to:

- Allow the tag cloud to be populated and sent to the client
- Allow selected tags to be used to filter the messages and files

Make the following changes to the `MessageController`:

```
package app

class MessageController {
    def tagService
    def contentService
    def userService

    def create = {//do not change...}

    def save = {//do not change...}

    def list = {
        def messages = Message.list(sort: 'lastUpdated',
                order: 'desc',
                fetch: [user: 'eager', tags: 'eager'])
        return [messages: messages,
                tagCloudData: tagService.cloudData(Message)]
    }

    def filterByTag = {
        def messages = Message.withTag( params.selectedTag )
                .sort( contentService.lastUpdatedSort )
        render(view: 'list', model: [
                messages: messages,
                tagCloudData: tagService.cloudData(Message)])

    }

}
```

Here we have injected `tagService` and `contentService`. We have created the list action to retrieve all messages as well as the tag cloud data for messages. Also, we have added a new `filterByTag` action that will be called when a tag is selected from the tag cloud. The list action is very simple. All we have to do is just load all the messages, which are ordered in a descending date order. Note that we also perform an eager fetch on the tags relationship as well as the user relationship to stop separate request to the database for each tag.

The `filterByTag` action is also kept extremely simple by reusing the `withTag` method we have already implemented on `Taggable` and `Message`. The `withTag` method does not perform any sorting, so we have had to inject the `ContentService` class to allow us to sort the list of results by descending date order.

We need to change the `FileController` in a similar way:

```
package app

import org.springframework.web.multipart.MultipartFile
import org.hibernate.FetchMode
```

```
class FileController {
    def tagService
    def contentService
    def fileService

    def newVersion = {//no change...}
    def create = {//no change...}
    def save = {//no change...}
    def extractExtension(MultipartFile file) {//no change...}
    def download = {//no change...}

    def list = {
        def c = File.createCriteria()
        def files = c.listDistinct {
            currentVersion {
                order('dateCreated', 'desc')
                fetchMode('user', FetchMode.EAGER)
                fetchMode('tags', FetchMode.EAGER)
            }
        }
        return [files: files,
                tagCloudData: tagService.cloudData(File)]
    }

    def filterByTag = {
        def files = File.withTag( params.selectedTag )
                .sort( contentService.lastUpdatedSort )
        render(view: 'list', model: [
                files: files,
                tagCloudData: tagService.cloudData(File)])
    }

}
```

The list action in FileController uses **criteria** to fetch the full list of uploaded files.

 Interestingly, here we are using the listDistinct method on the CriteriaBuilder to ensure that distinct results are returned by the query. If we did not use a distinct query, we could end up with duplicate results because of the Hibernate 'eager' fetch we are performing on tags. In the database, Hibernate uses an outer join to perform eager fetches on multiple cardinality relationships. This means files with more than one tag would be duplicated in the results list, if we did not perform a listDistinct call.

As with the MessageController class, we reuse the hasTag method on File and Taggable to allow all files with a given tag to be returned.

Rendering the tag cloud

Now comes the really easy part. We want to render the tag cloud from the new data we are supplying and make it filter the page when we click on one of our tags. To do this, we need to update the message and file list views, `views/message/list.gsp` and `views/file/list.gsp` respectively.

The body element of the message's `list.gsp` file changes in the following way:

```
<body>
<h2>View All Message</h2>
<div class="singlepanel">
    <g:render template="message"
        collection="${messages}" var="message"/>
</div>
<div class="tagcloudpanel">
    <h3>Tags</h3>
    <richui:tagCloud values="${tagCloudData}"
            controller="message" action="filterByTag"
            sortOrder="asc" minSize="6" maxSize="40"
            linkClass="taglink"/>
</div>
</body>
```

```
While the body tags of  the files list.gsp becomes:
<body>
<h2>View All Files</h2>
<div class="singlepanel">
    <g:render template="file" collection="${files}" var="file"/>
</div>
<div class="tagcloudpanel">
    <h3>Tags</h3>
    <richui:tagCloud values="${tagCloudData}"
            controller="file" action="filterByTag"
            sortOrder="asc" minSize="6" maxSize="40"
            linkClass="taglink"/>
</div>
</body>
```

We specify the tag cloud data as the value passed into the view model. We also give the controller and the action to be used to filter the messages and files by the tag selected, as well as specifying the sort order and some styling information.

Load up the application and add a number of messages with different tags. The result should be similar to the screenshot shown below:

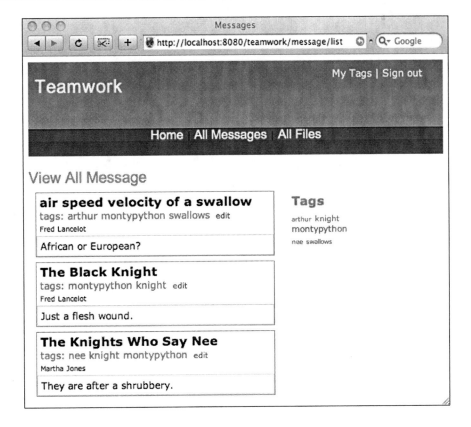

Summary

Our users aren't going to know what hit them! We have really been able to bring tagging to life and make it a useful mechanism for users to control and manage the information they want to share with other team members.

By leveraging the built-in support for AJAX in Grails, users are now able to edit tags inline, thus making this a very quick and painless operation. This is a preferred alternative to sending the user off to a new page to edit the tags for a message or file.

We then took our tagging support to new heights by implementing an auto-complete feature that allows users to select from an existing set of tags, while still being able to create new tags, if they wish to do so. This will help stop the proliferation of meaningless tags across the application.

Finally, we introduced tag clouds as a means of filtering content, as well as to show users which tags are becoming an integral part of the *folksonomy* being built-up by the whole team together.

The RichUI plug-in was invaluable when implementing these UI design patterns. It provides seamless support for enhancing Grails applications, with components that implement some of the most popular UI design patterns around. Take a look at the plug-in page for RichUI to see what else it has to offer: `http://grails.org/plugin/richui`.

In the next chapter, we are going to look at how we can make it easier for our users to find messages and files that they are interested in, by adding a search feature to the application. We will also add some Restful APIs to allow other developers to integrate with the application.

12

Searching, RSS, and REST Services

After our last increment of providing editable inline tagging, the users have been making good use of the application. There are now hundreds of posts and quite a few files in our application. Sometimes activity has been so fast that users have reported their messages are "getting lost" and people aren't seeing the information they need.

It is great news that our application is being used so much, but we need to address some new user goals that have arisen due to the usage of the application. Namely, to easily search for previous messages and keep up-to-date with the increased levels of activity.

It sounds like our users need to be able to search the content of the application, and given the high frequency of messages they would probably benefit from some sort of unobtrusive notification system for new content. An RSS feed springs to mind.

We have also received some requests to send messages into the application via email. Who knows where else we will need to receive data from in the future? We had better put some web services onto the application to allow other applications to add content in the future.

Searching

Adding full-text searching to a site is often not a trivial task. We have the following challenges:

- Indexing the content
- Converting the user input into search terms
- Performing the search

Make our objects searchable

This is starting to sound familiar, but thank goodness for plug-ins. Of course, there is a Grails plug-in that makes adding a search to our application trivial. The plug-in is called Searchable and is built on top of Lucene (`http://lucene.apache.org/java/docs/index.html`) and the Compass Search Engine framework (`http://www.compass-project.org/`). The core features provided by the Searchable plug-in are as follows:

- The domain classes that are marked as being searchable are mapped to the underlying search index.

- The changes made to domain objects through GORM are automatically synchronized to the search index.

- A **SearchableService** is provided to enable searching across multiple domain classes.

- Dynamic methods are added to `searchable` domain classes for easy searching over an individual domain class.

We can install the plug-in by running the following command from the command line:

```
grails install-plugin searchable
```

Once the plug-in is installed, we must modify the domain objects to be searched over (messages and files), and then we can start performing some basic searches in our application.

```
class Message extends Taggable {
    static searchable = true
    ...
}
class FileVersion implements Comparable {
    static searchable = true
    ...
}
```

Now, start the application, go to the link `http://localhost:8080/teamwork/searchable`, enter the text **knight** into the input field provided, and submit the form. This will find one of the messages created in the `BootStrap` class.

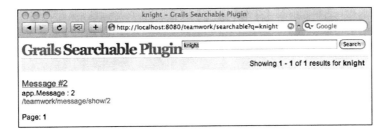

That's searching done then! Well, not quite. At the moment, there are a few problems:

- The search is not integrated into our site. Our users need to be able to search from every page.
- The results displayed show very little about the items that have been found.

Despite these two issues, the difficult part of searching is already done for us. Our domain objects are now searchable.

Integrate searching

To integrate searching into our application we need to do the following:

1. Add a search box to the layout so that users can search from any page.
2. Create an action that will perform the search.
3. Create a view for search results.
4. Update our existing view templates for messages and create a file version view template.

Site-wide search

The first step is to make search available from every page in the site so that users do not need to go off to a separate page to perform a search. This is achieved by a simple change to the layout `main.gsp`:

```
<div id="profileActions">
    <g:form controller="search" method="post">
        <input type="text" name="q"/>
        <input type="submit" value="Search"/>
    </g:form>
    <span class="signout">
        <g:link controller="profile" action="myTags">My Tags</g:link>
        <g:link controller="auth" action="signOut">Sign out</g:link>
    </span>
</div>
```

The search box is now available on every page in our site, as shown in the following screenshot:

Create the search controller

The input box that we added to the layout submits the search term to a `search` controller. We must now create this controller, with a default `index` action that will perform the search. The code for this action has already been copied directly from the default `SearchableController` that comes with the plug-in. Create the Groovy class `SearchController.groovy` in the `grails-app/controllers/app` folder. Add the following code:

```groovy
package app

import org.compass.core.engine.SearchEngineQueryParseException

class SearchController {

    def searchableService

    def index = {
        if (!params.q?.trim()) {
            return [:]
        }
        try {
            return [searchResult:
                searchableService.search(params.q, params)]
```

```
    } catch (SearchEngineQueryParseException ex) {
        return [parseException: true]
    }
  }
}
```

The plug-in provides a service class called `SearchableService`. We ask Spring to inject this service into our `searchableService` property. The `index` action takes the search query off the request parameters and calls `search` on the `searchableService` class. The `searchResult` object that is put in the model to be rendered contains the following properties:

- `results` — a list of all of the domain objects that match the search query.
- `scores` — a list of the match scores. There is one entry for each match.
- `total` — the total number of results for the search.
- `offset` — the 0-based result offset, for pagination.
- `max` — the maximum number of results that were requested.
- `suggestedQuery` — a suggested query that the user might like to try, based on spelling mistakes. It is only provided if suggested queries are requested in the search.

View the search results

The next step is to display the results that come back from the search action. We need to create a GSP in the `views/search` folder called `index.gsp` that will show the results of a search:

```
<html>
<head>
    <meta http-equiv="Content-Type" content="text/html; charset=UTF-8"/>
    <meta name="layout" content="main"/>
    <title>Search Results</title>
</head>
<body>
<h1>Welcome to Teamwork</h1>
<div>
    <h2>Search Results</h2>
    <g:if test="${searchResult}">
        <div class="searchsummary">
            <g:message code="search.summary"
                args="[searchResult.total, params.q]"/>
        </div>
    </div>
```

```
        <g:render template="/shared/item"
            collection="${searchResult.results}" var="data"/>
    </g:if>
    <g:else>
        <g:message code="search.noquery"/>
    </g:else>
</div>
</body>
</html>
```

The results of a search can contain a list of mixed type domain objects. Therefore, it makes sense to reuse the _item.gsp template that we had already created for handling lists of mixed type objects when performing polymorphic queries on Taggable.

Update the templates

Now we have two final changes to make:

- Create a template to render FileVersion objects.

- Stop the _message.gsp template from relying on user data.

Create the rendering template (_fileVersion.gsp) for FileVersion in the views/file folder and add the following code:

```
<div class="afile">
    <div class="filename">
        <a href="${g.createLink(controller: 'file',
            action: 'download', id: fileVersion.id)}">
            <g:message code="${fileVersion.name}" encodeAs="HTML"/>
        </a> -
    <g:message code="file.size" args="${[fileVersion.size]}"/>
    </div>
    <div class="filenamesupplimentary">
        <g:if test="${fileVersion.user}">
            <g:message code="file.name.supplementary"
                args="${[g.formatDate( format: 'hh:mm dd-MMM-yyyy',
                date: fileVersion.dateCreated),
                fileVersion.user.fullName]}"/>
        </g:if>
    </div>
    <div class="filebody">
        <g:message code="${fileVersion.description}"
                encodeAs="HTML"/>
    </div>
</div>
```

Now that we have this template in place, we need to allow the _item.gsp template to pass off execution for FileVersion objects:

```
<%@ page import="app.Message" contentType="text/html;charset=UTF-8" %>
<%@ page import="app.File" contentType="text/html;charset=UTF-8" %>
<%@ page import="app.FileVersion" contentType="text/html;charset=UTF-
8" %>
<g:each in="${data}" var="item">
    <g:if test="${item.class == File}">
        <g:render template="/file/file" bean="${item}" var="file"/>
    </g:if>
    <g:if test="${item.class == FileVersion}">
        <g:render template="/file/fileVersion" bean="${item}"
                var="fileVersion"/>
    </g:if>
    <g:if test="${item.class == Message}">
        <g:render template="/message/message" bean="${item}"
var="message"/>
    </g:if>
</g:each>
```

Users aren't searchable

The Searchable plug-in will only populate domain objects that are marked with the searchable = true static property. We have not added this property onto users or tags. So, we need to add logic to the _message.gsp file to avoid errors that would be caused by missing user data. If we want to allow users to be searchable in the future, then we would need to add the searchable property to the User domain class. We would then create a template file that could be used to render a user on the search results page.

The last change we need to make is to allow the _message.gsp template to render messages on the search results page, as well as the other areas of the site:

```
<div class="amessage">
    <div class="messagetitle">
        <g:message code="message.title" args="${[message.title]}"
            encodeAs="HTML"/>
    </div>
    <g:if test="${message.user}">
        <div class="tagcontainer" id="tags${message.id}">
            <g:render template="/taggable/showTags"
                model="[taggable: message]"/>
        </div>
        <div class="messagetitlesupplimentary">
            <g:message code="message.user"
```

if there is a user show tags show user info end-if

```
                args="${[message.user.firstName,
                    message.user.lastName]}"/>
        </div>
    </g:if>
    <div class="messagebody">
        <g:message code="message.detail" args="${[message.detail]}"
            encodeAs="HTML"/>
    </div>
</div>
```

The two checks we have added will stop the template from rendering the user information and tags if the user relationship is missing from the Message object.

If we run the application, then we should be able to see our **Search Results** page handling mixed content types, as shown in the following screenshot:

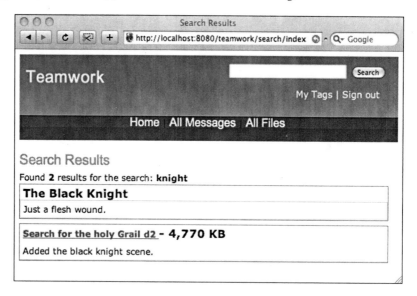

More searching

This is as far as we need to go for our simple application. The Searchable plug-in provides a lot more flexibility and power than it is possible to do justice here. Full documentation for the Searchable plug-in can be found on the Grails site at `http://grails.org/plugin/searchable`.

RSS

Having addressed the issue of old content being hard to find, we need to add a mechanism to allow users to keep track of all the new content being added to the site. A very simple way to allow this is to create an RSS feed that users can subscribe to if they want. We saw in the last chapter how to return XML from a controller. We can reuse this approach to quickly create a simple RSS feed for the application.

There is a Grails plug-in to help with writing feeds for Grails applications. This is called the Feeds plug-in (`http://grails.org/plugin/feeds`) and it is built on the ROME API (`https://rome.dev.java.net/`). Our feed is very simple. Therefore, we can use this as an opportunity to become more familiar with Groovy builders, rather than installing another plug-in.

[handwritten margin note: feed is simple in this app] using builders rather than the plugin]

A note about builders

Whenever producing anything but the simplest XML structure, we must be sure to build the XML in a separate class to the controller class. There are two reasons for this:

- Good design—encapsulating the construction of XML outside of the controller allows us to test and modify it independently from the controller.

- Grails injects many dynamic methods onto the controllers. If we need an element in the XML with the same name as one of these methods, then the builder will execute the method rather than adding the XML element we intended.

The first of these reasons is hopefully self-explanatory, while the second is a little subtler. If a node called on a builder exists as a method within the scope that the builder is being called from, then the method with the name is executed rather than a node being added to the builder. The following test illustrates the primacy of methods over node names:

```
package app

import groovy.xml.MarkupBuilder
import org.junit.Test

class BuilderNodeMethodTest extends GroovyTestCase {

    @Test
    public void testMethodNamesTakePriority() {
        def writer = new StringWriter()
        def builder = new MarkupBuilder( writer )
        builder.root {
```

```
            called()
            notCalled()
        }
        def root = new XmlSlurper().parseText( writer.toString() )
        assertEquals(0, root.called.size() )
        assertEquals(1, root.notCalled.size() )
    }
    def called() {
        println 'method called'
    }
}
```

We can see from the test that when the `called` node is executed within the builder, the method `called` is executed, instead of an element with the name 'called' being added to the XML. This is verified in our assertion that no elements exist with the name of `called`.

We would certainly have problems trying to construct our RSS XML in the controller as we need to produce a `link` element as part of RSS. This would conflict with the dynamically added `link` method that is added to controllers.

Create the RSS feed

To get round the problem posed by the dynamic methods on a controller, we can create a class to handle the XML construction for us. This class will live in the **src** folder as a utility class. The **src** folder is at the same level as the **grails-app** folder, and is then further split into **groovy** and **java** folders as shown in the following screenshot:

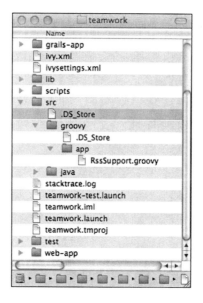

We are going to create the app package in the **groovy** source folder and create our `RssSupport` class that is constructed with a collection of items and defines a closure that can be used with a `MarkupBulder` to construct an RSS formatted XML document.

The implementation of `RssSupport` looks like:

```groovy
package app
class RssSupport {
    def content
    def build = {
        rss(version: '2.0' ) {
            channel {
                title('TeamWork updates')
                description('What do your team members want you to know?')
                    link('/teamwork/home')
                    language('en-us')
                    content.each {contentItem ->
                        item {
                            guid( "home#${contentItem.id}" )
                            pubDate( contentItem.lastUpdated )
                            title( contentItem.title )
                            description( contentItem.detail )
                        }
                    }
            }
        }
    }
}
```

A public property called `build` is declared on `RssSupport`, the value of this property is a closure. This closure can be passed into the Grails `render` method and it will be executed against an instance of `MarkupBuilder`. The result of executing the closure on the `MarkupBuilder` will then be written onto the HTTP response.

Here is the implementation of `RssController` that uses our `RssSupport` class:

```groovy
package app
import tagging.Taggable
import app.RssSupport
class RssController {
    def index = {
        def content = Taggable.list(sort: 'lastUpdated',
            order: 'desc')
        RssSupport rssBuilder = new RssSupport( content: content )
        render( contentType: 'text/xml', rssBuilder.build )
    }
}
```

We retrieve all of the instances of Taggable, sorted by the last updated date, instantiate an instance of RssSupport with the data and then pass the closure defined by the build property on RssSupport to the render method.

Remove authorization check

The final step is to remove the authorization check for the RSS feed. We need RSS readers to be able to go directly to the feed without any authentication. Remember that in Chapter 5, our authentication rules are declared as a filter called SecurityFilters.groovy in the grails-app/conf folder. We need to make a simple modification in order to allow requests made to RssController to pass through without requiring authentication.

```groovy
class SecurityFilters {
    def filters = {
        auth(controller: "*", action: "*") {
            before = {
                if( controllerName == 'rss' ) return true
                accessControl { true }
            }
        }

        userRoleManagement(controller: "(role|user)", action: "*") {
            before = {
                accessControl {
                    role("Administrator")
                }
            }
        }
    }
}
```

In the auth definition we can put a simple check in that tells JSecurity if the name of the controller being accessed is rss. If it is, then we can skip authentication.

Now if we fire up our application and access the URL http://localhost:8080/teamwork/rss in our favorite RSS reader, we should see a window that resembles the following screenshot:

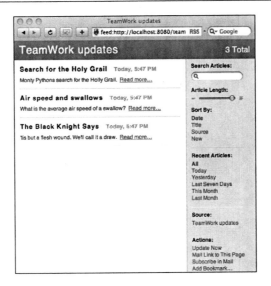

Now that we have our simple RSS feed implemented, we'll take a look at creating a REST service to allow other applications to create new messages.

REST services

Grails provides support for SOAP web services and REST web services. SOAP web service support is provided by either the XFire (`http://grails.org/plugin/xfire`) or Axis2 (`http://grails.org/plugin/axis2`) plug-ins. We are going to implement our services using the REST approach.

REST overview

REST is an architectural pattern where the URLs represent resources in the application. The HTTP method is then used to determine what action should be taken for that particular resource.

For example, we will create a REST resource for messages under `http://localhost:8080/api/message`. Clients will be able to perform three operations for this resource by using different HTTP methods and adding an ID to the URL as shown below:

- Get all messages — GET `http://localhost:8080/teamwork/api/message`
- Get a particular message, by id — GET `http://localhost:8080/teamwork/api/message/101`
- Create a new message - POST `http://localhost:8080/teamwork/api/message`

When retrieving a resource, the client will send a GET request to the URL and will expect the response to be XML formatted. When trying to create a new resource (a new message), the client must send a POST request that contains the data for the new resource in the body of the request. The client will expect to receive the details of the resource that has been created in the response.

To implement our REST service we need to:

- Add URL mappings so that we can respond to the HTTP method correctly
- Create controllers that are capable of handling XML data on the request and returning XML responses
- Configure security so that the client programs can have access to our secure resources

URL mapping

We know that Grails can map URLs to actions by using a default convention where the controller name and the name of the action are used to construct the URL, so that our URLs look like `controller/action/id`. This default mapping can be overridden using the `UrlMappings.groovy` class in the `grails-app/conf` folder. The default mappings for this file should look something like:

```
class UrlMappings {
    static mappings = {
        "/$controller/$action?/$id?" {
            constraints {
                // apply constraints here
            }
        }
        "500"(view: '/error')
    }
}
```

We can see that the first mapping sets up the default mapping that we are familiar with. There is also a mapping for server errors (HTTP response code 500) that is used to select a view for server errors.

Grails provides a number of different mechanisms that can be used for URL mapping. They are as follows:

- Mapping to variables
- Mapping to HTTP response codes
- Mapping to HTTP methods
- REST service mappings

- Mapping to wildcards
- Applying constraints

Mapping to variables

The default Grails pattern uses this approach to map the third token in a URL to the id parameter. Imagine that we wanted to provide a more readable URL when people search for messages by tag. Currently we have the URL: `http://localhost:8080/teamwork/message/filterByTag`. If we added the following URL mapping:

```
"/$selectedTag/message"(controller: "message") {
    action = "filterByTag"
}
```

then our users would be able to access all of the messages for a particular tag via the URL `http://localhost:8080/teamwork/message/filterByTag`. In addition, there would be no need to change the controller, as it already expects a request parameter called `selectedTag`.

Mapping to HTTP response codes

We have seen from the default mappings that there is a mapping to the HTTP 500 response code. We can specify a mapping to any response code that we wish to handle. For example, if we wanted to handle the situation where URLs are requested but don't have any resource associated, then we would add the following to our mapping class:

```
"404"(view:"/notFound")
```

This will execute a `notFound.gsp` view in the root of the views folder.

Mapping to HTTP methods

In version 1.0 of Grails, this is the approach that was used for mapping RESTful requests to the controllers.

```
"/api/message/$id?"(controller: "api") {
    action = [GET: "view", POST: "save"]
}
```

Mapping a request to HTTP methods allows specific actions to be called, which are based on the HTTP method that was used for the request. In the example above:

- A GET request to `/api/message` will be handled by the `view` action in `ApiController`.
- A POST request to `/api/message` will be handled by the `save` action in `ApiController`.

REST service mappings

Since Grails 1.1, a new type of URL mapping has been added specifically for use with REST web services. It uses the `resource` keyword shown in the mapping below:

```
"/api/message/$id?"(resource: "api")
```

This will map requests for the `/api/message` URL to the `ApiController`. The HTTP request methods GET, PUT, POST, and DELETE are mapped to the actions `show`, `update`, `save`, and `delete` respectively.

Mapping to wildcards

Grails also allows mapping of URLs with wildcards, by using single and double asterix and optional parameter binding as shown below:

```
"/javascript/*.js"(controller:"js")
```

will match `/javascript/application.js`.

```
"/javascript/${fileName}.js"(controller:"js")
```

will match `/javascript/application.js` and will add the parameter `fileName` to the request parameters with the value application.

```
"/javascript/**.js"(controller:"js")
```

will match `/javascript/ajax/actionBinder.js`.

```
"/javascript/$fileName**.js"(controller:"js")
```

will match `/javascript/ajax/actionBinder.js` and will add the parameter filename to the request parameters with the value `ajax/actionBinder`.

Applying constraints

One problem with displaying legible URLs to the users is that they may be tempted to modify the URLs themselves. In this case we could end up with invalid data coming in for simple view requests as well as the usual user input actions provided by an application. To address this concern, Grails allows us to apply constraints to a URL mapping. These constraints take the same form as the domain class constraints that we have already seen in Chapter 2.

Here is an example of applying constraints to a popular blog URL format taken from the Grails online documentation:

```
"/$blog/$year?/$month?/$day?/$id?" {
    controller = "blog"
    action = "show"
    constraints {
        year(matches:/d{4}/)
        month(matches:/d{2}/)
        day(matches:/d{2}/)
    }
}
```

Here we are verifying that the year, month, and day parameters are correctly formatted so we don't need to worry about this when processing the parameters in the action.

For more information on Grails URL mapping, take a look at the online documentation: http://grails.org/doc/1.1.x/guide/6.%20The%20Web%20Layer.html#6.4%20URL%20Mappings.

Our Message API mapping

After our brief introduction to mapping, let's set up the mapping that we will need in place to publish our REST interface for messages. Add the mapping to the UrlMappings.groovy class as shown below:

```
class UrlMappings {
    static mappings = {
        "/$controller/$action?/$id?" {
            constraints {
                // apply constraints here
            }
        }
        "500"(view: '/error')
        "/api/message/$id?"(resource: "api")
    }
}
```

Implementing the RESTful controller

From the URL mapping we have created above, it should be obvious that we need to implement a new controller (ApiController) with two actions: show and save. Both actions on the controller will need to be able to return XML for the respective requests. In addition, the save action needs to be able to take XML data off the request to construct a Message object.

Retrieving messages

We have already seen that it is fairly simple to return XML from an action by passing a closure into the `render` method that is then applied to a `MarkupBuilder`. However, if we do not need to format data according to an existing schema, like the RSS schema, then Grails provides a more convenient mechanism for XML marshaling with the use of converters. This approach makes it trivial to return an XML response for our domain objects:

```
package app

import grails.converters.XML

class ApiController {

    def show = {
        if( params.id ) {
            render Message.get( params.id ) as XML
        } else {
            def messages = Message.list( orderBy: 'lastUpdated',
                order: 'desc' )
            render messages as XML
        }
    }
}
```

Here we have implemented the `show` action that allows a client to retrieve either a list of all of the messages or an individual message, if a message id is specified. In either scenario, we can render the domain objects in XML format using the `as XML` notation.

The response for a single `Message` object will look like:

```
<message id="1">
    <dateCreated>2008-12-18 18:03:01.753</dateCreated>
    <detail>&apos;tis but a flesh wound. We&apos;ll call it a draw.</
detail>
    <lastUpdated>2008-12-18 18:03:02.141</lastUpdated>
    <tags>
        <tagger id="1"/>
    </tags>
    <title>The Black Knight Says</title>
    <user id="2"/>
</message>
```

While the output for a list of `Message` objects will look like:

```
<list>
    <message id="1">
        <dateCreated>2008-12-18 18:03:01.753</dateCreated>
```

```
        <detail>&apos;tis but a flesh wound. We&apos;ll call it a
            draw.</detail>
        <lastUpdated>2008-12-18 18:03:02.141</lastUpdated>
        <tags>
            <tagger id="1"/>
        </tags>
        <title>The Black Knight Says</title>
        <user id="2"/>
    </message>
    <message id="2">
        <dateCreated>2008-12-18 18:03:01.99</dateCreated>
        <detail>What is the average air speed of a swallow?</detail>
        <lastUpdated>2008-12-18 18:03:02.145</lastUpdated>
        <tags>
            <tagger id="2"/>
        </tags>
        <title>Air speed and swallows</title>
        <user id="2"/>
    </message>
</list>
```

Although using the XML converter allows us to get a RESTful API up and running quickly, we are missing a certain level of control. If our domains object structure changes, the interface to the client will change. We need to be careful about changing published interfaces once we are supporting real clients. While XML converters are very convenient for getting the service up and running, we must think carefully about the interfaces that we provide for clients.

Creating new messages

We also need to allow clients to create new messages in the system. This will be achieved by receiving the data for a message in an XML format in the body of a request. We know that Grails supports binding request parameters into our domain objects. It also allows us to bind XML data in a request to our domain objects. The prerequisite for enabling this binding is that the request has its *accept* header set to *text/html*. If the request comes in with this header set, then we can bind the following XML into our domain object:

```
<message>
    <title>Message from client</title>
    <detail>This message has been sent from a remote client!</detail>
</message>
```

In order to perform this binding, we must instantiate the domain class with the data from the `params` map, where the name corresponds to the root XML element:

```
def message = new Message(params.message)
```

We can now add the action to allow clients to create a new message:

where did view come for(com ? [handwritten annotation]

```
class ApiController {
    def userService
    def view = {...}
    def save = {
        def message = new Message(params.message)
        message.user = userService.getAuthenticatedUser()
        if( message.save() ) {
            render message as XML
        } else {
            def errors = message.errors.allErrors.collect {
                g.message(error:it)
            }
            render(contentType:"text/xml") {
                error {
                    for(err in errors) {
                        errorMessage(err)
                    }
                }
            }
        }
    }
}
```

Here we are binding the XML on the request into a new `Message` object, setting the authenticated user, saving the object and then returning the new `Message` as XML to the client. If there is an error when trying to save, we construct an error XML response so that the client can parse it and handle the validation error in some way.

Notice that in the `save` action we need to set the user that creates the message. When a human user creates a message through the web interface, we know who it is because they have authenticated themselves through the login form. When a client program calls our API to create a new message, it can't go through the normal authentication mechanism of logging in through a web form. We need to add another authentication route for the clients of our API.

Authentication for REST API

We have already put a special authentication rule in for RSS that negated the need for authentication. However, for access to the API, we allow clients to modify data. Therefore, it is essential that they provide valid credentials in some way or another. The approach we will take is quite naive, as it requires the client to provide the username and password for a real user in the system. In a real-world application it would be more secure to either:

- Allow users to generate a key that could be used for API access, or
- Create specific API users that only had an access key and could not log onto the applications web interface.

We are expecting the client to pass the username and password of a system user in the header of the request, which can be used to authenticate the request explicitly.

We will need to modify the SecurityFilters class to enable authentication for REST clients. To do this we will implement a method called `restAuth` that takes the username and password of the client off the request headers and authenticates against the JSecurity security manager service. Unfortunately, Grails does not inject services into a filter. However, it does provide the Spring application context as a dynamic property, so that we are able to get any services we need from the Spring context. This means we are able to request the JSecurity security manager service from the Spring context manually.

Add the following implementation to the `SecurityFilters.groovy` class in the `grails-app/conf` folder.

```
import org.jsecurity.authc.UsernamePasswordToken

class SecurityFilters {
    def filters = {
        auth(controller: "*", action: "*") {
            before = {
                if( controllerName == 'rss' ) return true
                if( controllerName == 'api' ) {
                    return restAuth( request,
                        applicationContext.getBean(
                            'jsecSecurityManager' ) )
                }
                accessControl {
                    return true
                }
            }
        }
    }
}
```

```
        def restAuth( request, jsecSecurityManager ) {
            def username = request.getHeader( 'username' )
            def password = request.getHeader( 'password' )
            def authToken = new UsernamePasswordToken(username, password)
            jsecSecurityManager.login( authToken )
        }
    }
```

A test script

Everything should be in place now for clients to access the API that we have
provided. Let's create a simple client and test script in order to check that our API is
performing as expected. In the `scripts` folder, create a file called RestTests.groovy
with the code shown below:

```
import groovy.xml.MarkupBuilder
class RestClient {
    def baseUrl
    def getMessages() {
        return doAction( "/message", 'GET' )
    }
    def getMessage( id ) {
        return doAction( "/message/${id}", 'GET' )
    }
    def createMessage( msgTitle, msgDetail ) {
        return doAction( "/message", 'PUT' ) { xml ->
            xml.message {
                title( msgTitle )
                detail( msgDetail )
            }
        }
    }
    def doAction( uri, method ) {
        return doAction( uri, method, null )
    }
    def doAction( uri, method, messageBody ) {
        def httpConnection = new URL( "${baseUrl}/api${uri}"
    ).openConnection()
        httpConnection.addRequestProperty( 'username', 'flancelot' )
        httpConnection.addRequestProperty( 'password', 'password' )
        httpConnection.setRequestProperty('CONTENT-TYPE', 'text/xml' )
        httpConnection.requestMethod = method
        httpConnection.doOutput = true
        if( messageBody ) {
            httpConnection.outputStream.withWriter( 'ASCII' ) {
                def writer = new StringWriter()
                messageBody( new MarkupBuilder( writer ) )
```

```
                    it << writer.toString()
            }
        }
        if( httpConnection.responseCode == httpConnection.HTTP_OK ) {
            return new XmlSlurper().parse( httpConnection.inputStream
)
        } else {
            throw new RuntimeException( 'Got a response of type: ' +
httpConnection.responseCode )
        }
    }
}
```

The code that is listed above is quite long, but it basically creates a client library with three public methods:

- `getMessage( id )` —retrieve the XML data for a message with the given ID
- `getMessages()` —retrieve all of the messages in an XML format
- `createMessage( title, detail )` —create a new message with the title and details supplied

We then have a utility method, `doAction`, to handle the HTTP communication with the server. This method optionally accepts a closure that will be executed against a `MarkupBuilder` instance to construct the data for the body of the request.

Now that the client is in place to talk to our REST services, we need to write the code to call the client. In `RestTest.groovy`, under the `RestClient` class, add the code shown below:

```
void readAllMessages( client ) {
    def messages = client.getMessages()
    messages.message.each { message ->
        def messageXml = client.getMessage( message.'@id' )
        println messageXml
    }
}
void createNewMessage( client ) {
    def createdMessage = client.createMessage(
        'from api',
        'can you believe it was that easy!' )
    println( "id of the created message is: ${createdMessage.'@id'}" )
}
target(default:"run our client test") {
    def client = new RestClient(
        baseUrl: 'http://localhost:8080/teamwork' )
    createNewMessage( client )
    readAllMessages( client )
}
```

If we run the application in one terminal window and open another terminal window, then we can run this script by going to the `teamwork` folder and executing:

```
grails rest-test
```

We should get some output that is similar to the following:

```
id of the created message is: 4
```

```
2008-12-18 20:07:51.557'tis but a flesh wound. We'll call it a draw.2008-
12-18 20:07:51.772The Black Knight Says
```

```
2008-12-18 20:07:51.682What is the average air speed of a swallow?2008-
12-18 20:07:51.775Air speed and swallows
```

```
2008-12-18 20:07:56.477can you believe it!2008-12-18 20:07:56.477from api
```

Summary

In this chapter, we really finished off our application in style! We:

- Introduced a site-wide search
- Provided an RSS feed for new content
- Implemented a RESTful API so that other systems can interact with our application.

By using the Searchable plug-in we were able, in no time at all, to give the users a powerful search that will allow them to find useful messages and files as the content of the application grows. We were able to respond quickly to the users request to keep an eye on messages and files that were posted by providing an RSS feed. We did this by using the built-in support that is provided by Grails for rendering a custom XML response. Finally, we have also allowed other developers to add value to our application by providing a RESTful API for messages.

We have finished adding new features to our application for now. Next we will look into making some of our work available for reuse by extracting the tagging implementation to a plug-in that will allow other teams to add tagging to their applications.

13
Build your own Plug-in

Now that you have finished with the implementation of your application, it is time to look at the code and see what can be pulled out into a separate component for reuse in future projects. The feature that stands out as being the most reusable is tagging. This feature will be useful on many different projects. Simplifying the implementation of tagging for future projects by using a plug-in will be a great benefit. In this chapter you will see how to:

- Create and package your own plug-in
- Enhance the plug-in by using dynamic method support in Groovy and Grails

The tagger plug-in

Grails plug-ins are developed in almost exactly the same way a regular application is. They can even be run as an application so that they can be tested independently from a real application. You can create a plug-in by using the `create-plugin` script in the command line. In your terminal window, go to the folder above the `teamwork` folder, where the application is present, and run:

```
grails create-plugin tagger
```

Notice that your plug-in has almost exactly the same structure as your application ,
as shown in the following screenshot:

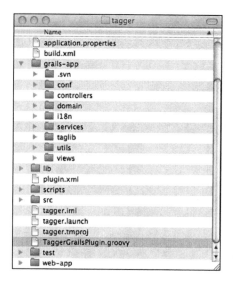

The only difference is the presence of a plug-in descriptor file called
`TaggerGrailsPlugin.groovy`. This is the main descriptor and configuration file for
the plug-in. It contains version information, author details, and a number of hooks
for Grails lifecycle events that your plug-in can participate in.

Fill in the version information and author details now:

```
def version = 0.1 //the version of the plugin

def grailsVersion = GrailsPluginUtils.grailsVersion //the version
of Grails the plugin is for

def author = "<your_name>"
def authorEmail = "<your_email>"
def title = "Allow domain classes to be tagged"
def description = '''\
Enable tagging of domain classes and provide UI tools to work with
tags.
'''

// URL to the plugin's documentation
def documentation = "http://grails.org/Tagger+Plugin"
```

All of the lifecycle hooks that are available are optional. You will not need to use
them for the first iteration of the plug-in, but they will be required later to make the
plug-in more flexible.

Extract the tagging code

In the first instance, you will take all of the tagging specific code out of your application and put it into the `Tagger` plug-in. This means moving the following folders from the `teamwork/grails-app` folder into the `tagger/grails-app` folder:

- controllers/tagging
- domain/tagging
- services/tagging
- views/taggable

Now run the `grails clean` command and then try to run the Teamwork application. You should see lots of compile errors. This is because the domain classes for tagging have disappeared.

In order to allow the application to run again, you need to compile the Tagger plug-in and reference it from the Teamwork application. In the command line, go to the `tagger` folder and run:

```
grails compile
```

To reference the Tagger plug-in from the Teamwork application, go to `BuildConfig.groovy` in the `grails-app/conf` folder. Make the following change:

```
grails.plugin.location.tagger = "../tagger"
grails.project.plugins.dir="/tools/grails-plugins"
```

Run the Teamwork application again. This time the application should compile and start. However, if you try to log into the application you will see that our plug-in isn't quite working yet. You will see an error when the `_file.gsp` template tries to use the `_showTags.gsp` template. This is because you have moved the `_showTags.gsp` template to a different folder in the plug-in, and the application does not know where to find it.

Accessing plug-in templates through Tag Libraries

In order to make the templates available to applications, we will need to expose them in some way. The simplest way is to provide a Tag Library with the plug-in that is able to render the templates. Since the tag is within the context of the plug-in, it will know where to look for the templates.

So far you have used tags provided by the Grails framework and some plug-ins, but you have not needed to implement one. If you have worked with the JSP Tag Libraries, you are in for a pleasant surprise.

Tag libraries are defined by the convention that they must go in the `grails-app/taglib` folder and must end in with `TagLib`. Create the file `tagger/TaggerTagLib.groovy` in the `grails-app/taglib` folder in your Tagger plug-in project. Add the following code to the new Groovy class:

```groovy
package tagger

class TaggerTagLib {

    static namespace = 'tagger'
    def showTags = { attrs ->
        renderTemplate( '/taggable/showTags', attrs.bean )
    }

    def editTagsForm = { attrs ->
        renderTemplate( '/taggable/editTagsForm', attrs.bean )
    }

    def renderTemplate( template, bean ) {
        out << g.render( template: template,
            model: ['taggable': bean],
            contextPath: pluginContextPath )
    }
}
```

[handwritten: s/b tagging   downloaded source says tagging]

Notice that this class has a static `namespace` property, two closure properties (`showTags` and `editTagsForm`), and a utility method called `renderTemplate`. Each closure property on a Tag library creates a tag definition that is callable from within a GSP. The `namespace` property defines the namespace that is used in the GSP to access the tag. The code shown above has created two new tags that can be called as follows:

```
<tagger:showTags bean="${message}"/>
<tagger:editTagsForm bean="${message}"/>
```

The `attrs` parameter declared on each of the closures will contain a `Map` of all of the attributes defined when the tag is called from a GSP. You can see that both of the tags are expecting to receive an object as the value of the `bean` attribute.

The `renderTemplate` method is simply a utility that renders the specified template and lets Grails know that the context path of the template should be the same as the context path of the plug-in. This means that Grails knows to look for the template under the plug-in rather than in the main application.

Notice that the `renderTemplate` method makes a call to a `render` method on a `g` object. This is actually calling the Grails `render` tag, which we have used many times before, but only from a GSP. Grails makes all Tag libraries available to other Tag libraries by injecting an object for each Tag library namespace into all Tag library classes. Therefore, all Tag libraries that we implement will have an object available with the name of `g` that exposes each of the available Grails Tag libraries as closures. Now, restart the Teamwork application and you will be able to modify the `_message.gsp` and `_file.gsp` templates to use the new `showTags` Tag library, like so:

```
<tagger:showTags bean="${message}"/>
```

and

```
<tagger:showTags bean="${file}"/>
```

Calling tags from controllers

Your GSP templates are not the only places that need to render tag view and edit templates. The `TaggableController`, which we have moved into the plug-in, must also be able to render tags in the view and edit states. The current line of code that handles this rendering looks something like:

```
render(template: "editTagsForm", model: [taggable: taggable])
```

When the plug-in is loaded into the Teamwork application, the call to this `render` method will look for the template within the context of the application rather than the plug-in. This means that the `editTagsForm` template will not be found as we have moved it to our plug-in.

There are two approaches that we can take in order to deal with this. The first is to modify the existing call to the `render` method to include a `plugin` attribute. This is used by the `render` method to look up the location of the plug-in based on the name. At first glance, this looks like the simplest solution, but what happens if we need to change the name of our plug-in? We would need to find all of the places that we have statically referenced the name of the plug-in and change it to the new name. A better solution would be to reuse the Tag libraries that we have already created that do not hard code the plug-in name.

As with tags, Grails dynamically adds all tags to controllers by creating a property on the controller for each tag namespace that is defined. All of the tags declared within that namespace are then added to the object and can be called from within the controller. This means that your showTags and editTagsForm Tag libraries will be made available in the controller through the tagger property. In order to call the Tag libraries from the TaggableController, you will need to modify the actions in the following way:

```
def editTags = {
    def taggable = Taggable.get(params.id)
    render tagger.editTagsForm( bean: taggable )
}

def saveTags = {
    def taggable = Taggable.get(params.id)
    taggable.clearTags()
    taggable.addTags(params.tags)
    render tagger.showTags( bean: taggable )
}

def showTags = {
    def taggable = Taggable.get(params.id)
    render tagger.showTags( bean: taggable )
}
```

The highlighted code shows how to call the necessary tag libraries from within the controller.

Current limitations

We have a fully functioning plug-in that can be used to add tagging to any future Grails application. This is sufficient for now, but the current implementation does have one quite serious limitation. When using this plug-in, any domain class that is to support tagging must extent the Taggable class. This is quite a serious design flaw, as it greatly reduces the flexibility of future applications using the plug-in, because they will not be able to extend any other class. For this reason, we need to take a closer look at how other plug-ins enhance the behavior of domain classes without forcing the use of inheritance.

Packaging a plug-in

Before we improve the design of the plug-in, let's take a quick look at how we can package our plug-in. Go to the command line in the tagger folder and run:

```
grails package-plugin
```

This will create a distributable ZIP file called `grails-tagger-0.1.zip`. The filename is constructed from the name of the plug-in plus the current version of the plug-in. The plug-in can now be installed into any Grails application by specifying the filename of the plug-in when running the `grails install-plugin` command. For example:

```
grails install-plugin grails-tagger-0.1.zip
```

Using plug-in events

When we installed the Searchable plug-in to make a domain class searchable, we added a static property (`static searchable = true`) to the domain class and it became searchable. This approach is possible in Groovy and Grails because Groovy allows methods and properties to be added to classes at run-time. The Grails plug-in architecture provides hooks into the lifecycle of a plug-in so that dynamic behavior can be added on startup.

The goal for the rest of this chapter is to convert the Taggable plug-in so that domain classes can be made taggable by defining the property (`static taggable = true`). You will achieve this through dynamically adding methods to domain classes at runtime.

Grails plug-in lifecycle events

Before moving on to the implementation details it is worth having a brief look at the lifecycle events that are made available by the Grails plug-in architecture.

There are two types of lifecycle events that are available to Grails plug-ins:

- Build events
- Runtime events

The following build events are available:

- Plug-in installation, through the `scripts/_Install.groovy` script file.
- Plug-in upgrade, through the `scripts/_Upgrade.groovy` script file.
- General scripting events, of which there are a large number of pre-defined events and a potentially infinite number of custom plug-in events. See the online Grails documentation for more details about these events: `http://grails.org/doc/1.1/guide/single.html#4.3 Hooking into Events`.

The available runtime events are:

- doWithSpring — where the plug-in is able to inject objects into the Spring application context
- doWithWebDescriptor — where the plug-in can participate in the dynamic generation of the web.xml file for the application
- doWithApplicationContext — where the plug-in is able to perform some runtime configuration after the Spring application context has been created
- doWithDynamicMethods — where the plug-in is able to add dynamic methods to classes within the application
- onChange — where the plug-in can perform runtime operations based on changes to specified monitored resources
- onConfigChange — where the plug-in can respond to changes in the configuration files at run time

Handlers for runtime events are provided in the *Plugin class in the root folder for the plug-in. In our case, this will be the TaggerGrailsPlugin.groovy file. To enable a plug-in to respond to each of the runtime events, a closure is declared with the relevant name in the *Plugin descriptor class.

doWithSpring

This closure takes no arguments and the contents of the closure will be executed against the Spring Bean Builder that is used by Grails in order to construct the Spring context of an application. The basics of this builder are:

- Each node represents the id of a bean in the Spring context
- Each node takes an argument that is the class of the object to be constructed
- Properties for the bean are defined within the node

For example, if we needed to manually inject a service into Spring that was a client wrapper around a remote service, then we might create a doWithSpring closure as shown below:

```
def doWithSpring = {
    remoteService(OurServiceClient) {
        endPoint = 'http://www.aservice.com'
    }
}
```

This would register an object in the Spring context with the id of remoteService. When this object is constructed, it will be a new instance of the OurServiceClient class and the endPoint property will be set to http://www.aservice.com.

A full description of how to use the Spring Bean Builder can be found on the Grails site (http://grails.org/doc/1.1/guide/single.html#14.4) along with the explanation of the BeanBuilder DSL.

doWithWebDescriptor

This closure receives the web.xml file as an XMLSlurper GPathResult. The closure is then able to use the GPathResult to find and manipulate the necessary elements for the plug-in. This happens when the application is started up. The web.xml file cannot be modified as a result of this closure, only the resulting behavior a loaded application.

doWithApplicationContext

This closure receives the fully constructed Spring ApplicationContext (http:// static.springframework.org/spring/docs/2.5.x/api/org/springframework/ context/ApplicationContext.html). At this point, it is too late to modify the context. The aim of this closure is to perform runtime configuration based on the final state of the context.

doWithDynamicMethods

This closure allows plug-in developers to add dynamic behavior to applications. No other runtime lifecycle event handlers are allowed to add dynamic methods to Grails classes. This closure also receives a fully constructed Spring ApplicationContext, which allows us to create dynamic methods that can interact with the Spring context.

onChange and onConfigChange

Both of these events are fired in reaction to a watched resource being modified. In order to handle these events, the *Plugin class must declare a watchedResources property, which is either a String or a List of String objects. When one of these resources is changed and reloaded by Grails, either the onChange or the onConfigChange closure will be executed, depending on the type of the changed object.

```
def watchedResources = "file:./grails-app/controllers/*Controller.
groovy"

def onChange = { event
    //do something when a controller changes.
}
```

In the example above, all of the controller files are being watched for changes. The event object that is passed into the onChange and onConfigChange closures has the following properties:

- source—the source of the event, being either a re-loaded class or a spring resource
- ctx—the Spring ApplicationContext object
- plugin—the plug-in object that manages the resource
- application—the GrailsApplication object

We will implement the handler for the doWithDynamicMethods and doWithSpring events in order to remove the design constraint with the Tagging plug-in. For more details on how to use the other runtime events, take a look at the plug-in section in the Grails on-line documentation: http://grails.org/doc/1.1/guide/12.%20Plug-ins.html.

Inspecting Grails artifacts

Go back to the TaggerGrailsPlugin.groovy class in the root of your Tagger plug-in. This is where we had added author and version information previously. There are a number of closures defined in the body of this class, one for each of the runtime events that were described above.

Apart from the arguments declared, each of the closures has an instance of GrailsApplication (http://grails.org/doc/1.1/api/org/codehaus/groovy/grails/commons/GrailsApplication.html) injected into its scope. This is the key to inspecting specific Grails class types (for example, domain classes) in order to see if your plug-in should add dynamic behavior.

The GrailsApplication class

The GrailsApplication class represents a running Grails application. It can be used to return information regarding classes that match Grails conventions, as well as providing runtime configuration information. Each class within a Grails application is referenced by an instance of the GrailsClass interface. In order to see all the classes in a Grails application you can use the GrailsApplication interface in the following way:

```
application.allClasses.each { println it.name }
```

Here `application` is the instance of the `GrailsApplication` interface that is provided to all plug-in event handling closures. To see all of the classes that follow a particular convention in a Grails application, you can use the `*Classes` dynamic method convention:

```
application.controllerClasses.each { println it.name }
```

The following table defines the dynamic method conventions that are available in the `GrailsApplication` class:

Dynamic Method	Description
`*Classes`	All classes of a particular type, for example, `domainClasses`
`get*Class`	Retrieves a GrailsClass instance for the short name of a class for example, `getControllerClass('MyController')`
`is*Class`	Determines if a Class is of a particular artifact type for example, `isControllerClass( MyController.class )`
`add*Class`	Adds a class for a particular artifact type for example, `addControllerClass( MyController.class )`

Find Taggable domain classes

Now that we can list all of the classes that are adhering to a particular Grails convention, it is time to check each domain class to see if it has the `taggable` property. Open the `TaggerGrailsPlugin.groovy` class and add the following implementation to the `doWithDynamicMethods` closure:

```
def doWithDynamicMethods = { ctx ->
    application.domainClasses.each { domainClass ->
        def isTaggable = GrailsClassUtils.getStaticPropertyValue(
            domainClass.clazz, 'taggable' )
        if( isTaggable ) {
            println "Make ${domainClass} taggable"
        }
    }
}
```

In the code above, we iterate over all of the domain classes, and retrieve the value of the static property `taggable` for each class. If a class does not have a static property with the given name, then `GrailsClassUtils` will return **null**. For the moment, if the domain class has the `taggable` property set, then we just print the name of the class. Notice that we are using a utility class provided by Grails called `GrailsClassUtils`. This class has lots of useful methods for finding out information about classes in Grails. We must be sure to import it into the plug-in class:

```
import org.codehaus.groovy.grails.commons.GrailsClassUtils
```

Now, add the `taggable` property to the `Message` and `File` domain classes and restart the application. The following output will be displayed in the console:

```
Make Artefact > Message taggable
Make Artefact > File taggable
```

Re-modeling tag relationships

It is necessary to re-model the relationship between a domain object and its tags as we wish to remove the dependency on the `Tagger` superclass. Create a new package called `tagger` in the Tagger plug-in in the `grails-app/domain` folder to work on the new domain structure. We need a new class to represent tags in the new structure. Create the class `TagData` as shown below:

```
package tagger
class TagData {
    String name
    static constrains = {
        name( blank: false )
    }
}
```

We also require a class to store the relationship between tags and domain objects, as before. Create the new `TagRelationship` domain class shown as follows:

```
package tagger
class TagRelationship {
    long taggedItem
    Class taggedType
    TagData tag
    Date dateCreated
    static constraints = {
        tag( nullable: false )
    }
    public String toString() {
        return tag.name
    }
}
```

This looks very similar to the previous incarnation of the domain class that held relationships between tags and domain classes. The big difference is the two new properties:

- `taggedItem`—this will store the id of the domain object that has a particular tag (for example, the id of a `Message`).
- `taggedType`—this holds the `Class` of the domain object that is related to the tag (for example, `File`).

These properties should provide all the information you need to be able to retrieve tags for a given domain object and to retrieve the domain objects for a particular tag.

Adding Taggable behavior

It is time to look at adding the dynamic behavior to the domain classes. Previously, by virtue of extending the `Taggable` class, domain classes would inherit the following:

- `tags` — the property containing a list of the tags that the domain class instance was associated with
- `tagsAsString` — a property to return tags for a domain class instance as a space delimited `String`
- `addTags` — allows a list of tags to be added to a domain class instance
- `addTag` — allows a single tag to be added to a domain class instance
- `hasTag` — determines if a class has a particular tag
- `clearTags` — removes all of the tags from a domain class instance
- `withTag` — retrieves all of the instances of either all of the children of `Taggable` or a given child type that had a specific tag
- `withTags` — retrieve all of the instances of any child of `Taggable` that has any one of a supplied list of tags

To add the properties and methods dynamically, you will have to create a Groovy class to take responsibility for applying the dynamic behavior to a particular domain class. Create the `tagger` package under the `src/groovy` folder and a new Groovy class called `TaggablePrototype` under this package.

There is quite a lot of code to rewrite to add the properties and methods dynamically to our taggable classes, so let's take it in small steps.

Groovy MetaClass

Before you start adding dynamic behavior to the domain classes, it is necessary to understand a little more about metaprogramming in Groovy. We saw in Chapter 4 that all Groovy classes are constructed by the `GroovyClassGenerator`, which is responsible for adding the `GroovyObject` interface, along with an implementation of this interface to your class. The methods provided by the `GroovyObject` interface are:

- `invokeMethod`
- `getProperty`
- `setProperty`
- `getMetaClass`
- `setMetaClass`

Calling the `getMetaClass` method on the class retrieves the `MetaClass` implementation for a class. There is a specific implementation of the `MetaClass` interface called `ExpandoMetaClass`, which is returned by default. The beauty of `ExpandoMetaClass` is that it provides an incredibly simple syntax for adding dynamic methods and properties to a class. By creating a simple test class, we can see some examples of how to use `ExpandoMetaClass` to dynamically add the following to a class:

- Read-only properties
- Read/write properties
- Simple stateless methods
- Methods that interact with the state of the object

In the tagger plug-in, in the `test/unit` folder, create a groovy unit test class called `MetaProgrammingTests` under a package called `metatest`, shown as follows:

```
package metatest

class MetaProgrammingTests extends GroovyTestCase {
    // tests to go here
}

class ExtendMe {
    def myName
}
```

The `ExtendMe` class is a simple class that we will add dynamic behavior to during the tests. Add the following test that demonstrates how to add a read-only property to the `ExtendMe` class:

```
public void testAddingAReadOnlyProperty() {
    ExtendMe.metaClass.getInterest = {->return 'skiing'}
    def extended = new ExtendMe()
    assertEquals( 'skiing', extended.interest )
    assertEquals( 'skiing', extended.getInterest() )
}
```

In the example above, we get access to the `MetaClass` instance for the `ExtendMe` class and add a read-only property called `interest` to the class. A closure, that returns the `String` 'skiing', is assigned to the `interest` property on the `ExtendMe` instance and is executed when this property is called.

It is critical to specify that the closure has no arguments through use of the -> notation, otherwise Groovy will not recognize the method as a property when it is added to the class.

The following code shows how to add a read/write property dynamically to a class:

```
public void testAddingAReadWriteProperty() {
    ExtendMe.metaClass.interest = null
    def extended = new ExtendMe()

    assertNull( extended.interest )
    extended.interest = 'shopping'
    assertEquals( 'shopping', extended.interest )
}
```

You simply have to assign a value to the property that you wish to add on the MetaClass of the class and the property will be created with the specified default value.

When adding properties in this manner beware that the property is stored in a WeakHashMap on ThreadLocal. Therefore, if your object has a long lifetime, the value of the dynamic property may not survive for the duration of the object's lifetime.

The following example shows how to add a stateless method to an object:

```
public void testAddingAMethod() {
    ExtendMe.metaClass.greet = { name ->
        def greeting = "Hi ${name}, how are you?"
        println greeting
        return greeting
    }
    def extended = new ExtendMe()

    assertEquals( 'Hi fred, how are you?', extended.greet( 'fred' ) )
}
```

The syntax for adding a method is the same as adding a read-only property. In the example above, we have specified that the greet method should take a single name argument.

The last example will add another method that can interact with the existing state of the class that it is added to:

```
public void testAddingMethodToInteractWithObjectState() {
    ExtendMe.metaClass.introduceTo = { name ->
        def introduction = "Hi ${name},
            my name is ${delegate.myName}."
        println introduction
        return introduction
    }
    def extended = new ExtendMe( myName: 'Jon' )
    assertEquals( 'Hi fred, my name is Jon.', extended.introduceTo(
'fred' ) )
}
```

In the example above, the definition of the introduceTo method uses the object represented by the delegate property to get the value of the myName property from our extended object. All closures have a delegate property created within their scope. This is, by default, the declaring context of the closure. However, the ExpandoMetaClass sets the delegate property for closures that represent methods on an object to the object itself. This is so that we can interact with the state of the object.

That is the introduction you need for Groovy metaprogramming to be able to add dynamic behavior to your taggable domain classes. So let's move on to the implementation.

Getting the home page working

The first thing we need to do is to remove the dependency on the old style of making a domain class taggable and switch over to the new style. Stop the Message and File domain classes from extending the Taggable class and remove the withTag implementations from each of these classes shown as follows:

```
package app

class Message {
    static taggable = true
    //properties and constraints will remain the same
}
```

And your File domain class:

```
package app

class File {
    static taggable = true
    //properties and constraints will remain the same
}
```

At this point, if we try running the application everything will be broken! To fix the application to the point where users can log in and go to the home page, we need to:

- Allow tags to be added to a taggable class using the `addTag` method, this is required by the `Bootstrap` class
- Add the `hasTag` method, required by the `addTag` method
- Add the `tags` property, required by the `hasTag` method
- Add the `tagsAsString` property so that tags can be rendered on the home page

Let's take a look at the first pass of `TaggablePrototype` that will add these methods onto the domain classes. Create the `TaggablePrototype.groovy` file in the `tagger/src/groovy/tagger` folder and add the code shown below:

```groovy
package tagger

class TaggablePrototype {
    def addMethodsTo(domainClass) {
        ExpandoMetaClass metaClass = domainClass.metaClass
        //add properties
        metaClass.getTags = getTags
        metaClass.getTagsAsString = getTagsAsString

        //add instance methods
        metaClass.hasTag = hasTag
        metaClass.addTag = addTag
    }
    def getTags = {->
        def taggedItem = delegate
        return TagRelationship.withCriteria {
            eq('taggedItem', taggedItem.id)
        }.findAll { tagRelationship ->
            tagRelationship.taggedType == taggedItem.class
        }
    }
    def getTagsAsString = {->
        return delegate.tags.collect {it.tag.name}.join(' ')
    }
    def hasTag = {String tagName ->
        return delegate.tags.find {it.tag.name == tagName}
    }
    def addTag = {String tagName ->
        def tag = TagData.findByName(tagName)
```

```
        if( !tag ) {
            tag = new TagData(name: tagName).save()
        }
        if( !delegate.hasTag(tagName) ) {
            def tagRel = new TagRelationship(tag: tag, taggedItem:
    delegate.id, taggedType: delegate.class)
            tagRel.save()
        }
    }
}
```

The first method in the listing (addMethodsTo) determines which methods are added dynamically to the provided class. You can see that two properties (tags and tagsAsString) and two instance methods (addTag and hasTag) are being added. All of the closures that are to be used as implementations for the dynamic methods and properties are declared separately as properties of the TaggablePrototype class. This allows us to separate adding the dynamic behavior from the implementation of the dynamic behavior.

The first dynamic property we provide is tags, which allows the object to return its list of tags. The behavior of the tags property is implemented by the getTags closure. This closure queries the TagRelationship class for all of the items where the taggedItem property equals the id of the delegate object. It then filters out any TagRelationship instances that are for a different class other than the delegate object. Notice that the delegate object has been assigned to another variable (taggedItem). This is necessary because we need to have access to the delegate object for the getTags closure inside the withCriteria closure. If you try accessing the delegate property from within the withCriteria closure, then you will find that it is set to HibernateCriteriaBuilder. This is because the withCriteria closure uses the HibernateCriteriaBuilder.

The next property (tagsAsString) is much simpler, but it relies on the existence of the tags property. It simply calls the tags property on the delegate, collects all of the names of the tags and then joins them into a space-delimited string.

The hasTag method is declared next. This method takes a tag as a string and checks if the tag exists in the list of tags for the delegate object.

Finally, the addTag method is declared. It checks if the tag name exists and creates the tag if it does not. Then the delegate is checked to make sure it does not have the specified tag already. If the delegate does not have a relationship with the tag, a new relationship is created.

We now have a class that is capable of adding dynamic tagging behavior to the domain classes. The next step is to use this class in the plug-in initialization. Go to the `TaggerGrailsPlugin` class and update the `doWithDynamicMethods` in the following way:

```
def doWithDynamicMethods = { applicationContext ->
    def prototype = new TaggablePrototype()
    application.domainClasses.each { domainClass ->
        def isTaggable = GrailsClassUtils.getStaticPropertyValue
                        ( domainClass.clazz, 'taggable' )
        if( isTaggable ) {
            prototype.addMethodsTo( domainClass )
        }
    }
}
```

Don't forget to import the `TaggablePrototype` class:

```
import tagger.TaggablePrototype
```

Now, restart the Teamwork application. Users will be able to log in and see the bootstrap data on the home page with any tags being displayed. This is shown in the following screenshot:

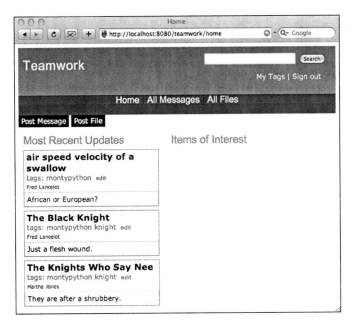

Unfortunately, that is about as far as you will be able to go. We now need to go through and add support for the features provided in the rest of the application.

Items of Interest

Currently, if a user attempts to register interest in a tag it will have no effect. That is, nothing will be displayed on the home page in the **Items of Interest** section. Here are the steps necessary to get this feature working again with the new tagging plug-in:

- Delete the tagging package under the domain folder for the plug-in. This will create errors making it easier to spot where the old domain classes are being used.

- Modify the structure of the `User` domain class so that watched tags can be handled in the new structure.

- Add a method to the existing the `TagService` class in the plug-in that will allow applications to query all of the tagged items for a set of tags.

- Update the `ContentService` class in the Teamwork application to use the new method on the `TagService` class.

The first task is fairly straightforward. The second task, to remodel the `User` domain class, is a bit trickier. We need to implement a unidirectional many-to-many relationship between the `User` class and the `TagData` class. We don't want to use the `TagRelationship` class to do this, as we could end up getting users in our results when searching for messages and files via tags. Therefore, in order to create the relationship, we need to create a new `WatchedTag` domain class in the Teamwork application:

```
package app

import tagger.TagData

class WatchedTag {
    TagData tag

    public String toString() {
        return tag.name
    }
}
```

Once this class is in place, make the changes to `User`, as shown below:

```
package app

import tagger.TagData

class User {
    static hasMany = [watchedTags: WatchedTag]
    //no change to the properties
    static constraints = {//no change}
    def needToHash(String password) {//no change}
```

used groovy version

```groovy
def overrideTags(String tags) {
    watchedTags.each {it.delete()}
    watchedTags = []
    watchedTags.addAll( tags?.split(' ')?.collect {
        tagName ->
            def tagData = TagData.findByName( tagName )
                ?:new TagData( name: tagName )
            new WatchedTag( tag: tagData )
    } )
}
def getTagsAsString() {//no change}

def getTags() {
    return (watchedTags?:[]).collect{it.tag}
}
}
```

We have made two basic changes here. We have made the watchedTags property
a relationship to the new WatchedTag class. We have had to re-implement the
overrideTags method to work with this new class.

Let's now add the new method to the TagService class that will allow us to query
all of the taggable items that are related to one or more of the entries in the tags list.
Also, we no longer need the createTagRelationship methods that were previously
on the service, so let's remove them.

```groovy
package tagging

import tagger.TagRelationship

class TagService {

    boolean transactional = true

    def allWithTags( tags ) {
        return TagRelationship.withCriteria {
            inList( 'tag', tags )
        }.collect { it.taggedType.get( it.taggedItem ) }
    }
    def cloudData(type) {//no change yet}
}
```

The allWithTags method above provides the implementation necessary to find
all tagged items of any type that have a relationship to one of the tags supplied.
The withCriteria method is called on the TagRelationship class to return all
TagRelationship instances that have a tag in the supplied list. The tagged item is
then collected from each of the matching TagRelationship instances. Remember
that both the class of the tagged item and the id of the tagged item are stored in the
TagRelationship class.

Finally, we must update the `allWatchedItems` method on the `ContentService` class in the Teamwork application as shown below:

```
class ContentService {
    def userService
    def tagService
    def allWatchedItems() {
        def watchedTags = userService.authenticatedUser.tags
        return watchedTags ?
                tagService.allWithTags( watchedTags ) : []
    }
    //no other changes...
}
```

When the application is restarted, users will be able to set the tags they wish to watch again.

[handwritten marginalia: Watched Tag, not inserted but UserWatchedTag]

[handwritten note: Not sure it worked? → exception, Data Integrity Violation Error: not null prop references a null or transient value...]

[handwritten note: get stack trace upon entering a tag → MissingMethodException: No signature of method static tagging. Tag.findAllByNameLike().]

Create messages and files

Now onto making the create messages and files features work again. You will need to:

- Make the `addTags` method part of the dynamic behavior of a `Taggable` class.
- Make sure that the tags are added to messages and files after the object has been saved, because you need the `id` of the object to be populated before it can have a `TagRelationship`.

To make the `addTags` method part of our taggable behavior, you will need to create a closure in the `TaggablePrototype` class that implements the behavior of the `addTags` method. Add the following closure property to the `TaggablePrototype` class:

```
def addTags = {String spaceDelimitedTags ->
    if( spaceDelimitedTags ) {
        spaceDelimitedTags.split(' ') each {
            addTag(it)
        }
    }
}
```

[handwritten note: use Groovy version]

Now update the `addMethodsTo` method to add the new behavior to the `Taggable` domain classes:

```
def addMethodsTo(domainClass) {
    ExpandoMetaClass metaClass = domainClass.metaClass
    //add properties
    metaClass.getTagsAsString = getTagsAsString
    metaClass.getTags = getTags

    //add instance methods
    metaClass.addTag = addTag
    metaClass.hasTag = hasTag
    metaClass.addTags = addTags
}
```

The last change is to update `MessageController` and `FileService` to make the call to `addTags`. This takes place after the message or file object has been successfully saved. Remember that the `TagRelationship` class has the property `taggedItem`. This is the hibernate-generated `id` of the `taggable` object. If the `addTags` method is called before the `taggable` object is saved, the `id` property will not be populated and an invalid id of 0 will be given to the `TagRelationship` instance.

Here is the updated `save` action for `MessageController`:

```
def save = {
    def message = new Message(params)
    message.user = userService.getAuthenticatedUser()
    if (!message.hasErrors() && message.save()) {
        message.addTags(params.userTags)
        flash.toUser = "Message [${message.title}] has been added."
        redirect(action: 'create')
    } else {
        render(view: 'create', model: [message: message,
            userTags: params.userTags])
    }
}
```

And the updated `saveNewVersion` method for `FileService`:

```
def saveNewVersion( params, multipartFile ) {
    def version = createVersionFile( params, multipartFile )
    def file = applyNewVersion( params.fileId, version )
    file.save()
    file.addTags( params.userTags )
    return file
}
```

Update tags

You may have noticed that the in-line editing that allows users to update tags is also broken now. This is because we are calling the GORM `get` method on the `Taggable` class in order to retrieve an instance of either `Message` or `File`. We have now deleted the `Taggable` class, so we need a mechanism that will allow us to get an instance of the correct class for a given id. We can solve this problem by registering a lookup table in Spring that uses the short name of the `taggable` domain object as the key and the `Class` of the object as the value. Requests to plug-in actions can then pass a key for the lookup table and the `TaggableController` will use the supplied key to determine which object type to use.

This means you get to see how to make a plug-in add new objects to the Spring context on start up. First though, modify the `doWithDynamicMethods` closure in the `TaggerGrailsPlugin` class as follows:

```
def doWithDynamicMethods = { applicationContext ->
    def prototype = new TaggablePrototype()
    def taggedClasses = applicationContext.getBean('taggedClasses')
    application.domainClasses.each { domainClass ->
        def isTaggable = GrailsClassUtils.getStaticPropertyValue(
            domainClass.clazz, 'taggable' )
        if( isTaggable ) {
            prototype.addMethodsTo( domainClass )
            taggedClasses[domainClass.shortName] = domainClass.clazz
        }
    }
}
```

You can see that we pull an object from the Spring application context with the name `taggedClasses`. This object is the lookup table and is implemented as a `Map`. Each domain class that is marked as taggable is added to the map with a key determined by the short name of the class.

How did the `taggedClasses` `Map` get into the Spring context?

```
def doWithSpring = {
    taggedClasses(HashMap)
}
```

You need to modify the `doWithSpring` closure to register a `HashMap` in the Spring context with the name `taggedClasses`. When the plug-in is started, the `doWithSpring` closure is executed against the Spring Bean Builder that Grails uses to create the Spring context for an application.

The next change is to stop the `TaggableController` actions from using the
`Taggable` class and instead use the `taggedClasses` lookup table.

```
package tagger
import grails.converters.JSON
class TaggableController {
    def taggedClasses // injected by Spring
    def editTags = {
        def taggable = taggableFromType( params )
        render tagger.editTagsForm( bean: taggable )
    }
    def saveTags = {
        def taggable = taggableFromType( params )
        taggable.clearTags()
        taggable.addTags(params.tags)
        render tagger.showTags( bean: taggable )
    }
    def showTags = {
        def taggable = taggableFromType( params )
        render tagger.showTags( bean: taggable )
    }
    def suggestTags = { ... }
    def renderAsXml(tags) { ... }
    def taggableFromType( params ) {
        def clazz = taggedClasses[ params.type ]
        return clazz.get( params.id )
    }
}
```

[handwritten annotation: this method still references Tagg & the distribution source concurs. It cannot be right.]

As with services, the `taggedClasses` object will be injected because its property
has the same name as the object in the Spring context. Each action that used to call
`Taggable.get( params.id )` has been updated to load the taggable object through
the `taggableFromType` utility method. This method takes the request `params` map
and assumes a parameter called `type`, which contains the key to a taggable class has
been sent on the request. The `Class` that is retrieved from the `taggedClasses` map is
then used to load the taggable object from the database.

The last step to hook up this mechanism is to make sure that all of the links to these actions will send the `type` parameter. Modify the `_showTags` template as follows:

```
<%@ page import="org.codehaus.groovy.grails.commons.
DefaultGrailsDomainClass" %>
<%
    def taggableShortName = new DefaultGrailsDomainClass( taggable.
class ).shortName
    def moreParams = [type: taggableShortName]
%>
<span class="tags">${taggable.getTagsAsString()}</span>
<g:remoteLink controller="taggable" action="editTags"
    id="${taggable.id}" update="tags${taggable.id}"
    params="${moreParams}">edit</g:remoteLink>
```

[handwritten note: this does not match downloaded source, nor when I have coded]

And the `_editTagsForm` template:

```
<%@ page import="org.codehaus.groovy.grails.commons.
DefaultGrailsDomainClass" %>
<%
    def taggableShortName = new DefaultGrailsDomainClass( taggable.
class ).shortName
    def moreParams = [type: taggableShortName]
%>
<g:formRemote name="tagForm" url="[controller:'taggable',action:'save
Tags']"
        update="tags${taggable.id}" class="inlineedit">
    <input type="hidden" name="id" value="${taggable.id}"/>
    <input type="hidden" name="type"
        value="${taggableShortName}"/>
    <fieldset>
        <dl>
            <dt>Tags</dt>
            <dd>
                <richui:autoComplete name="tags"
                    action="${createLinkTo('dir':
                            'taggable/suggestTags')}"
                    delimChar=" " value="${taggable.
                                    getTagsAsString()}"
                    forceSelection="false"/>
            </dd>
        </dl>
    </fieldset>
```

```
    <input type="submit" value="Save"/> |
    <g:remoteLink controller="taggable" action="showTags"
        id="${taggable.id}" update="tags${taggable.id}"
        params="${moreParams}">Cancel</g:remoteLink>
</g:formRemote>
```

The important part about both of these templates is the code at the top that extracts the key to be sent on the `type` parameter from the `taggable` object. An instance of `DefaultGrailsDomainClass` is instantiated, passing in the `taggable` object. An instance of this class represents a domain class in Grails and implements the `GrailsClass` interface. Therefore, you can be sure that it will extract the `shortName` from our `taggable` object in the same way as the plug-in initialization code.

The final change we need to make is adding the `clearTags` method to our `taggable` domain classes. In `TaggablePrototype` class, add the following closure property:

```
def clearTags = {
    delegate.tags.each { tagRel ->
        tagRel.delete( flush: true )
    }
}
```

Make sure this implementation is bound to the `clearTags` method on `taggable` classes by adding the following highlighted code:

```
def addMethodsTo(domainClass) {

    ExpandoMetaClass metaClass = domainClass.metaClass
    //add properties
    metaClass.getTagsAsString = getTagsAsString
    metaClass.getTags = getTags

    //add instance methods
    metaClass.addTag = addTag
    metaClass.hasTag = hasTag
    metaClass.addTags = addTags
    metaClass.clearTags = clearTags
}
```

Not only have we fixed in-line editing for the new plug-in structure, but we have also seen how a plug-in can register objects into the Spring context. Now, let's take a look at listing messages and files.

List messages and files

If you remember, there are two actions related to listing messages and files. The first is to list all by last modified date, while the second is to list a filtered subset by a tag selected from the tag cloud. The problem we have when listing all of the messages or files is that a tag cloud is displayed on that page. So we need to modify the implementation of the `cloudData` method on the `TagService` to handle our new domain structure.

[handwritten: downloaded source is not static]

```
def static cloudData( type ) {
    def data = [:]
    Tag.list().each { tag ->
        def count = TagRelationship.withCriteria {
            eq( 'tag', tag )
        }.findAll { it.taggedType == type }.size()
        if( count ) {
            data.put( tag.name, count )
        }
    }
    return data
}
```

[handwritten margin notes: references non-existent domain? too downloaded book source, uses TagData, TagRelationship, TagDb too]

This method simply iterates over all of the tags in the application, counting how many `TagRelationship` instances with the specified `type` exists for each tag. The logic is the same as before, just updated for the new tagger domain structure. This change should be enough to get the list pages working for messages and files.

To enable filtering by a specific tag requires the following changes:

- Two new `TagService` methods, one to return all of the items with a single specified tag and the other to return all of the items of a particular type, that have a single specified tag
- Update the `MessageController` class to use the new service methods
- Update the `FileController` class to use the new service methods

The two new service methods are very simple and are built on the existing method of finding tagged items, given a list of tags:

```
package tagging

class TagService {

    def allWithTags( tags ) { ... }

    def allWithTag( String tagName ) {
        return allWithTags( [TagData.findByName( tagName )] )
    }
}
```

```
    def withTag( String tagName, Class type ) {
        return allWithTag( tagName ).findAll {
            it.class == type
        }
    }

    def cloudData(type) { … }
}
```

Now, we must update the `filterByTag` implementation to use `TagService`:

```
package app

import tagger.Tag

class MessageController {

    def tagService
    def contentService
    def userService

    def post = { … }
    def save = { … }
    def list = { … }

    def filterByTag = {

        def messages = tagService.withTag(
                params.selectedTag, Message )
                .sort( contentService.lastUpdatedSort )
        render(view: 'list', model: [
                messages: messages,
                tagCloudData: tagService.cloudData(Message)])
    }
}
```

The updates to `FileController` are very similar:

```
package app

class FileController {

    def tagService
    def contentService
    def fileService

    def post = { … }
    def save = { … }
    def download = { … }
    def newVersion = { … }
    def list = { … }

    def filterByTag = {
```

```
        def files = tagService.withTag(
                params.selectedTag, File )
                .sort( contentService.lastUpdatedSort )
        render(view: 'list', model: [
                files: files,
                tagCloudData: tagService.cloudData(File)])
    }
}
```

RSS

Finally, the RssController must be modified to allow the RSS feed to continue to work with the new tagger plug-in. Rather than relying on polymorphic querying by simply calling Taggable.list(), it is necessary to build the list from the individual classes that are to be published via RSS. The RssController must be modified as follows:

```
package app

class RssController {

    def contentService

    def index = {
        def content = Message.list()
        content.addAll( File.list() )
        content.sort( contentService.lastUpdatedSort )

        RssSupport rssBuilder = new RssSupport( content: content )
        render( contentType: 'text/xml', rssBuilder.build )
    }
}
```

Summary

Not only have we built a valuable application for our users, we have now significantly reduced the development costs of future Grails projects that wish to make use of tagging behavior.

We have seen that creating a basic plug-in is a fairly simple business, but there are a few issues ready to trip up the unwary developer, such as referencing views and templates through the correct context path.

We have also seen that creating flexible and functional plug-ins requires a bit more thought, as well as a slightly deeper understanding of metaprogramming in Groovy. The benefit of taking the time to build a plug-in in such a way is that the design choices of developers who use the plug-in will not be limited. If we had left the plug-in in its original incarnation, where a domain class had to extend the `Taggable` class, then the plug-in would only be useful in the very simplest of applications. Consider how limiting it would be if you had to extend a `Searchable` class to make your domain classes work with the searchable plug-in.

In the next chapter, we will prepare the application for a production environment and go through a sample installation with a MySQL database server and a Tomcat application server. We will also briefly cover some of the real world concerns when building applications in Grails and the options that are available to deal with them.

14

Deployment and the Real World

The final stage in the delivery of the application is to deploy it to a stable production environment, running in a hosted servlet container and against a permanent database that will not be cleared out every time the application is restarted or redeployed. We will see just how simple it is to package a Grails project into a deliverable web archive (WAR) file and set up the Grails configuration for a production environment.

Once the application is up and running, we will review some of the next steps that are worth investigating to learn more about working with Grails.

Set up the environment

First of all, we will set up an environment on our local machine that will work in the same way as a production environment. This will involve setting up a database and application server. You will be using MySQL and Tomcat.

Install MySQL

Download and install MySQL from `http://dev.mysql.com/downloads/`. Once you have installed MySQL, create a database for the application by logging on as the root user and creating a new database. By default, the password for the `root` user is blank. You obviously need to change this if you are running in a real production environment!

Log on as the root user:

```
mysql -u root -p
```

Create the new database:

```
create database teamwork;
```

Now, create a user that the application will use to access the database:

```
create user teamwork@localhost identified by 'workteam';
grant all on teamwork.* to 'teamwork'@'localhost';
```

Install Tomcat

Now, you need to install your servlet container. Tomcat is a fairly standard choice. Go to the Tomcat site, `http://tomcat.apache.org`, and download the latest 6.0 release. Follow the installation instructions from the Tomcat site for your operating system.

In order to create a data source that will allow your application to connect to the MySQL teamwork database, you will need to configure a JNDI resource. The simplest way to do this for Tomcat is to include a `context.xml` file in the `META-INF` folder of your web application.

Create the `context.xml` file in the `teamwork/web-app/META-INF` folder as shown below:

```xml
<?xml version="1.0" encoding="UTF-8"?>
<Context>
    <Resource name="teamwork/dataSource"
              auth="Container"
              type="javax.sql.DataSource"
              username="teamwork"
              password="workteam"
              driverClassName="com.mysql.jdbc.Driver"
              url="jdbc:mysql://localhost:3306/teamwork"
              maxActive="8"
              maxIdle="4"/>
</Context>
```

When the application is packaged as a WAR file and deployed to Tomcat, the `context.xml` file will be used to create a JNDI data source resource that is only available for this application.

This is the simplest way to configure a JNDI resource for your application. However, it is certainly *not* the best. The problem here is that our web application needs to know too much information about the production database. Managing this file within the web application means that the application is tied to one database when running in production mode and all developers will know how to connect to the production database. The benefit of a JNDI data source is that you can deploy an application to any servlet container that has a DataSource configured with the relevant JNDI name. When setting up on a real production environment, the context.xml file should be taken out of the application source and managed independently by server administrators.

Configure Grails

Now that you have the Servlet container and database ready to go, let's take a look at the steps you need to take in order to configure the application to use the database and deploy it to the Tomcat server.

Set up the DataSource

Given that Grails is built on the Java platform, it should come as no great surprise that it uses JDBC to communicate with databases. Therefore, it is necessary to install the correct driver for your database. Download the Connector/J driver for MySQL and put the JAR file in the lib folder of your project.

DataSource configuration

The configuration for a particular DataSource can be found under the grails-app/conf folder in the DataSource.groovy file. Grails uses the builder syntax of nested closures in order to declare DataSource configuration, so the declaration of a DataSource that connects directly to a MySQL database would look something like:

```
dataSource {
    pooled = true
    dbCreate = "update"
    url = "jdbc:mysql://localhost/appDB"
    driverClassName = "com.mysql.jdbc.Driver"
    username = "appDBUser"
    password = "apDBPassword"
}
```

The options that are available for a `DataSource` through this builder are:

Property	Description
driverClassName	The full name of the driver class for the database.
username	The database username that is used to connect.
password	The database password that is used to connect.
url	The URL to connect to the database with.
dbCreate	Determines the control Grails has over the database when an application starts. The options are `create-drop`, `create` and `update`. These will be covered in more depth shortly.
pooled	Whether a connection pool should be used, `true` is the default.
logSql	Whether to enable SQL logging, `false` is the default.
dialect	The Hibernate dialect to be used to communicate with the database.
jndiName	The JNDI name of a `DataSource` in the servlet container to be used.

Of course, we will be using the `jndiName` property because we have declared the JNDI entry in the `context.xml` file.

Environmentally aware

Grails has a built-in notion of runtime environments. There are three default environments. These are:

- Development—used by default when you call the `run-app` script. This allows dynamic reloading of your code.
- Test—used by default when you call the `test-app` script.
- Production—used by default when you package your application.

We can use these environments to declare different configurations for different environments. This allows us to use a database that can be trashed and reloaded on every restart when developing, but keep a persistent state across re-deploys to the production environment.

In your `DataSource.groovy` file, you should already see the following that has been generated by default when you created the project:

```
dataSource {
    pooled = false
    driverClassName = "org.hsqldb.jdbcDriver"
    username = "sa"
    password = ""
}
// environment specific settings
```

```
environments {
    development {
        dataSource {
            dbCreate = "create-drop" // one of 'create', 'create-
drop','update'
            url = "jdbc:hsqldb:mem:devDB"
        }
    }
    test {
        dataSource {
            dbCreate = "update"
            url = "jdbc:hsqldb:mem:testDb"
        }
    }
    production {
        dataSource {
            dbCreate = "update"
            url = "jdbc:hsqldb:file:prodDb;shutdown=true"
        }
    }
}
```

The first dataSource node defines the base configuration to be used by all environments. Under this node, there is an environments node containing three other nodes: development, test, and production. Each of these corresponds to the default runtime environments provided by Grails. When the application runs in one of these modes, it will use the additional configuration information that is defined within the relevant environment closure. Using this mechanism, we can declare that the application should use the correct database for the correct environment.

Database management

We have seen that Grails is able to construct a database schema automatically when the application starts from the structure of the domain classes. You'll be glad to know that we can control this behavior, as we don't want a production application to be rebuilding the database each time it is redeployed! The control that an application is given over the database is determined by the dbCreate property, as mentioned earlier. The available options for this property are:

- create-drop—this option is used for development by default. It will drop the entire database schema and recreate it from the current domain classes when the application is started.

- create—this option will create the database schema if it does not already exist, and will not alter the schema if it does exist. However, it will delete all of the data within an existing schema.

- update — this option will create the schema if it does not already exist and will update an existing schema to represent the latest domain classes.

It is no surprise then that the default setting for production is update, as both of the other options clear out any existing data on startup!

Update your DB configuration

We can now change the configuration of the dataSource property so that when the application runs in production mode, it will look up the DataSource from the JNDI entry that we created in the context.xml file. Change the configuration of the dataSource nodes in the DataSource.groovy file, as shown below:

```
environments {
    development {
        dataSource {
            pooled = false
            driverClassName = "org.hsqldb.jdbcDriver"
            username = "sa"
            password = ""
            dbCreate = "create-drop" // one of 'create', 'create-
drop','update'
            url = "jdbc:hsqldb:mem:devDB"
        }
    }
    test {
        dataSource {
            pooled = false
            driverClassName = "org.hsqldb.jdbcDriver"
            username = "sa"
            password = ""
            dbCreate = "create-drop"
            url = "jdbc:hsqldb:mem:testDb"
        }
    }
    production {
        dataSource {
            jndiName = "java:comp/env/teamwork/dataSource"
            dbCreate = "update"
        }
    }
}
```

The code above configures the production environment to use a JNDI DataSource and stops the database from being wiped out on each redeploy.

Control the bootstrap

The final change to be made before we can look at packaging the application for deployment is to modify the `BootStrap` class so that the application does not create test data in production mode. If we do not do this, the bootstrap data will be added again every time the application is deployed in production.

The production environment will need some base data to be created when it is installed for the first time. When installing the application for the first time, we need to ensure the following:

- There will always be an Administrator role
- There will always be a User role
- There will always be at least one user with the Administrator role

Modify the `BootStrap` class to contain the following code:

```
import app.Role
import org.jsecurity.crypto.hash.Sha1Hash
import app.User
import app.Message
import grails.util.Environment
class BootStrap {
    def user
    def admin
    def mjones
    def flancelot
    def init = {servletContext ->
        if( Environment.current == Environment.PRODUCTION ) {
            productionData()
        }
        if( Environment.current == Environment.DEVELOPMENT ||
            Environment.current == Environment.TEST ) {
            createUsersAndRoles()
        }
        if( Environment.current == Environment.DEVELOPMENT ) {
            createMessages(flancelot, mjones)
        }
    }
    def destroy = {
    }
    private def productionData() {
        def adminRole = Role.findByName( 'Administrator' )
        if( !adminRole ) {
            adminRole = new Role(name: 'Administrator').save()
        }
```

```
        if ( !Role.findByName( 'User' ) ) {
            new Role(name: 'User').save()
        }
        if ( !User.findByUsername( 'sysadmin' ) ) {
            new User(username: 'sysadmin',
                title: 'Mr',
                firstName: 'System',
                lastName: 'Administrator',
                password: new Sha1Hash("teamwork_admin").toHex(),
                role: adminRole).save()
        }
    }
    private def createUsersAndRoles() {
        user = new Role(name: 'User').save()
        admin = new Role(name: 'Administrator').save()
        mjones = new User(username: 'mjones',
                title: 'Miss',
                firstName: 'Martha',
                lastName: 'Jones',
                password: new Sha1Hash("admin").toHex(),
                role: admin).save()

        flancelot = new User(username: 'flancelot',
                title: 'Mr',
                firstName: 'Fred',
                lastName: 'Lancelot',
                password: new Sha1Hash("password").toHex(),
                role: user).save()
    }
    private def createMessages(flancelot, mjones) {
        def message1 = new Message(title: 'The Knights Who Say Nee',
                detail: 'They are after a shrubbery.',
                user: mjones).save()
        message1.addTag('montypython')
        message1.addTag('knight')
        def message2 = new Message(title: 'The Black Knight',
                detail: 'Just a flesh wound.',
                user: flancelot).save()
        message2.addTag('montypython')
        message2.addTag('knight')
        def message3 = new Message(title: 'air speed velocity
                                            of a swallow',
                detail: "African or European?",
                user: flancelot).save()
        message3.addTag('montypython')
    }
}
```

We have extracted the existing logic into two methods:

- `createUsersAndRoles` — creates the users and roles that are needed for testing
- `createMessages` — creates the messages that we use for our manual test data.

We have also created a new method called `productionData` that will ensure that the data we require in production is loaded once and only once. Finally, we have simplified the `init` closure so it is clear what data is being set up in each environment.

Package the WAR file

Now that the application is configured to behave properly in a production environment, we need to package it into a WAR file. Once this is complete, we can deploy the application to any servlet container. Grails provides a command to package an application into a WAR file. In the command line, go to the `teamwork` folder and run:

```
grails war teamwork.war
```

The `war` command will create the specified `teamwork.war` file in the current folder. The environment used by default when executing the `war` command is `production`. So whenever the deployed application is executed, it will run under the `production` environment configuration.

If we don't specify a file name, a WAR file will be created with the project name and the version number of the application, from `application.properties`, as a suffix to the file name.

When running the `grails war` command, Grails will package all of the required libraries (JAR files), so that the application can be deployed to a servlet container with minimum fuss. However, this does mean that all of the Hibernate and Spring classes are also packaged up in this WAR file, which makes it quite big. By running the `grails war` command with the `nojars` argument (`grails war teamwork.war --nojars`), you can create a much smaller WAR file (around 5MB instead of 30MB). This is helpful if you have a slow connection to your hosting environment, and is absolutely critical if you are hosting a number of applications in the same servlet container, due to the memory consumption of loading all of the Hibernate and Spring classes into memory for each application. If you decide to package your application with the `nojars` option, then you will, of course, have to remember to add all of the necessary JAR files to the shared classpath of your servlet container.

Deploy

Take the WAR file that was generated by Grails, copy it to your Tomcat webapps folder, and start Tomcat. Your application will be deployed!

Hosting options

The hosting options are the same with Grails as with any other Java web application. So as long as the hosting provider has a servlet container option, you will be able to deploy your web application.

Next steps

That's it! Well, not quite. You now know enough to start building web applications with Grails and you will get some serious productivity benefits using the standard approaches of controllers, domain classes, GSPs, and services that have been outlined in this book. However, there is always more to learn. Go ahead and wow your colleagues by producing slick web applications in record time, but at the same time, take a look at some of the following options that will help when implementing larger and more complicated web applications.

Java Hibernate classes with GORM

In this book, you have seen the default Grails convention for declaring domain classes, that is, Groovy classes located in the domain folder. Grails also supports using Java Hibernate classes as domain classes for your application. This means you can code your domain objects in Java and use Hibernate XML configuration, or Hibernate annotations, to define the persistent properties of your domain classes.

It is worth becoming familiar with this approach as it can provide a number of benefits over using Groovy domain classes:

- You can reuse existing domain classes from other projects. For example, you may be building a web interface to an existing project.

- The persistent domain model you produce will be reusable by non-Grails applications. This is a serious consideration for web applications that are not simple standalone applications.

- Being able to use the Hibernate configuration directly gives you more flexibility and control over the persistence of your domain model than is provided by default with the GORM.

- Other developers in your department may be skeptical of relatively new technologies and so having a good chunk of your application and domain logic in Java Hibernate classes that can be reused under another web framework will reduce the risk of adopting Grails.

- Many classical developers are not entirely comfortable with dynamic languages. By keeping your domain classes in a static, strongly-typed language you may find Grails is more palatable to others.

- Groovy is slower than Java. If you have complex algorithms in your domain classes, they will run faster in Java.

- When Grails uses Java domain classes, it still adds all of the useful GORM methods so that your web application continues to work as if the domain classes were in Groovy.

It is also important to recognize the overheads that will occur by using Java Hibernate objects as your domain model:

- You will lose the ability to specify constraints for domain classes by using the simple builder syntax on a static constraints property.

- You will have to use the more verbose Hibernate declarations to create simple relationships between domain classes.

- You will lose the power and flexibility of the Groovy syntax in your domain model.

Whether to use Java or Groovy for your domain model is up to you, but if you know how to do both, then you will at least be able to switch between the two approaches if you need to.

Integrating with other presentation frameworks

By default, Grails uses GSP and GSP Tags as its view technology. The first positive thing about GSP is that it looks a lot like JSP, so most web developers will be very familiar with the syntax. The great thing about GSP is that tags are incredibly easy to implement. This makes componentizing views a lot easier.

My main concern with GSP, just like JSP, is that it is hard to test. There is no way to perform a unit test on a GSP. This means that any presentation logic residing in GSPs must either be tested by automated functional tests or tested manually. Neither of these approaches is ideal.

Fortunately, the Grails community has been busy. There are a number of plug-ins to support different presentation frameworks. Two plug-ins that might be of particular interest are:

- Google Web Toolkit
- Wicket

Both of these frameworks are object–based, and hence should prove to be much simpler to unit test than GSPs. Alternatively, with the introduction of the Testing plug-in in Grails 1.1, tag libraries are much easier to test. So if you can keep as much presentation logic as possible in tag libraries, then you may be able to test them sufficiently so that the need for testing GSPs is reduced.

Data migration

As you saw earlier in this chapter, Grails provides three different strategies for your application to manage the schema of its database. While Grails can update the schema for your application, it does not manage any data migration as a result of modifying the schema. You could get yourself into a lot of trouble if you go changing the structure of the database without thinking about how it will affect existing data in the production environment!

There are currently three plug-ins that support migrating schemas changes:

- dbmigrate Plugin
- LiquiBase Plugin
- Autobase Plugin

The dbmigrate plug-in (`http://code.google.com/p/dbmigrate/wiki/Grails`) provides two scripts. The first script generates a migration file that will transform your database schema from the current version to match the schema required by your current domain classes.

The LiquiBase plug-in (`http://www.liquibase.org/manual/grails`) allows you to manage changes to an existing database structure by defining a number of change sets in an XML format. The XML commands available are the same as if you were using the LiquiBase framework on any other project. A number of Grails commands are supplied by the plug-in to perform operations such as:

- `migrate`—apply change sets to the database
- `rollback`—specify a tag, a number of change sets, or a date to roll the database back to
- `tag`—apply a tag for the current database schema that can be used for a rollback

The Autobase plug-in (`http://wiki.github.com/RobertFischer/autobase`) provides a Grails-style wrapper around LiquiBase. Change sets are defined in Groovy code as a Builder DSL, rather than XML. This makes complicated change sets much easier to write and repetitive changes can be encapsulated. When an application is deployed, any change sets that have not already been applied to the database are executed.

Summary

Throughout this book, we have seen how Grails can speed up and simplify development of real-world Java web applications. In this chapter we have seen, as with most other things, how Grails simplifies packaging your application so that it can be deployed to any standard Java servlet container.

If this book has given you a taste for web development in Grails, then you will find looking at the suggestions in this chapter useful for expanding your Grails knowledge. The goal of these pointers is to prepare you to handle some of the real-world challenges that come during and after initial development of any web application.

Hopefully, Grails will ease the pain of your next web application development so that you can spend more time focusing on your users and building great software.

Index

OutputStream 150

P

password encryption, JSecurity plug-in 97
password property 286
plug-in
  installing 86, 87, 88
  list, searching 86
  password encryption 98, 99
plug-in events, using 257
Polymorphic queries 182
pooled property 286
principal tag 105
production environment 286
ProfileController 194
prototype, service scope 167
prototype library 211

Q

queryDelay attribute 216
QuickStart script 88

R

range constraint 28
ranges, Groovy feature 75, 76
realms
  authenticate(authToken) method 89
  authenticate, implementing 91
  authTokenClass property 89
  creating 90, 91
  dynamic finders 92
  hasRole(principal, roleName) method 90
  hasRole, implementing 94
  isPermitted(principle, permission) method
    90
  methods 89
  properties 89
redirect method 44, 45
registerMetaClass method 123
relationship
  fields, ordering through constraints 31
  role class, associating with user class 29, 30
  user class, associating with role class 30
relationship, types
  many-to-many 29

many-to-one 29
one-to-many 29
one-to-one 29
remoteLink tag 206
remoteLink tag, attributes
  action attribute 206
  after attribute 206
  asynchronous attribute 206
  before attribute 206
  controller attribute 206
  id attribute 206
  method attribute 206
  on<ErrorCode> attribute 206
  onComplete attribute 206
  onFailure attribute 206
  onLoaded attribute 206
  onLoading attribute 206
  onSuccess attribute 206
  onUninitialized attribute 206
  update attribute 206
renderAsXml method 215
render method 45
renderTemplate method 255
request, service scope 167
REST
  overview 239
REST API
  authentication 247, 248
RESTful controller, implementing
  messages, retrieving 244, 245
  new messages, creating 245, 246
REST service mappings, URL mapping 242
REST services
  about 239
  implementing, requisites 240
  REST, overview 239
  REST API, authentication 247, 248
  RESTful controller, implementing 243
  test script 248, 249
  URL mapping 240, 241
results property 231
RichUI autoComplete widget 215-218
Rich UI tag cloud component 219
Role.groovy class 29, 30
Role.groovy file 20
role class
  associating, with user class 29, 30

Packt Open Source Project Royalties

When we sell a book written on an Open Source project, we pay a royalty directly to that project. Therefore by purchasing Grails 1.1 Web Application Development, Packt will have given some of the money received to the Grails project.

In the long term, we see ourselves and you—customers and readers of our books—as part of the Open Source ecosystem, providing sustainable revenue for the projects we publish on. Our aim at Packt is to establish publishing royalties as an essential part of the service and support a business model that sustains Open Source.

If you're working with an Open Source project that you would like us to publish on, and subsequently pay royalties to, please get in touch with us.

Writing for Packt

We welcome all inquiries from people who are interested in authoring. Book proposals should be sent to author@packtpub.com. If your book idea is still at an early stage and you would like to discuss it first before writing a formal book proposal, contact us; one of our commissioning editors will get in touch with you.

We're not just looking for published authors; if you have strong technical skills but no writing experience, our experienced editors can help you develop a writing career, or simply get some additional reward for your expertise.

About Packt Publishing

Packt, pronounced 'packed', published its first book "Mastering phpMyAdmin for Effective MySQL Management" in April 2004 and subsequently continued to specialize in publishing highly focused books on specific technologies and solutions.

Our books and publications share the experiences of your fellow IT professionals in adapting and customizing today's systems, applications, and frameworks. Our solution-based books give you the knowledge and power to customize the software and technologies you're using to get the job done. Packt books are more specific and less general than the IT books you have seen in the past. Our unique business model allows us to bring you more focused information, giving you more of what you need to know, and less of what you don't.

Packt is a modern, yet unique publishing company, which focuses on producing quality, cutting-edge books for communities of developers, administrators, and newbies alike. For more information, please visit our website: www.PacktPub.com.

Apache Struts 2 Web Application Development

ISBN: 978-1-847193-39-1   Paperback: 300 pages

A beginner's guide for Java developers

1. Design, develop, test, and deploy your web applications using Struts 2 framework

2. No prior knowledge of JavaScript and CSS is required

3. Apply the best of agile development techniques and TDD techniques

4. Step-by-step instructions and careful explanations with lots of code examples

Tapestry 5: Building Web Applications

ISBN: 978-1-847193-07-0   Paperback: 280 pages

A step-by-step guide to Java Web development with the developer-friendly Apache Tapestry framework

1. Latest version of Tapestry web development framework

2. Get working with Tapestry components

3. Gain hands-on experience developing an example site

4. Practical step-by-step tutorial

Please check **www.PacktPub.com** for information on our titles

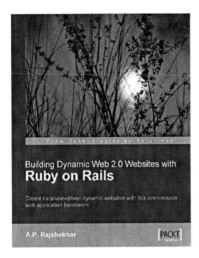

Printed in the United States
149132LV00001B/49/P

9 781847 196682